Fodor's InFocus

PORTLAND

2nd Edition

**Where to Eat and Stay
for All Budgets**

**Must-See Sights
and Local Secrets**

Ratings You Can Trust

Fodor's Travel Publications New York, Toronto, London, Sydney, Auckland
www.fodors.com

FODOR'S IN FOCUS PORTLAND

Series Editor: Douglas Stallings

Editor: John Rambow

Editorial Production: Carolyn Roth

Editorial Contributor: Janna Mock-Lopez

Maps & Illustrations: David Lindroth, *cartographer*; Bob Blake and Rebecca Baer, *map editors;* William Wu, *information graphics*

Design: Fabrizio LaRocca, *creative director*; Guido Caroti, *art director*; Ann McBride, *designer*; Melanie Marin, *senior picture editor*

Cover Photo: (Multnomah Falls, Columbia River Gorge National Scenic Area): Ron Niebrugge/Alamy

Production/Manufacturing: Amanda Bullock

COPYRIGHT

2nd Edition

ISBN 978-1-4000-0454-6

ISSN 1941-0255

SPECIAL SALES

This book is available for special discounts for bulk purchases for sales promotions or premiums. Special editions, including personalized covers, excerpts of existing books, and corporate imprints, can be created in large quantities for special needs. For more information, write to Special Markets/Premium Sales, 1745 Broadway, MD 6-2, New York, NY 10019, or e-mail specialmarkets@randomhouse.com.

AN IMPORTANT TIP & AN INVITATION

Although all prices, opening times, and other details in this book are based on information supplied to us at press time, changes occur all the time in the travel world, and Fodor's cannot accept responsibility for facts that become outdated or for inadvertent errors or omissions. **So always confirm information when it matters,** especially if you're making a detour to visit a specific place. Your experiences—positive and negative—matter to us. If we have missed or misstated something, **please write to us.** We follow up on all suggestions. Contact the Portland editor at editors@fodors.com or c/o Fodor's at 1745 Broadway, New York, NY 10019.

PRINTED IN THE UNITED STATES OF AMERICA

10 9 8 7 6 5 4 3 2 1

Be a Fodor's Correspondent

Your opinion matters. It matters to us. It matters to your fellow Fodor's travelers, too. And we'd like to hear it. In fact, we *need* to hear it. When you share your experiences and opinions, you become an active member of the Fodor's community. Here's how you can help improve Fodor's for all of us.

Tell us when we're right. We rely on local writers to give you an insider's perspective. But our writers and staff editors also depend on you. Your positive feedback is a vote to renew our recommendations for the next edition.

Tell us when we're wrong. We update most of our guides every year. But things change. If any of our descriptions are inaccurate or inadequate, we'll incorporate your changes in the next edition and will correct factual errors at fodors.com *immediately*.

Tell us what to include. You probably have had fantastic travel experiences that aren't yet in Fodor's. Why not share them with a community of like-minded travelers? Share your discoveries and experiences with everyone directly at fodors. com. Your input may lead us to add a new listing or a higher recommendation.

Give us your opinion instantly at our feedback center at www. fodors.com/feedback. You may also e-mail editors@fodors.com with the subject line "Portland Editor." Or send your nominations, comments, and complaints by mail to Portland Editor, Fodor's, 1745 Broadway, New York, NY 10019.

Happy Traveling!

Tim Jarrell, Publisher

CONTENTS

ABOUT THIS BOOK

Our Ratings

We wouldn't recommend a place that wasn't worth your time, but sometimes a place is so experiential that superlatives don't do it justice: you just have to be there to know. These sights, properties, and experiences get our highest rating, **Fodor's Choice**, indicated by orange stars throughout this book. Black stars highlight sights and properties we deem **Highly Recommended**, places that our writers, editors, and readers praise again and again for consistency and excellence.

Credit Cards

Want to pay with plastic? **AE, D, DC, MC, V** after restaurant and hotel listings indicate whether American Express, Discover, Diners Club, MasterCard, and Visa are accepted.

Restaurants

Unless we state otherwise, restaurants are open for lunch and dinner daily. We mention dress only when there's a specific requirement and reservations only when they're essential or not accepted—it's always best to book ahead.

Hotels

Unless we tell you otherwise, you can assume that the hotels have private bath, phone, TV, and air-conditioning. We always list facilities but not whether you'll be charged an extra fee to use them, so when pricing accommodations, find out what's included.

Many Listings
- ★ Fodor's Choice
- ★ Highly recommended
- ⊠ Physical address
- ⊹ Directions
- ⌖ Mailing address
- ☎ Telephone
- 🖷 Fax
- ⊕ On the Web
- ✉ E-mail
- ☝ Admission fee
- ☉ Open/closed times
- Ⓜ Metro stations
- ⊟ Credit cards

Hotels & Restaurants
- ⌗ Hotel
- ↩ Number of rooms
- ⚲ Facilities
- ❢❢ Meal plans
- ✕ Restaurant
- ⚑ Reservations
- ⚐ Smoking
- ⑅ BYOB
- ✕⌗ Hotel with restaurant that warrants a visit

Outdoors
- ⚑ Golf
- ⛺ Camping

Other
- ☺ Family-friendly
- ⇨ See also
- ⊠ Branch address
- ☞ Take note

WHEN TO GO

Portland's mild climate is best from June through September. Hotels are often filled in July and August, so it's important to book reservations in advance. Spring and fall are also excellent times to visit. The weather usually remains quite good, and the prices for accommodations, transportation, and tours can be lower (and the crowds much smaller!) in the most popular destinations. In winter, snow is uncommon in the city but abundant in the nearby mountains, making the region a skier's dream.

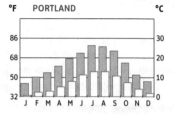

Climate

Average daytime summer highs are in the 70s; winter temperatures are generally in the 40s. Rainfall varies greatly from one locale to another. In the coastal mountains, for example, 160 inches of rain fall annually, creating temperate rain forests. Portland has an average of only 36 inches of rainfall a year—less than New York, Chicago, or Miami—however, in winter the rain may never seem to end. More than 75% of Portland's annual precipitation occurs from October through March. Portland is equally gray and drizzly in winter.

Forecasts National Weather Service (⊕ www.wrh.noaa.gov). **Weather Channel** (⊕ www.weather.com).

Welcome to Portland

WORD OF MOUTH

"Go to Powells . . . a city of books. Go to the Japenese Gardens regardless of weather. . . . Ride the Streetcar to get around town."

—Scarlett

By Janna
Mock-
Lopez

WHAT DISTINGUISHES PORTLAND, OREGON, from the rest of America's cityscapes? Or from the rest of the world's urban destinations for that matter? In a Northwest nutshell: everything. For some, it's the wealth of cultural offerings and never-ending culinary choices; for others, it's Portland's proximity to the ocean and mountains, or simply the beauty of having all these attributes in one place. Strolling through downtown or within one of Portland's numerous neighborhoods, there's an unmistakable vibrancy to this city—one that is encouraged by clean air, infinite trees, and a blend of historic and modern architecture.

Portland's various nicknames—Rose City, Bridgetown, Beervana, Brewtopia—tell its story in a nutshell as well. For a more involved explanation of what "everything" means, though, do what Portlanders would do to immerse themselves in a topic: grab a robust cup of coffee, a pot of steaming tea, or a sudsy mug of microbrew, and read on.

HISTORY

Portland's first inhabitants were bands of Native Americans. More than 10,000 years ago, indigenous tribes created complex thriving communities where they lived off and traded the various natural resources. Thanks to the networks of rivers, including the mighty Columbia, there was an abundance salmon here. Tribes such as the Chinook based their entire economies and cultures upon the cycles of salmon runs.

By the late 1700s into the early 1800s, the findings of the Lewis and Clark expedition began to draw settlers from the East. The British Hudson Bay Company, looking to build a fur-trading operation, founded Fort Vancouver, a settlement that's now within present-day Portland's metropolitan area.

As interest in the beauty and bounty of the West grew, both the Oregon Trail and the Barlow Road passages enabled the first large wave of pioneers to create settlements in the early 1840s. Two such pioneers, William Overton and Asa Lovejoy, were the joint founders of Portland. Overton was particularly impressed by the region's commercial prospects and set his sights on obtaining land. Unable to round up the 25¢ needed to file a land claim for a 640-acre site, he borrowed the quarter from Lovejoy in return for half of

1

TOP REASONS TO GO

■ Unleash your inner foodie in a city that has become a hot culinary destination, and experience an amazingly textured range of global delights created with fresh, locally harvested ingredients.

■ Beer "hop" (pun intended) between more than 40 local microbrews and sample offbeat varieties with such names as Hallucinator, Doggie Claws, and Sock Knocker.

■ Get up close and personal with Portland's true quirky nature by staying at or visiting one of the many beautifully restored McMenamins properties in and around

town, such as a renovated elementary school turned hotel.

■ Spend the day at Washington Park, where you can stroll through the International Rose Test Garden, Japanese Garden, Oregon Zoo, World Forestry Center, and Children's Museum—all within a short distance of one another.

■ Peruse the aisles filled with more than a million new and used books at Powell's City of Books in the Pearl District. Top off hours of literary wanderlust with a fresh mocha or ginseng tea downstairs at World Cup Coffee and Tea House.

the claim. They cleared trees, built roads, and constructed this area's first buildings.

The next phase of the region's evolution came after Overton left for Texas—he sold his portion of their joint claim to former shopkeeper and would-be developer Frances Pettygrove. When it came time to name their new settlement in 1845, Lovejoy and Pettygrove disagreed on what they wanted. Lovejoy, a Massachusetts native wanted to call it "Boston," while Pettygrove, from Maine, preferred "Portland." To settle the matter, legend claims that they did a coin toss—best of three—in which Pettygrove prevailed.

Development occurred quickly after Pettygrove and Lovejoy built a log store on the southeast corner of Front and Washington. Tanneries, saw mills, and even an oxen-driven mill wagon serving as the first public transportation system had been established. By the end of that decade, Portland had 800 residents. The Oregon Territory was officially formed in 1848. It was a vast chunk of real estate that included land north of California all the way south of Canada. Through the help of Congress and the passage of the Oregon Land act, every man or woman became entitled to 320 acres.

With the first of three transcontinental railroads reaching Portland in 1883, the city's was well on the way to becoming a major trading hub. In 1887 the Morrison Bridge—not the one visible today, which replaced the original in 1958—had been built across the Willamette River. With more arrivals came more neighborhoods and annexations: by 1900 Portland had become the Northwest's largest city, with a population of nearly 100,000. However, it was the nearly 1.5 million visitors that came over the course of several months to take part in 1905's Lewis and Clark Centennial Exposition that spurred the next major growth wave. Portland's population doubled in the next five years.

Drive around the city, particularly in the Northeast or Northwest areas, and you'll see beautiful houses built in this time, done in Victorian, Edwardian, and Colonial styles. The Pittock Mansion, a massive French chateau that's one of the most notable buildings in town, is now a public museum furnished with period artifacts. Finished in 1914 for the lumber, real estate, and publishing magnate Henry Pittock and his wife Georgiana, the house and its 46-acre estate is in the West Hills area, 1,000 feet above the city.

Portland continued to grow rapidly through the first half of the 20th century. Remarkably, by the mid-1920s, nine of Portland's existing bridges had already been built, including the Steel, Hawthorne, Broadway, Interstate, Sellwood, Burnside, Ross Island, Vista bridges, and BNSF Railway Bridge. The need for more than 100,000 workers at the Kaiser Company, one of the largest shipbuilding operations in the world, kept Portland prosperous during both world wars.

More than 40,000 of these workers came to live in Vanport, in what amounted to the largest public housing project ever built in the United States. Unfortunately a flood later destroyed Vanport and left many of its residents displaced. Both this and continued regional growth over the next decade prompted an expansion into suburbia. Portland's largest suburbs—Gresham, Beaverton, and Hillsboro—saw the biggest increases in residents.

By the late 1960s into the early 1970s, Portland began the preservation efforts for which it is known today. Under Governor Tom McCall, an urban growth boundary was adopted. Under this policy, high-density development was allowed only in designated urban areas, and strict use restrictions were placed on farmland. This approach of restricting growth ran counter to what most cities across America of this size and growth rate were experiencing: as automobile use became more common, most people were abandoning city centers.

Those in favor of this political approach say it has preserved precious farmland, provided an economic base for the farmers, and forced the creation of public transportation. Over time this has meant that Portland has less overall traffic than other cities its size. Though hardly congestion-free today, Portland is a vibrant, clean destination whose urban planning, sustainability practices, and transportation efficiency make it a model for other cities.

GETTING AROUND

In general, it's easy to get around Portland. The Willamette River is Portland's east–west dividing line. Burnside Street separates north from south. The city's 200-foot-long blocks are highly walkable, but you can also explore the downtown core and Nob Hill by MAX light rail, the Portland Streetcar, or TriMet buses (⇨ *Portland Essentials*). Closer to the downtown core are the Pearl District and Old Town/Chinatown. Both the Pearl District and Nob Hill have many restaurants, specialty shops, and nightspots.

Note that you can explore the entire downtown for free through TriMet's "fareless square" system. Fare is not required when boarding buses, MAX light-rail, or streetcars when traveling within this designated area. Just say "fareless" as you board, and be sure to get off before you pass into a fare zone; drivers really do take note of who is riding for free, and may ask you to get off.

PORTLAND LIFE

Rich cultural offerings, prime historic and modern architecture, endless recreational activities, and a friendly feel make Portland alluring for just about everyone. But it seems that Portland's food scene is one of its biggest attractions these days. It's true that Portland's filled with amazing restaurants—though it's not necessarily the recipes that are causing all the commotion. Rather, it's the "locavore" movement—using ingredients that are raised, grown, or foraged within a reasonable distance—that's got diners and chefs excited. Often, diners experience savory fish, fowl, or pasta dishes made with seasonal fruit and veg-

Portland by Bike

In the mid-1990s the City of Portland adopted a 20-year Bicycle Master Plan for improvements that encourage more bicycles. Thanks to this plan, locals and travelers alike can take advantage of Portland's bicycle-friendliness. There are now more than 150 mi of bicycle boulevards, lanes, and off-street paths. Add to that thorough, accessible maps, specialized tours, and parking capacity (including lockers and racks downtown), and bicycling becomes not only a feasible but a sought-after mode of transportation.

Educators, advocates, riding groups, and businesses, along with the government, are working toward making Portland even more bike-friendly and safe. According to TriMet, whose entire bus fleet is equipped with bicycle racks, more than 80,000 bicycles are taken on MAX or bus each year. An intended 400-plus mi of bike paths are to be added over the next decade.

For more on bicycle transportation resources and information, visit ⊕ www.portlandonline. com/transportation.

etable accompaniments that have just been plucked from the vine or ground.

After you're done with a delicious meal, you may find yourself at one of the many unique coffeehouses or local breweries sipping on something satisfying. Dozens of options blanket the city. Stumptown Coffee Roasters is a local favorite for a cup of joe; for microbrew possibilities, check out a McMenamins, BridgePort, or Widmer brewery. These sites are frequented by locals, too, and make great hangouts to people-watch or as a pit stop for determining the day's or evening's activities.

Portland has a thriving cultural community with ballet, opera, symphonies, theater, and art exhibitions both minor and major in scope. Whatever you choose, you can count on several things: relatively affordable ticket prices and crowds dressed in everything from tennis shoes to tuxedos. Portlanders are sometimes accused by outsiders of being "too casual" when it comes to showing up for performances. But it might be this "lower-brow" approach to arts and culture that is why many events are well-attended.

One arts attraction that pulls in locals as well as tourists is the Portland Art Museum. Its two large buildings house paintings by old-world masters, an impressive collection of Native American art (much of it from the Northwest)—and an expanding collection of modern and contemporary art. Across the street from the art museum is the Oregon Historical Society, which has more than 85,000 artifacts, including ancient objects from the earliest settlements. Exhibitions bring to life what their mission statement proclaims is, "preserving and interpreting Oregon's past in thoughtful, illuminating, and provocative ways."

If smaller galleries are more of your thing, Portland has plenty. Lots of galleries and studios are in the swanky Pearl District, on the fringe of downtown. Print art, fiber art, contemporary art, and photography as well as glass, video art, and 3-D art, are all represented here.

IF YOU LIKE

BIKING

Portland has been called the best city in the country for biking, and with bike lanes galore, mild weather year-round, and a beautiful waterfront to ride along, it's no wonder. With all this encouragement, cyclists in Portland have gotten creative: not only does cycling provide an excellent form of transportation around here, it also has evolved into a medium of progressive politics and public service. Riders gather at least once every month on the last Friday to ride together through the streets of the city. The event, called Critical Mass (⊕ *www.rosecitycriticalmass.org*), is meant to publicize bike riding as a powerful alternative to cars, and members have also been known to gather together for political protest. In addition, several bike co-ops in the city are devoted to providing used bikes at decent prices to members of the community, as well as to teaching bike maintenance and the economic and environmental benefits of becoming a commuter on two wheels.

PUB THEATERS

Sipping a pint of local brew is one of Oregon's favorite pastimes, but Portlanders have taken this a step further with so-called pub theaters—movie theaters showing second-run, classic, or cult films for $3 or so that let you can buy a pitcher of good locally brewed beer and a slice of pizza to enjoy while watching. The McMenamin brothers are largely to thank for this phenomenon, being the masterminds behind such popular spots as the Bagdad Theatre, the Mission Theatre, and the St. John's Pub. In addition, unaffiliated establishments like the Laurelhurst Theatre

Portland Parks It

Portlander artists are known for their innovation when it comes to creating work reflective of the region. One such artist, Brian Mock (⊕ www.brianmock. com), creates curvaceous women's figures and jumping salmon nearly 7 feet tall by welding recycled nuts, bolts, forks, and hinges. Curious onlookers are left to ponder what better fate might have met Aunt Thelma's toaster than the Dumpster. Mock's work is represented by two area galleries: Exit 21 and Onda galleries

Many of the best things about Portland aren't inside the city's restaurants or museums but outside—in its parks. If the weather cooperates—and in Portland that isn't always a given—you need to do as city residents do and head outdoors.

When looking toward the hills on the west side of town it's hard to miss the tree-blanketed 5,155 acres of Forest Park. The nation's largest urban wilderness, Forest Park, is a car-free haven for runners, hikers, bikers, and nature enthusiasts. The park is home to more than 60 mammals, including elk, deer, and bobcats, and more than 110 bird species.

Another popular park is Washington Park—one of Oregon's oldest, acquired in 1871—which has picnic areas, playgrounds, and hiking trails; within the park are Hoyt Arboretum and the International Rose Test and Japanese Gardens. Waterfront Park is right downtown, on the west bank of the Willamette River. This local favorite hosts many of Portland's major annual festivals and concerts, including the Rose Festival and Waterfront Blues Festival.

A few other natural havens: Mt. Tabor Park, an extinct volcanic cinder cone, has miles of trails that meander through forest to the top, where impressive downtown and Mt. Hood views are the reward. Another, Laurelhurst Park, is a wonderful mix of large shady trees and open green spaces. There are plenty of spots for sunny afternoon picnics, admiring nature and letting kids run around.

If you have kids in tow you'll appreciate that, in addition to plenty of outdoor parks, there are scores of indoor family-friendly activities. Landmark destinations to spend a few hours or an entire day are the Oregon Zoo—in the same area as the Portland Children's Museum and World Forestry Center Discovery Museum—and the Oregon Museum of Science and Industry (fondly referred to as OMSI), on the east side of the Willamette River across from downtown and the Clinton Street Theater have managed to get in on the action as well.

BRIDGES

With a river running through the center of the city, Portland has one of the most interesting urban landscapes in the country, due in no small part to the several unique bridges that span the width of the Willamette River. Five of the city's 10 bridges are drawbridges that must be frequently raised to let barges go through, and there's something awe-inspiring and anachronistic in watching a portion of a city's traffic and hubbub stand still for several minutes as a slow-moving vessel floats through still water. Each bridge is beautiful and different: the St. John's Bridge has elegant 400-foot towers, the Broadway Bridge is a rich red hue, the arches of the huge two-level Fremont Bridge span the river gracefully, and the Steel Bridge has a pedestrian walkway just 30 feet above the water, allowing walkers and bikers to get a fabulous view of the river.

Exploring
Portland

WORD OF MOUTH

"[T]he Pittock Mansion grounds are a good place to view Mt. Hood and Mt. St. Helens if the sky is clear. It's free to visit the grounds just for the view, but you do have to drive up—no public transit unless you want to walk about ½-mile from a bus stop. Of course, you could visit the mansion too—it's pretty cool."

—Andrew

Updated
by Janna
Mock-
Lopez

ONE OF THE GREATEST THINGS ABOUT PORTLAND is that there's so much to explore. This city rightfully boasts that there's something for everyone. What makes discovering Portland's treasures even more enticing is that its attractions, transportation options, and events are all relatively accessible and affordable.

Portland has long been considered a hub for indie music. Hundreds of bands flock to become part of the creative flow of alternative, jazz, blues, and rock, which dominate the nightclub scene seven nights a week. Factor in an outrageous number of independent brewpubs and coffee shops—with snowboarding, windsurfing, or camping within an hour's drive—and it's easy to see why so many younger singles take advantage of Portland's eclectic indoor and outdoor offerings.

Couples can double the romance and intrigue, with strolls through never-ending parks, dimmed dining rooms for savoring innovative regional cuisine, and gorgeous cruises along the Willamette River aboard the *Portland Spirit*. As for hiking, climbing, biking, running, paired people have a built-in playground to renew their shared interests in Portland's natural bounty.

Families can explore first-rate museums and parks, including the Children's Museum, the Oregon Museum of Science and Industry, and Oaks Park. Many of these attractions offer permanent displays as well as nationally touring exhibits. At most libraries, parks, and recreational facilities, expect to find hands-on activities, music, story times, plays, and special performances for children. Many restaurants in and around Portland are family-friendly, and with immediate access to the MAX light rail and streetcars, toting kids around downtown is easy.

DOWNTOWN

Portland has one of the most attractive, inviting downtown centers in the United States. It's clean, compact, and filled with parks, plazas, and fountains. Architecture fans find plenty to admire in its mix of old and new. Hotels, shops, museums, restaurants, and entertainment can all be found here, and the entire downtown area is part of the Tri-Met transit system's Fareless Square, within which you can ride MAX, the Portland Streetcar, or any bus for free.

PORTLAND TOP 5 EXPERIENCES

■ Gaze at Portland's gorgeous skyline in the afternoon light, while gently gliding down the Willamette River aboard the *Portland Spirit*.

■ Walk around downtown (or ride the streetcar) to see the interesting mix of contemporary and historic buildings.

■ Take in the true cultural and social flavor of Portland by participating in either the First Thursday Gallery Walk in the Pearl District or the Last Thursday art event on Alberta Street. The galleries, open late, attract thousands of people.

■ Have some homespun fun by sauntering from craft to craft at the Portland Saturday Market.

■ Eat like a locavore by trying one of the many eco-conscious restaurants serving dishes made from locally harvested ingredients.

Numbers in the text correspond to numbers in the margin and on the Downtown, the Pearl District, and Old Town/ Chinatown map.

WHAT TO SEE

② Central Library. The elegant, etched-graphite central staircase and elaborate ceiling ornamentation make this no ordinary library. With a gallery space on the second floor and famous literary names engraved on the walls, this building is well worth a walk around. ⊠ *801 S.W. 10th Ave., Downtown* ☎ *503/988–5123* 🖂 *Free* ⊙ *Mon. and Thurs.–Sat. 10–6, Tues. and Wed. 10–8, Sun. noon–5.*

⑯ Chapman and Lownsdale squares. During the 1920s, these parks were segregated by sex: Chapman, between Madison and Main streets, was reserved for women, and Lownsdale, between Main and Salmon streets, was for men. The elk statue on Main Street, which separates the parks, was given to the city by David Thompson, mayor from 1879 to 1882. It honors the elk that grazed in the area in the 1850s.

⑲ City Hall. Portland's four-story, granite-faced City Hall, which was completed in 1895, is an example of the Renaissance Revival style popular in the late 19th century. Italian influences can be seen in the porch, the pink scagliola (faux marble) columns, the cornice embellishments, and other details. Much beauty was restored when the building was renovated in the late 1990s. The ornate interior—with

GREAT ITINERARIES

IF YOU HAVE 1 DAY

Spend the morning exploring downtown. Visit the Portland Art Museum or the Oregon History Center, stop by the historic First Congregational Church and Pioneer Court-house Square, and take a stroll along the Park Blocks or Waterfront Park. Eat lunch and do a little shopping along Northwest 23rd Avenue in the early afternoon, and be sure to get a look at the beautiful historic homes in Nob Hill. From there, drive up into the northwest hills by the Pittock Mansion, and finish off the afternoon at the Japanese Garden and the International Test Rose Garden in Washington Park. If you still have energy, head across the river for dinner on Hawthorne Boulevard; then drive up to Mt. Tabor Park for Portland's best sunset.

IF YOU HAVE 3 DAYS

On your first day, follow the itinerary above, but stay on the west side for dinner, and take your evening stroll in Waterfront Park. On your second morning, visit the Portland Classical Chinese Garden in Old Town, and then head across the river to the Sellwood District for lunch and antiquing. Stop by the Crystal Springs Rhododen-dron Garden; then head up to Hawthorne District in the afternoon. Wander through the Hawthorne and Belmont neighborhoods for a couple hours, stop by Laurelhurst Park, and take a picnic dinner up to Mt. Tabor Park. In the evening, catch a movie at the Bagdad Theatre, or get a beer at one of the east side brew-pubs. On Day 3, take a morn-ing hike in Hoyt Arboretum or Forest Park; then spend your afternoon exploring shops and galleries in the Pearl District and on northeast Alberta Street. Drive out to the Grotto, and then eat din-ner at the Kennedy School or one of the other McMenamins brewpubs.

IF YOU HAVE 7 DAYS

With a full week, you have time to slow down and take your time in the city. Follow the suggestions outlined above, but spread them out over four days instead of three. Then it's time to get out of town. Whether you drive through the beautiful Columbia Gorge, head to the coast, or explore the Oregon wine country, there's plenty to see within a few hours' drive. See Chapter 8, "Easy Side Trips from Portland," for inspi-ration and help in planning the rest of your week.

Downtown, The Pearl District and Old Town/Chinatown

Central Library, **2**
Chapman and Lownsdale squares, **16**
Chinatown Gate, **26**
City Hall, **19**
First Congregational Church, **4**
Governor Tom McCall Waterfront Park, **12**
Jamison Square Park, **29**
Japanese-American Historical Park, **24**
Jean Vollum Natural Capital City, **28**
Justice Center, **17**
Keller Auditorium, **10**
KOIN Center, **11**
Mark O. Hatfield U.S. Courthouse, **15**
Old Church, **7**
Oregon Historical Society, **5**
Oregon Maritime Center and Museum, **23**
Pioneer Courthouse Square, **1**

Portland Art Museum, **6**
Portland Building, **20**
Portland Center for the Performing Arts, **3**
Portland Classical Chinese Garden, **25**
Portland Farmer's Market, **9**
Portland Saturday Market, **22**
Portland State University, **8**
Powell's City of Books, **31**
Skidmore Fountain, **21**
Tanner Springs Park, **30**
Terry Schrunk Plaza, **18**
Union Station, **27**
World Trade Center, **14**
Yamhill National Historic District, **13**

KEY
○ Max Light Rail

Willamette River

Burnside Bridge
Morrison Bridge
Hawthorne Bridge

TO CHILDREN'S MUSEUM AND BERRY BOTANIC GARDEN

GOVERNOR TOM McCALL WATERFRONT PARK

MAX LIGHT RAIL

CENTRAL CITY STREETCAR

SKIDMORE OLD TOWN NATIONAL HISTORIC DISTRICT

CHINATOWN

0   1/4 mile
0   1/4 kilometer

intricate scrollwork, decorative tile, sunny atrium, and art exhibits—provides a fine shortcut between Southwest 4th and 5th avenues. ✉ *1220 S.W. 5th Ave., Downtown* ☎ *503/823–4000* ☉ *Weekdays 8–5.*

❹ First Congregational Church. This Venetian Gothic church, modeled after Boston's Old South Church, was completed in 1895, and you still can hear its original bell, purchased in 1871, ringing from its 175-foot tower. The church provided much of the land on which the Portland Center for the Performing Arts was built. ✉ *1126 S.W. Park Ave., Downtown* ☎ *503/228–7219* ✏ *Free* ☉ *Weekdays 9–2.*

⓬ Governor Tom McCall Waterfront Park. Named for a former governor revered for his statewide land-use planning initiatives, this park stretches north along the Willamette River for about a mile to Burnside Street. Broad and grassy, Waterfront Park's got a fine ground-level view of downtown Portland's bridges and skyline. Once an expressway, it's now the site for many events, among them the Rose Festival, classical and blues concerts, and the Oregon Brewers Festival. The four-day **Cinco de Mayo Festival** in early May celebrates Portland's sister-city relationship with Guadalajara, Mexico. Next to the Rose Festival, this is one of Portland's biggest get-togethers. Food and arts-and-crafts booths, stages with mariachi bands, and a carnival complete with a Ferris wheel line the riverfront for the event. Bikers and joggers enjoy the area year-round. The arching jets of water at the **Salmon Street Fountain** change configuration every few hours and are a favorite cooling-off spot during the dog days of summer. ✉ *S.W. Naito Pkwy. (Front Ave.) from south of Hawthorne Bridge to Burnside Bridge, Downtown.*

⓱ Justice Center. This modern building houses the jail, county courts, and police support offices. Visitors are welcome to browse the **Police Museum** (☎ *503/823–0019* ✏ *Free* ☉ *Tues.–Fri. 10–3*) on the 16th floor, which has uniforms, guns, and badges worn by the Portland Police Bureau. There's a security check to get in, and photo ID is required. ✉ *1111 S.W. 2nd Ave., Downtown.*

⓾ Keller Auditorium. Home base for the Portland Opera, the former Civic Auditorium also hosts traveling musicals and other theatrical extravaganzas. The building itself, part of the Portland Center for the Performing Arts, is not particularly distinctive, but the **Ira Keller Fountain,** a series of 18-foot-high stone waterfalls across from the front entrance, is worth a look. ⊠ *S.W. 3rd Ave. and Clay St., Downtown* ☎ *503/274–6560* ⊕ *www.pcpa.com.*

⑪ **KOIN Center.** An instant landmark after its completion in 1984, this handsome pink tower with a tapering form and a pyramidal top takes its design cues from early art deco skyscrapers. Made of brick with limestone trim and a blue metal roof, the tower has offices (including those of the CBS-TV affiliate and a radio station) and, on its top floors, expensive condominiums. ⊠ *S.W. Columbia St. and S.W. 3rd Ave., Downtown.*

⑮ **Mark O. Hatfield U.S. Courthouse.** The sophisticated exterior of this 1997 skyscraper is clad in Indiana limestone, and the courtroom lobbies have expansive glass walls. Whimsical bronze critters make light of the justice system in Tom Otterness's "Law of Nature," the centerpiece of a ninth-floor sculpture garden that has grand city views. Visitors must pass through a security screening and show photo ID. ⊠ *S.W. 3rd Ave. between Main and Salmon Sts., Downtown* ☜ *Free* ☉ *Weekdays.*

❼ **Old Church.** This building erected in 1882 is a prime example of Carpenter Gothic architecture. Tall spires and original stained-glass windows enhance its exterior of rough-cut lumber. The acoustically resonant church hosts free classical concerts at noon each Wednesday. If you're lucky you'll get to hear one of the few operating Hook and Hastings tracker pipe organs. ⊠ *1422 S.W. 11th Ave., Downtown* ☎ *503/222–2031* ⊕ *www.oldchurch.org* ☜ *Free* ☉ *Weekdays 11–3.*

❺ **Oregon Historical Society.** Impressive eight-story-high trompe ★ l'oeil murals of Lewis and Clark and the Oregon Trail cover two sides of this downtown museum, which follows the state's story from prehistoric times to the present. A pair of 9,000-year-old sagebrush sandals, a covered wagon, and an early chainsaw are displayed inside "Oregon My Oregon," a permanent exhibit that provides a comprehensive overview of the state's past. Other spaces host large traveling exhibits and changing regional shows. The center's research library is open to the public; its bookstore is a good source for maps and publications on Pacific Northwest history. Every month the Oregon Historical Society has a day on which kids are admitted for free. Check the Web site for dates. ⊠ *1200 S.W. Park Ave., Downtown* ☎ *503/222–1741* ⊕ *www.ohs.org* ☜ *$11* ☉ *Mon.–Sat. 10–5, Sun. noon–5.*

❶ Pioneer Courthouse Square. In many ways the living room, public heart, and commercial soul of downtown, Pioneer Square is not entirely square but rather centered in this amphitheatrical brick piazza. Special seasonal, charitable, and festival-oriented events often take place in this premier people-watching venue. On Sunday **vintage trolley** (☎ 503/323–7363) cars run from the MAX station here to Lloyd Center, with free service every half hour between noon and 6 PM. Call to check on the current schedule. You can pick up maps and literature about the city and the state here at the **Portland/Oregon Information Center** (☎ 503/275–8355 ⊕ *www.travelportland.com* ⊙ *Weekdays 8:30–5:30, Sat. 10–4, Sun. 10–2*). Directly across the street is one of downtown Portland's most familiar landmarks, the classically sedate **Pioneer Courthouse.** Built in 1869, it's the oldest public building in the Pacific Northwest. ✉ *701 S.W. 6th Ave., Downtown.*

❻ Portland Art Museum. The treasures at the Pacific Northwest's
★ oldest arts facility span 35 centuries of Asian, European, and American art. A high point is the Center for Native American Art, with regional and contemporary art from more than 200 tribes. The **Jubitz Center for Modern and Contemporary Art** contains six floors devoted entirely to modern art, with the changing selection chosen from than 400 pieces in the Museum's permanent collection. The film center presents the annual Portland International Film Festival in February and the Northwest Film Festival in early November. Also take a moment to linger in the peaceful outdoor sculpture garden. Kids under 18 are admitted free. ✉ *1219 S.W. Park Ave., Downtown* ☎ *503/226–2811, 503/221–1156 film schedule* ⊕ *www.pam.org* ✑ *$12* ⊙ *Tues., Wed., and Sat. 10–5, Thurs. and Fri. 10–8, Sun. noon–5.*

❷⓿ Portland Building. *Portlandia,* the second-largest hammered-copper statue in the world, surpassed only by the Statue of Liberty, kneels on the second-story balcony of one of the first postmodern buildings in the United States. Built in 1982 and architect Michael Graves's first major design commission, this 15-story office building is buff color, with brown-and-blue trim and exterior decorative touches. A huge fiberglass mold of Portlandia's face is exhibited in the second-floor Public Art Gallery, which provides a good overview of Portland's 1% for Art Program, and the hundreds of works on display throughout the city. ✉ *1120 S.W. 5th Ave., Downtown* ✑ *Free* ⊙ *Weekdays 8–6.*

3 Portland Center for the Performing Arts. The "old building" and the hub of activity here is the **Arlene Schnitzer Concert Hall,** host to the Oregon Symphony, musical events of many genres, and lectures. Across Main Street, but still part of the center, is the 292-seat **Delores Winningstad Theater,** used for plays and special performances. Its stage design and dimensions are based on those of an Elizabethan-era stage. The 916-seat **Newmark Theater** is also part of the complex. ⊠ *S.W. Broadway and S.W. Main St., Downtown* ☎ *503/274–6560* ⊕ *www.pcpa.com* ⊙ *Free tours Wed. at 11 AM, Sat. every ½ hr 11–1.*

9 Portland Farmer's Market. On Saturday from April through mid-December, local farmers, bakers, chefs, and entertainers converge at the South Park Blocks near the PSU campus for Oregon's largest open-air farmer's market. It's a great place to sample the regional bounty and to witness the local-food obsession that's revolutionized Portland's culinary scene. There's also a Wednesday market. ⊠ *South Park Blocks at S.W. Park Ave. and Montgomery St., Downtown* ☎ *503/241–0032* ⊕ *www.portlandfarmersmarket.org* ⊙ *Apr.–mid-Dec., Sat. 8:30–2; May–Oct., Wed. 10–2.*

8 Portland State University. The state's only university in a major metropolitan area takes advantage of downtown's South Park Blocks to provide trees and greenery for its 15,000 students. The compact campus, between Market Street and I–405, spreads west from the Park Blocks to 12th Avenue and east to 5th Avenue. Seven schools offer undergraduate, masters, and doctoral degrees. ⊠ *Park Ave. and Market St., Downtown* ☎ *503/725–3000* ⊕ *www.pdx.edu.*

18 Terry Schrunk Plaza. A terraced amphitheater of green lawn and brick, shaded by flowering cherry trees, the plaza is a popular lunch spot for the office crowd. Up by Southwest 4th Avenue there's a Suzhou stone, a valuable limestone boulder received as a sister-city gift from Suzhou, China. ⊠ *Between S.W. 3rd and 4th Aves. and S.W. Madison and Jefferson Sts., Downtown.*

14 World Trade Center. The three sleek, handsome World Trade Center buildings, designed by the Portland architectural firm Zimmer Gunsel Frasca, are connected by sky bridges. Banks, retail stores, a deli, coffee shops, and a hair salon occupy the ground floors. ⊠ *Salmon St. between S.W. 2nd Ave. and S.W. Naito Pkwy., Downtown.*

⑬ Yamhill National Historic District. Trains glide by many examples of 19th-century cast-iron architecture on the MAX line between the Skidmore and Yamhill stations, where the streets are closed to cars. Take a moment at the Yamhill station to glance around at these old buildings, which have intricate rooflines and facades. Nearby, on Southwest Naito Parkway at Taylor Street is **Mill Ends Park,** which sits in the middle of a traffic island. This patch of whimsy, at 24 inches in diameter, has been recognized by *Guinness World Records* as the world's smallest official city park. ⊠ *Between S.W. Naito Pkwy. and S.W. 3rd Ave. and S.W. Morrison and S.W. Taylor Sts., Downtown.*

THE BERRY BOTANIC GARDEN. There are no berries to pick at this public garden and research center, which contains an extraordinary collection of rare and native plants cultivated by accomplished gardener Rae Selling Berry. Tranquil paths wind through native plants, rhododendrons, and unusual alpine flora on the wooded 6¼-acre estate near Lewis & Clark College. Due to a local ordinance the garden can only receive visitors by appointment, so call a day ahead. ⊠ *15505 S.W. Summerville Ave., Downtown* ☎ *503/636–4112* ⊕ *www.berrybot.org* ⊠ *$5* ☉ *Daily by appointment only, dawn–dusk.*

PEARL DISTRICT AND OLD TOWN/ CHINATOWN

The Skidmore Old Town National Historic District, commonly called Old Town/Chinatown, is where Portland was born. The 20-square-block section, bounded by Oak Street to the south and Everett Street to the north, includes buildings of varying ages and architectural designs. Before it was renovated, this was skid row. Vestiges of it remain in parts of Chinatown; older buildings are slowly being remodeled and over the last several years the immediate area has experienced a surge in development. The Portland Classical Chinese Garden is also here. MAX serves the area with a stop at the Old Town/Chinatown station.

Bordering Old Town to the northwest is the Pearl District. Formerly a warehouse area along the railroad yards, the Pearl District is the fastest-growing part of Portland. Midrise residential lofts have sprouted on almost every block, and boutiques, outdoor retailers, galleries, and trendy restaurants border the streets. The Portland streetcar line passes through here on its way from Nob Hill to downtown and Portland State University, with stops at two new, ecologically themed city parks.

Numbers in the text correspond to numbers in the margin and on the Downtown, the Pearl District and Old Town/ Chinatown map.

2

WHAT TO SEE

㉖ Chinatown Gate. Recognizable by its 5 roofs, 64 dragons, and 2 huge lions, the Chinatown Gate is the official entrance to the **Chinatown District.** During the 1890s, Portland had the second-largest Chinese community in the United States. Today's Chinatown has shrunk to a handful of blocks with a few shops, grocery stores, and so-so restaurants (there are better places for Chinese outside the district). ⊠ *N.W. 4th Ave. and Burnside St., Old Town/Chinatown.*

㉙ Jamison Square Park. This gently terraced park surrounded by tony Pearl District lofts contains a soothing fountain that mimics nature. Rising water gushes over a stack of basalt blocks, gradually fills the open plaza, and then subsides. Colorful 30-foot tiki totems by pop artist Kenny Scharf stand along the park's west edge. Take the streetcar to Jamison Square. ⊠ *N.W. 10th Ave. and Lovejoy St., Pearl District.*

㉔ Japanese-American Historical Plaza. Take a moment to study the evocative figures cast into the bronze columns at the plaza's entrance; they show Japanese and Japanese-Americans before, during, and after World War II—living daily life, fighting in battle for the United States, and marching off to internment camps. Simple blocks of granite carved with haiku poems describing the war experience powerfully evoke this dark episode in American history. ⊠ *N.W. Naito Pkwy. and Davis St., in Waterfront Park, Old Town/ Chinatown.*

㉘ Jean Vollum Natural Capital Center. Known to most locals as the Ecotrust Building, this building has a handful of organic and environment-friendly businesses and other retail outlets, including Hot Lips Pizza, World Cup Coffee, and Patagonia (selling outdoor clothes). Built in 1895 and purchased by Ecotrust in 1998, the former warehouse has been adapted to serve as a landmark in sustainable, "green" building practices. Grab a "field guide" in the lobby and take the self-guided tour of the building, which begins with the original "remnant wall" on the west side of the parking lot; proceeds throughout the building; and ends on the "eco-roof," a grassy rooftop with a great view of the Pearl District. ✉ *721 N.W. 9th Ave., Pearl District* ☎ *503/227–6225* ⊕ *www.ecotrust.org/ncc* ✑ *Free* ☉ *Weekdays 7–6; ground-floor businesses also evenings and weekends.*

㉓ Oregon Maritime Museum. Local model makers created most
☾ of this museum's models of ships that once plied the Columbia River. Contained within the stern-wheeler steamship *Portland,* this small museum provides an excellent overview of Oregon's maritime history. ✉ *On steamship at end of S.W. Pine St., in Waterfront Park, Skidmore District* ☎ *503/224–7724* ⊕ *www.oregonmaritimemuseum.org* ✑ *$5* ☉ *Wed.–Sun. 11–4.*

★ **Fodor's Choice Portland Classical Chinese Garden.** In a twist on
㉕ the Joni Mitchell song, the city of Portland and private donors took down a parking lot and unpaved paradise when they created this wonderland near the Pearl District and Old Town/Chinatown. It's the largest Suzhou-style garden outside China, with a large lake, bridged and covered walkways, koi- and water lily–filled ponds, rocks, bamboo, statues, waterfalls, and courtyards. A team of 60 artisans and designers from China literally left no stone unturned—500 tons of stone were brought here from Suzhou—in their efforts to give the windows, roof tiles, gateways, including a "moongate," and other architectural aspects of the Garden some specific meaning or purpose. Also on the premises are a gift shop and a two-story teahouse overlooking the lake and garden. ✉ *N.W. 3rd Ave. and Everett St., Old Town/Chinatown* ☎ *503/228–8131* ⊕ *www.portlandchinesegarden.org* ✑ *$8.50* ☉ *Nov.–Mar., daily 10–5; Apr.–Oct., daily 10–6. Tours daily at noon and 1.*

★ **Fodor's Choice Portland Saturday Market.** On weekends from
㉒ March to Christmas, the west side of the Burnside Bridge and the Skidmore Fountain area has North America's largest open-air handicraft market. If you're looking for jewelry, yard art, housewares, and decorative goods made from every material under the sun, then there's an amazing collection of talented works on display here. Entertainers and food and produce booths add to the festive feel. ✉ *Under west end of Burnside Bridge, from S.W. Naito Pkwy. to Ankeny Sq., Skidmore District* ☎ *503/222–6072* ⊕ *www.saturdaymarket.org* ☉ *Mar.–Dec., Sat. 10–5, Sun. 11–4:30.*

★ **Fodor's**Choice **Powell's City of Books.** The largest independent
❸❶ bookstore in the world, with more than 1.5 million new and
used books, this Portland landmark can easily consume several hours. It's so big it has its own map, and rooms are
color-coded according to the types of books, so you can find
your way out again. Be sure to look for the pillar bearing
signatures of prominent sci-fi authors who have passed
through the store—the scrawls are protected by a jagged
length of Plexiglas. At the very least, stop into Powell's for a
peek or grab a cup of coffee at the adjoining branch of World
Cup Coffee. ⊠ *1005 W. Burnside St., Pearl District* ☎ *503/228–
4651* ⊕ *www.powells.com* ☉ *Daily 9* AM–*11* PM.

❷❶ **Skidmore Fountain.** This unusually graceful fountain, built
in 1888, is the centerpiece of **Ankeny Square,** a plaza
around which the Portland Saturday Market takes place.
Two nymphs uphold the brimming basin on top; citizens
once quenched their thirst from the spouting lions' heads
below, and horses drank from the granite troughs at the
base of the fountain. ⊠ *On MAX line at S.W. Ankeny St.
and 1st Ave., Skidmore District.*

❸❶ **Tanner Springs Park.** Tanner Creek, which once flowed
through the area, lends its name to Portland's newest park,
created in 2005. Today this creek flows underground, and
this quiet, manmade wetland and spring with alder groves
was built in the middle of the Pearl District as a reminder
of what the area was once like. ⊠ *N.W. 10th Ave. and
Marshall St., Pearl District.*

❷❼ **Union Station.** You can always find your way to Union Station by heading toward the huge neon GO BY TRAIN sign that
looms high above the station. The vast lobby area, with
high ceilings and marble floors, is worth a brief visit if you
hold any nostalgia for the heyday of train travel in the
United States. Amtrak trains stop here. ⊠ *800 N.W. 6th
Ave., Old Town/Chinatown.*

NOB HILL AND VICINITY

The showiest example of Portland's urban chic is Northwest
23rd Avenue—sometimes referred to with varying degrees
of affection as "trendy-third"—a 20-block thoroughfare
that cuts north–south through the neighborhood known as
Nob Hill. Fashionable since the 1880s and still filled with
Victorian houses, the neighborhood is a mixed-use cornu-
copia of old Portland charm and new Portland hip. With its

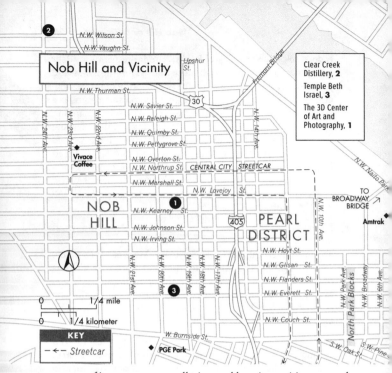

Nob Hill and Vicinity

Clear Creek
Distillery, **2**

Temple Beth
Israel, **3**

The 3D Center
of Art and
Photography, **1**

N.W. Wilson St.
N.W. Vaughn St.
N.W. Thurman St.
Upshur St.
N.W. Savier St.
N.W. Raleigh St.
N.W. Quimby St.
N.W. Pettygrove St.
N.W. Overton St.
Vivace Coffee
N.W. Northrup St.
CENTRAL CITY STREETCAR
N.W. Marshall St.
N.W. Lovejoy St.
NOB HILL
N.W. Kearney St.
N.W. Johnson St.
N.W. Irving St.
PEARL DISTRICT
N.W. Hoyt St.
N.W. Glisan St.
N.W. Flanders St.
N.W. Everett St.
N.W. Couch St.
W. Burnside St.
PGE Park

Fremont Bridge
N.W. Naito Pkwy.
TO BROADWAY BRIDGE
Amtrak
North Park Blocks
N.W. Park Ave.
N.W. Broadway
N.W. 6th Ave.
S.W. Oak St.
S.W. Pine

N.W. 24th Ave.
N.W. 23rd Ave.
N.W. 22nd Ave.
N.W. 21st Ave.
N.W. 20th Ave.
N.W. 19th Ave.
N.W. 18th Ave.
N.W. 17th Ave.
N.W. 14th Ave.
N.W. 10th Ave.

0   1/4 mile
0   1/4 kilometer

KEY
- ← - Streetcar

cafés, restaurants, galleries, and boutiques, it's a great place
to stroll, shop, and people-watch. More restaurants, shops,
and nightspots can be found on Northwest 21st Avenue, a
few blocks away. The Portland Streetcar runs from Legacy
Good Samaritan Hospital in Nob Hill, through the Pearl
District on 10th and 11th avenues, connects with MAX
light rail near Pioneer Courthouse Square downtown, and
then continues on to Portland State University and River-
Place on the Willamette River.

*Numbers in the text correspond to numbers in the margin
and on the Nob Hill and Vicinity map.*

WHAT TO SEE

❷ Clear Creek Distillery. The distillery keeps such a low profile
that it's practically invisible. But ring the bell and someone
will unlock the wrought-iron gate and let you into a dim,
quiet tasting room where you can sample Clear Creek's
world-famous Oregon apple and pear brandies and grap-
pas. ⊠*2389 N.W. Wilson, Nob Hill* ☎*503/248–9470*
⊕*www.clearcreekdistillery.com* ☉ *Weekdays 9–5, Sat.
11–5.*

NEED A BREAK? Vivace Coffee (⊠ *1400 N.W. 23rd Ave.* ☎ *503/228–3667*) is inside Pettygrove House, a restored Victorian gingerbread house built in 1892 that was once the home of Francis Pettygrove, the man who named Portland after winning a coin-toss. Today it's a creperie and coffeehouse with colorful walls and comfortable chairs.

❸ Temple Beth Israel. The imposing sandstone, brick, and stone structure with a massive domed roof and Byzantine styling was completed in 1928 and still serves a congregation first organized in 1858. ⊠ *1972 N.W. Flanders St., Nob Hill.*

❶ The 3D Center of Art and Photography. Half gallery and half museum, this center devoted to three-dimensional imagery exhibits photographs best viewed through red-and-blue glasses, in addition to artifacts on the history of stereoscopic art. A collection of rare Nazi-era stereocards is displayed next to View-Masters and 3-D snapshot cameras. A three-dimensional rendering of famous classical paintings is one of the many changing 3-D slide shows you might see in the backroom Stereo Theatre. ⊠ *1928 N.W. Lovejoy St., Nob Hill* ☎ *503/227–6667* ⊕ *www.3dcenter.us* ⊠ *$5* ☉ *Thurs.–Sat. 11–5, Sun. 1–5; also 1st Thurs. of month 6* PM*–9* PM.

WASHINGTON PARK AND FOREST PARK

The best way to get to Washington Park is via MAX light rail, which travels through a tunnel deep beneath the city's West Hills. Be sure to check out the Washington Park station, the deepest (260 feet) transit station in North America. Graphics on the walls depict life in the Portland area during the past 16.5 million years. There's also a core sample of the bedrock taken from the mountain displayed along the walls. Elevators to the surface put visitors in the parking lot for the Oregon Zoo, the World Forestry Center Discovery Museum, and the Children's Museum.

Numbers in the text correspond to numbers in the margin and on the Washington Park and Forest Park map.

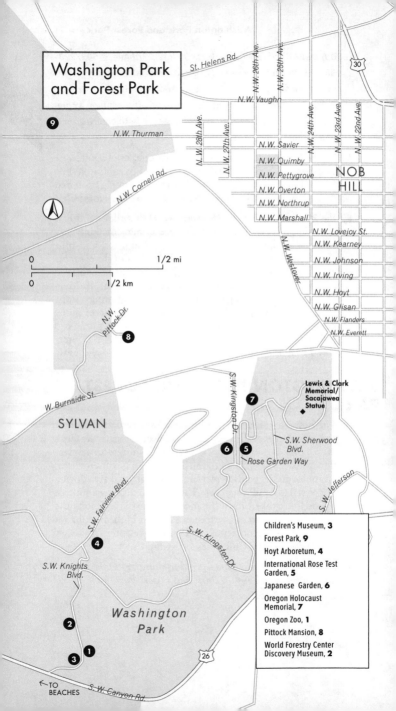

Washington Park and Forest Park

⑨

N.W. Thurman

N.W. Cornell Rd.

St. Helens Rd.

N.W. Vaughn

N.W. 28th Ave.
N.W. 27th Ave.
N.W. 26th Ave.
N.W. 25th Ave.
N.W. 24th Ave.
N.W. 23rd Ave.
N.W. 22nd Ave.

30

N.W. Savier
N.W. Quimby
N.W. Pettygrove
N.W. Overton
N.W. Northrup
N.W. Marshall

NOB
HILL

N.W. Lovejoy St.
N.W. Kearney
N.W. Johnson
N.W. Irving
N.W. Hoyt
N.W. Glisan
N.W. Flanders
N.W. Everett

N.W. Westover

0   1/2 mi
0   1/2 km

N.W. Pittock Dr.

⑧

W. Burnside St.

SYLVAN

S.W. Kingston Dr.

⑦

Lewis & Clark
Memorial/
Sacajawea
Statue

◆

S.W. Sherwood
Blvd.

⑥ ⑤

Rose Garden Way

S.W. Jefferson

S.W. Fairview Blvd.

④

S.W. Knights
Blvd.

S.W. Kingston Dr.

Washington
Park

②
③ ①

←TO
BEACHES

S.W. Canyon Rd.

26

Children's Museum, 3
Forest Park, 9
Hoyt Arboretum, 4
International Rose Test
Garden, 5
Japanese Garden, 6
Oregon Holocaust
Memorial, 7
Oregon Zoo, 1
Pittock Mansion, 8
World Forestry Center
Discovery Museum, 2

WHAT TO SEE

❸ Children's Museum. Colorful sights and sounds offer a feast
of sensations for kids of all ages where hands-on play is
the order of the day. Visit nationally touring exhibits, catch
a storytime, a sing-along, or a puppet show in the Play It
Again theater, create sculptures in the clay studio, splash
hands in the water works display, or make a creation from
junk in the Garage. To reach the museum's complex, take
the "Zoo" exit off U.S. 26. ⊠ *4015 S.W. Canyon Rd., Washington Park* ☎ *503/223–6500* ⊕ *www.portlandcm.org* ⊠ *$8*
⊙ *Tues.–Sat. 9–5, Sun. 11–5.*

❾ Forest Park. At 5,000 acres the nation's largest urban wilderness, this city-owned park, with more than 50 species of
birds and mammals, has more than 70 mi of trails. Running the length of the park is the 24½-mi Wildwood Trail,
which extends into Washington Park. The 11-mi Leif Erikson Drive, which picks up from the end of Northwest
Thurman Street, is a popular place to jog or ride a mountain
bike. The **Portland Audubon Society** (⊠ *5151 N.W. Cornell
Rd.* ☎ *503/292–6855*) supplies free maps and sponsors a
flock of bird-related activities, including guided bird-watching events. There's a hospital for injured and orphaned
birds as well as a gift shop stocked with books and feeders.
⊠ *Past Nob Hill in Northwest district. Take N.W. Lovejoy
St. west to where it becomes Cornell Rd. and follow to
park* ☎ *503/823–7529* ⊠ *Free* ⊙ *Daily dawn–dusk.*

❹ Hoyt Arboretum. Ten miles of trails wind through the arboretum, which has more than 1,000 species of plants and
one of the nation's largest collections of coniferous trees;
pick up trail maps at the visitor center. Also here are the
Winter Garden and a memorial to veterans of the Vietnam
War. ⊠ *4000 S.W. Fairview Blvd., Washington Park*
☎ *503/865-8733* ⊕ *www.hoytarboretum.org* ⊠ *Free* ⊙ *Arboretum daily dawn–dusk, visitor center daily 9–4.*

❺ International Rose Test Garden. Despite the name, these
★ grounds are not an experimental greenhouse laboratory
but three terraced gardens, set on 4 acres, where 10,000
bushes and 400 varieties of roses grow. The flowers, many
of them new varieties, are at their peak in June, July, September, and October. From the gardens, you can see highly
photogenic views of the downtown skyline and, on fine
days, the Fuji-shaped slopes of Mt. Hood, 50 mi to the
east. Summer concerts take place in the garden's amphitheater. Take MAX light rail to Washington Park station

and transfer to Bus No. 63. ⊠ *400 S.W. Kingston Ave., Washington Park* ☎ *503/823–3636* ⊕ *www.rosegardenstore. org* ⚑ *Free* ☉ *Daily dawn–dusk.*

★ **Fodor's Choice Japanese Garden.** The most authentic Japanese
❻ garden outside Japan takes up 5½ acres of Washington Park above the International Rose Test Garden. This serene spot, designed by a Japanese landscape master, represents five separate garden styles: Strolling Pond Garden, Tea Garden, Natural Garden, Sand and Stone Garden, and Flat Garden. The Tea House was built in Japan and reconstructed here. The west side of the Pavilion has a majestic view of Portland and Mt. Hood. Take MAX light rail to Washington Park station and transfer to Bus No. 63. ⊠ *611 S.W. Kingston Ave., Washington Park* ☎ *503/223–1321* ⊕ *www.japanesegarden.com* ⚑ *$8* ☉ *Oct.–Mar., Mon. noon–4, Tues.–Sun. 10–4; Apr.–Sept., Mon. noon–7, Tues.– Sun. 10–7.*

❼ **Oregon Holocaust Memorial.** This memorial to those who perished during the Holocaust bears the names of surviving families who live in Oregon and Southwest Washington. A bronzed baby shoe, a doll, broken spectacles, and other strewn possessions await notice on the cobbled courtyard. Soil and ash from six Nazi concentration camps is interred beneath the black granite wall. Take MAX light rail to Washington Park station, and transfer to Bus No. 63. ⊠ *S.W. Wright Ave. and Park Pl., Washington Park* ☎ *503/245– 2733* ⊕ *www.ohrconline.org* ⚑ *Free* ☉ *Daily dawn–dusk.*

❶ **Oregon Zoo.** This beautiful animal park in the West Hills is
☺ famous for its Asian elephants. Major exhibits include an
★ African section with rhinos, hippos, zebras, and giraffes. Steller Cove, a state-of-the-art aquatic exhibit, has two Steller sea lions and a family of sea otters. Other exhibits include polar bears, chimpanzees, an Alaska Tundra exhibit with wolves and grizzly bears, a penguin house, and habitats for beavers, otters, and reptiles native to the west side of the Cascade Range. In summer a 4-mi round-trip narrow-gauge train operates from the zoo, chugging through the woods to a station near the International Rose Test Garden and the Japanese Garden. Take the MAX light rail to the Washington Park station. ⊠ *4001 S.W. Canyon Rd., Washington Park* ☎ *503/226–1561* ⊕ *www.oregonzoo.org* ⚑ *$10.50, $2 2nd Tues. of month* ☉ *Mid-Apr.–mid-Sept., daily 9–6; mid-Sept.–mid Apr., daily 9–4.*

2

❽ Pittock Mansion. Henry Pittock, the founder and publisher
★ of the *Oregonian* newspaper, built this 22-room, castlelike
mansion, which combines French Renaissance and Victorian styles. The opulent manor, built in 1914, is filled with
art and antiques. The 46-acre grounds, north of Washington
Park and 1,000 feet above the city, have superb views of
the skyline, rivers, and the Cascade Range. There's a teahouse and a small hiking trail. ✉ *3229 N.W. Pittock Dr.,
from W. Burnside St. heading west, turn right on N.W.
Barnes Rd. and follow signs, North of Washington Park*
☎ *503/823–3623* ⊕ *www.pittockmansion.com* 🎫 *$7* ⊗ *June–
Aug., daily 11–4; Sept.–Dec. and Feb.–May, daily
noon–4.*

❾ World Forestry Discovery Center Museum. Visitors will find
☾ interactive and multimedia exhibits that teach forest sustainability. A white-water raft ride, smoke-jumper training
simulator, and Timberjack tree harvester all provide different perspectives on Pacific Northwest forests. On the
second floor the forests of the world are explored in various travel settings. A canopy lift ride hoists visitors to the
50-foot ceiling to look at a Douglas fir. A $1 parking fee
is collected upon entry. Or take MAX light rail to the
Washington Park station. ✉ *4033 S.W. Canyon Rd., Washington Park* ☎ *503/228–1367* ⊕ *www.worldforestry.org*
🎫 *$8* ⊗ *Daily 10–5.*

EAST OF THE WILLAMETTE RIVER

Portland is known as the City of Roses, but the 10 distinctive bridges spanning the Willamette River have also
earned it the name Bridgetown. The older drawbridges,
near downtown, open several times a day to allow passage
of large cargo ships and freighters. You can easily spend a
couple of days exploring the attractions and areas on the
east side of the river.

*Numbers in the text correspond to numbers in the margin
and on the East of the Willamette River map.*

WHAT TO SEE

❻ Crystal Springs Rhododendron Garden. For much of the year
this 7-acre retreat near Reed College is frequented mainly
by bird-watchers and those who want a restful stroll. But
starting in April, thousands of rhododendron bushes and
azaleas burst into flower. The peak blooming season for

these woody shrubs is May; by late June the show is over. ✉ *S.E. 28th Ave., west side, 1 block north of Woodstock Blvd., Sellwood/Woodstock area* ☏ *503/771–8386* ⊕ *www. portlandonline.com* 🎫 *$3 Mar.–Labor Day, Thurs.–Mon. 10–6; otherwise free* ☉ *Daily dawn–dusk.*

NEED A BREAK? At the **Bagdad Theatre and Pub** (✉ *3702 S.E. Hawthorne Blvd., Hawthorne District* ☏ *503/236–9234*) you can buy a pint of beer, a slice of pizza, and watch a movie in large classic theater complete with dining tables.

❸ **Hawthorne District.** This neighborhood stretching from the foot of Mt. Tabor to 30th Avenue attracts a more college-age, bohemian, crowd than downtown or Nob Hill. With many bookstores, coffeehouses, taverns, restaurants, antiques stores, and boutiques filling the streets, it's easy to spend a few hours wandering. ✉ *S.E. Hawthorne Blvd. between 30th and 42nd Aves., Hawthorne District.*

❺ **Laurelhurst Park.** Manicured lawns, stately trees, and a wild-fowl pond make this 25-acre southeast Portland park a favorite urban hangout. **Laurelhurst,** one of the city's most beautiful neighborhoods, surrounds the park. ✉ *S.E. 39th Ave. between S.E. Ankeny and Oak Sts., Laurelhurst* ⊕ *www.portlandparks.org* ☉ *Daily dawn–dusk.*

❹ **Mt. Tabor Park.** Dirt trails and asphalt roads wind through forested hillsides and past good picnic areas to the top of Mt. Tabor, an extinct volcano with a panoramic view of Portland's West Hills and Cascade mountains. This butte and the conical hills east of the park are evidence of the gigantic eruptions that formed the Cascade Range millions of years ago. One of the best places in the city to watch the sunset, the park is also a popular place to bike, hike, picnic, or just throw a Frisbee. ✉ *S.E. 60th Ave. and Salmon St., just east of Hawthorne District* ⊕ *www.portlandonline.com* ☉ *Daily dawn–dusk.*

THE GROTTO. Owned by the Catholic Church, the National Sanctuary of Our Sorrowful Mother, as it's officially known, displays more than 100 statues and shrines in 62 acres of woods. The grotto was carved into the base of a 110-foot cliff and has a replica of Michelangelo's *Pietà*. The real treat is found after ascending the cliff face via elevator, as you enter a wonderland of gardens, sculptures, and shrines, and a glass-walled cathedral with an awe-inspiring view of the Columbia River and the Cascades.

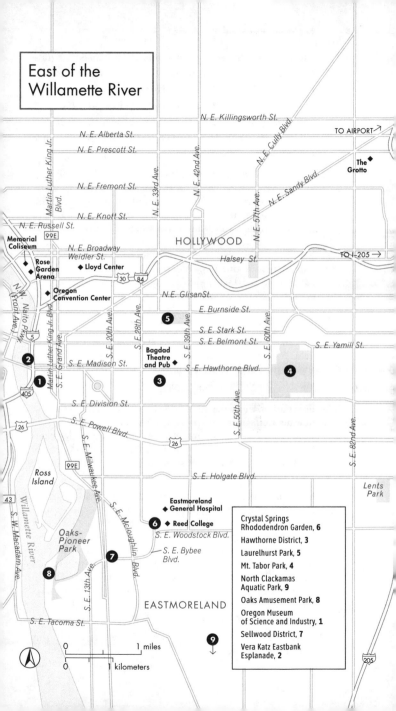

East of the Willamette River

N. E. Killingsworth St.

TO AIRPORT →

N. E. Alberta St.

N. E. Prescott St.

The Grotto

N. E. Fremont St.

N. E. Knott St.

N. E. Russell St.

99E

Martin Luther King Jr. Blvd.

Memorial Coliseum

Rose Garden Arena

HOLLYWOOD

N. E. Broadway

Weidler St.

Lloyd Center

Halsey St.

TO I-205 →

Oregon Convention Center

30 84

N.E. Glisan St.

E. Burnside St.

5

S. E. Stark St.

S. E. Belmont St.

S. E. Yamill St.

Bagdad Theatre and Pub

S. E. Madison St.

3

S. E. Hawthorne Blvd.

4

2

1

405

S. E. Division St.

S. E. Powell Blvd.

26

26

S. E. Holgate Blvd.

Lents Park

43

Ross Island

99E

Oaks-Pioneer Park

Eastmoreland General Hospital

6 Reed College

S. E. Woodstock Blvd.

7

S. E. Bybee Blvd.

8

EASTMORELAND

S. E. Tacoma St.

9

0   1 miles

0   1 kilometers

N. E. 33rd Ave.
N. E. 42nd Ave.
N. E. 57th Ave.
N. E. Cully Blvd.
N. E. Sandy Blvd.
S. E. Grand Ave.
S. E. 20th Ave.
S. E. 28th Ave.
S. E. 39th Ave.
S. E. 60th Ave.
S. E. 50th Ave.
S. E. 82nd Ave.
S. E. Milwaukie Ave.
S. E. McLoughlin Blvd.
S. E. 13th Ave.
S. W. Macadam Ave.
Willamette River
N. W. Naito Pkwy. (Front Ave.)

205

Crystal Springs Rhododendron Garden, **6**

Hawthorne District, **3**

Laurelhurst Park, **5**

Mt. Tabor Park, **4**

North Clackamas Aquatic Park, **9**

Oaks Amusement Park, **8**

Oregon Museum of Science and Industry, **1**

Sellwood District, **7**

Vera Katz Eastbank Esplanade, **2**

There's a dazzling Festival of Lights at Christmastime (late November and December), with 250,000 lights, and holiday concerts in the 600-seat chapel. Sunday masses are held here, too. ✉ *Sandy Blvd. at N.E. 85th Ave., Near Airport* ☎ *503/254–7371* ⊕ *www.thegrotto.org* ✐ *Plaza level free; elevator to upper level $3* ☾ *Mid-May–Labor Day, daily 9–8:30; Labor Day–late Nov. and Feb.–mid-May, daily 9–5:30; late Nov.–Jan., daily 9–4.*

❾ North Clackamas Aquatic Park. If you're visiting Portland with ☙ kids and are looking for a great way to cool off—especially on one of Portland's hot July or August days—check out this 45,000-square-foot, all-indoor attraction, whose main pool has 4-foot waves and three super slides. There's also a 25-yard-long lap pool, a wading pool, an adults-only hot whirlpool, and a café. Children under age 8 must be accompanied by someone 13 or older. ✉ *7300 S.E. Harmony Rd., Milwaukie* ☎ *503/557–7873* ⊕ *www.clackamas.us/ncprd/ aquatic* ✐ *$9.99* ☾ *Open swim mid-June–Labor Day, weekdays noon–4 and 7–9, weekends 11–3 and 4–8; Labor Day–mid-June, Sat. noon–7, Sun. noon–5.*

North Mississippi Avenue. Four blocks of old storefronts reinvented as cafés, collectives, shops, and music venues along this north Portland street showcase the indie spirit of the city's do-it-yourselfers and creative types. Bioswale planter boxes, found-object fences, and café tables built from old doors are some of the innovations you'll see around this hip new district. At the hub of it all is the ReBuilding Center, an outlet for recycled building supplies that has cob (clay-and-straw) trees and benches built into the facade. Take MAX light rail to the Albina/Mississippi station. ✉ *Between N. Fremont and Shaver Sts., off N. Interstate Ave.*

Northeast Alberta Street. Quirky handicrafts by local artists are for sale inside the galleries, studios, coffeehouses, restaurants, and boutiques lining this street in the northeast Portland neighborhood. It's a fascinating place to witness the intersection of cultures and lifestyles in a growing city. Shops unveil new exhibits during an evening event called the Last Thursday Art Walk. The Alberta Street Fair in September showcases the area with arts-and-crafts displays and street performances. ✉ *Between Martin Luther King Jr. Blvd. and 30th Ave., Alberta District.*

❽ Oaks Amusement Park. There's a small-town charm to this ☙ park that has bumper cars, thrill rides and roller-skating year-round. A 360-degree loop roller coaster and other high-velocity, gravity-defying contraptions border the mid-way, along with a carousel and Ferris wheel. The skating rink, built in 1905, is the oldest continuously operating one in the United States, and features a working Wurlitzer organ. There are outdoor concerts in summer. ⊠ *S.E. Spokane St. east of Willamette River; from S.E. Tacoma St. on east side of Sellwood Bridge, take S.E. 6th Ave. north and Spokane west, Sellwood* ☎ *503/233–5777* ⊕ *www.oakspark. com* ✇ *Park free, multiride bracelets $11.75–$14, individual-ride tickets $2.25* ⊙ *Mid-June–Labor Day, Tues.–Thurs. noon–9, Fri. and Sat. noon–10, Sun. noon–7; late-Apr.–mid-June and Labor Day–Oct., weekends noon–7; late-Mar.–late-Apr., weekends noon–5.*

❶ Oregon Museum of Science and Industry (*OMSI*). Hundreds of hands-on exhibits draw families to this interactive science museum, which also has an Omnimax theater and the Northwest's largest planetarium. The many permanent and touring exhibits are loaded with enough hands-on play for kids to fill a whole day exploring robotics, ecology, rockets, computers, animation, and outer space. Moored in the Willamette as part of the museum is a 240-foot submarine, the USS *Blueback*, which can be toured for an extra charge. ⊠ *1945 S.E. Water Ave., south of Morrison Bridge, under Hawthorne Bridge* ☎ *503/797–4000 or 800/955–6674* ⊕ *www.omsi.edu* ✇ *Full package $21, museum $11, planetarium $5.75, Omnimax $8.50, submarine $5.75* ⊙ *Mid-June–Labor Day, daily 9:30–7; Labor Day–mid-June, daily 9:30–5:30.*

❼ Sellwood District. The pleasant neighborhood that begins east of the Sellwood Bridge was once a separate town. Annexed by Portland in the 1890s, it retains a modest charm. On weekends the antiques stores along 13th Avenue do a brisk business. Each store is identified by a plaque that tells the date of construction and the original purpose of the building. More antiques stores, specialty shops, and restaurants are near the intersection of Milwaukie and Bybee. ⊠ *S.E. 13th Ave. between Malden and Clatsop Sts., Sellwood.*

❷ Vera Katz Eastbank Esplanade. A stroll along this 1½-mi pedestrian and cycling path across from downtown is one of the best ways to experience the Willamette River and Portland's bridges close-up. Built in 2001 the esplanade runs along the east bank of the Willamette River between the Hawthorne and Steele bridges, and features a 1,200-

foot walkway that floats atop the river, a boat dock, and public art. Pedestrian crossings on both bridges link the esplanade to Waterfront Park, making a 3-mi loop. Take MAX light rail to the Rose Quarter station. ⊠ *Parking at east end of Hawthorne Bridge, between Madison and Salmon Sts.*

Where to Eat

WORD OF MOUTH

"I tried Andina for the first time and LOVED it (Peruvian food, VERY popular) and also had lunch at Park Kitchen which I liked a lot as well (NW, eclectic). And the pastrami at Kenny & Zukes, which is right near Powell's, is absolutely fantastic (this is coming from an ex NY-er)."

—NWWanderer

Updated
by Janna
Mock-
Lopez

THESE DAYS, RISING-STAR CHEFS are flocking to Portland. In this playground of sustainability and creativity, lots of the city's hottest restaurants change menus weekly—sometimes even daily—depending upon the ingredients they have delivered to their door that morning from local farms. A combination of fertile soils, temperate weather, nearby waters, and an urban growth boundary means that a bountiful harvest (be it lettuces or hazelnuts, mushrooms or salmon) is within any chef's reach.

And these chefs are not shy about putting new twists on old favorites. Restaurants like Le Pigeon (yes, they serve "squab"), Beast, 50 Plates, Hoyt 23, and Paley's Place have all taken culinary risks by presenting an exciting blend of menu offerings based on sustainable ingredients. Because there's such a near-fanatical willingness for chefs to explore their creative boundaries, one's palate hardly knows what to expect from restaurant to restaurant, season to season.

The other benefit of this culinary craze is that menus extend across nations and continents. First-time visitors to Portland always seem to be impressed by the diversity of its restaurants. Lovers of ethnic foods have their pick of Chinese, French, Indian, Peruvian, Italian, Japanese, Polish, Middle Eastern, Tex-Mex, Thai, and Vietnamese specialties. Of course, Northwest cuisine is prevalent, taking advantage of the availability of fresh salmon, halibut, crab, oysters, and mussels from the rivers and the Pacific Ocean.

Most of the city's trendier restaurants and reliable classics are concentrated in Nob Hill, the Pearl District, and downtown. But a smattering of cuisines can also be found on the east side of town as well, near Fremont, Hawthorne Boulevard, Sandy Boulevard, Alberta Street, and tucked away in many neighborhoods in between. True food enthusiasts will be well rewarded by doing a little research to find some of the out-of-the-way places.

HOURS, PRICES, AND DRESS

Compared to other major cities, Portland restaurants aren't open quite as late, and it's unusual to see many diners after 11 PM even on weekends, though there are a handful of restaurants and popular bars that do serve late if you happen to be out on the town.

One aspect to Portland's dining scene that many locals and out-of-towners find appealing is how reasonably priced topnotch restaurants are. Particularly welcome in Portland

PORTLAND DINING BEST BETS

★ Fodor's Choice
Andina, El Gaucho, 50 Plates, Gracie's, Lemongrass

CHILD-FRIENDLY
Belly Restaurant, Kornblatt's, McMenamins Kennedy School Courtyard Restaurant, Mother's Bistro, Pastini

GOOD FOR GROUPS
Doug Fir, Lemongrass, Rheinlander, Serratto

HOT SPOTS
50 Plates, Andina, Departure

BEST HAPPY HOUR
23 Hoyt, Bo Restobar, Saucebox

ROMANTIC MEAL
Blue Hour, Gracie's, Salty's

SPECIAL OCCASION
El Gaucho, Genoa, Portland City Grill

3

is happy hour, when both inventive cocktails as well as small plates of food can be a good value; you can easily put together a fine early dinner by grazing from the happy hour menu at a restaurant that also has a bar scene.

In Portland, many diners dress casually for even higher-end establishments—a proclivity that's refreshing to some and annoying to others. In any case, jeans are acceptable almost everywhere.

WHAT IT COSTS				
¢	$	$$	$$$	$$$$
RESTAURANTS				
under $10	$10–$15	$16–$20	$21–$30	over $30

Restaurant prices are per person for a main course at dinner and do not include any service charges or taxes.

DOWNTOWN

Finding a fabulous place to dine downtown is almost as easy as closing your eyes and pointing on the map. One thing visitors appreciate about lunch downtown is the plethora of food carts lining the streets. Smells of Greek, Russian, Japanese, Lebanese, and Mexican food permeate the air as the noon hour approaches. Lines of workers hover

Where to Eat in Downtown Portland

KEY
—O— Max Light Rail
—←— Streetcar

Willamette River

NOB HILL

OLD TOWN

PEARL DISTRICT

Chinatown Gate

Civic Stadium

Portland Art Museum

Portland State University

Memorial Coliseum

Amtrak Station

Tom McCall Waterfront Park

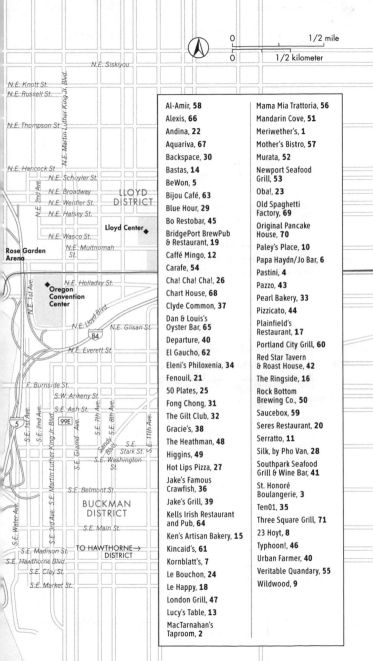

N.E. Siskiyou

N.E. Knott St.
N.E. Russell St.

N.E. Thompson St

N.E. Hancock St.
N.E. Schuyler St.
N.E. Broadway
N.E. Weidler St.
N.E. Halsey St.

LLOYD
DISTRICT

Lloyd Center

N.E. Wasco St.
N.E. Multnomah St.

Rose Garden
Arena

N.E. Holladay St.
Oregon
Convention
Center

N.E. Lloyd Blvd.
N.E. Glisan St.

N.E. Everett St.

E. Burnside St.
S.W. Ankeny St.
S.E. Ash St.

The Gilt Club, **32**

S.E. Stark St.
S.E. Washington St.

S.E. Belmont St.

BUCKMAN
DISTRICT

S.E. Main St.

TO HAWTHORNE→
DISTRICT

S.E. Madison St.
S.E. Hawthorne Blvd.
S.E. Clay St.
S.E. Market St.

0 — 1/2 mile
0 — 1/2 kilometer

Al-Amir, **58**
Alexis, **66**
Andina, **22**
Aquariva, **67**
Backspace, **30**
Bastas, **14**
BeWon, **5**
Bijou Café, **63**
Blue Hour, **29**
Bo Restobar, **45**
BridgePort BrewPub & Restaurant, **19**
Caffé Mingo, **12**
Carafe, **54**
Cha! Cha! Cha!, **26**
Chart House, **68**
Clyde Common, **37**
Dan & Louis's Oyster Bar, **65**
Departure, **40**
El Gaucho, **62**
Eleni's Philoxenia, **34**
Fenouil, **21**
50 Plates, **25**
Fong Chong, **31**
The Gilt Club, **32**
Gracie's, **38**
The Heathman, **48**
Higgins, **49**
Hot Lips Pizza, **27**
Jake's Famous Crawfish, **36**
Jake's Grill, **39**
Kells Irish Restaurant and Pub, **64**
Ken's Artisan Bakery, **15**
Kincaid's, **61**
Kornblatt's, **7**
Le Bouchon, **24**
Le Happy, **18**
London Grill, **47**
Lucy's Table, **13**
MacTarnahan's Taproom, **2**

Mama Mia Trattoria, **56**
Mandarin Cove, **51**
Meriwether's, **1**
Mother's Bistro, **57**
Murata, **52**
Newport Seafood Grill, **53**
Oba!, **23**
Old Spaghetti Factory, **69**
Original Pancake House, **70**
Paley's Place, **10**
Papa Haydn/Jo Bar, **6**
Pastini, **4**
Pazzo, **43**
Pearl Bakery, **33**
Pizzicato, **44**
Plainfield's Restaurant, **17**
Portland City Grill, **60**
Red Star Tavern & Roast House, **42**
The Ringside, **16**
Rock Bottom Brewing Co., **50**
Saucebox, **59**
Seres Restaurant, **20**
Serratto, **11**
Silk, by Pho Van, **28**
Southpark Seafood Grill & Wine Bar, **41**
St. Honoré Boulangerie, **3**
Ten01, **35**
Three Square Grill, **71**
23 Hoyt, **8**
Typhoon!, **46**
Urban Farmer, **40**
Veritable Quandary, **55**
Wildwood, **9**

around the makeshift kitchen trailers, waiting to get their fill of the inexpensive and authentic selection of food. For more info, check out one of the blogs about them (⊕ *www.foodcartsportland.com*), and for daily specials, check out the Twitter thread at @pdxfoodcarts.

$ ✕**Al-Amir.** *Middle Eastern.* After moving beyond this Middle Eastern restaurant's small front bar, you pass through an elaborately large and ornate gateway into a dark, stylish dining room. Choose between excellent broiled kebabs, falafel, hummus, tabbouleh, and baba ghanoush. There's live music and belly dancing on Friday and Saturday. ⊠ *223 S.W. Stark St.* ☎ *503/274–0010* ⊕ *www.alamirportland.com* ⊟ *AE, D, MC, V* ⊘ *No lunch weekends.*

¢ ✕**Bijou Cafe.** *American.* This spacious, sunny restaurant with high ceilings has some of the best breakfasts in town, and they're served all day: French-style crepes and oyster hash are both popular, as are fabulous pancakes and French toast. At lunch the breakfast dishes are joined by burgers, sandwiches, and soups. ⊠ *132 S.W. 3rd Ave., Downtown* ☎ *503/222–3187* ⊟ *MC, V* ⊘ *No dinner.*

$ ✕**Bo Restobar.** *Asian.* Combining the trend of tapas and chic cocktails, this hotel bar brings both to delicious heights. The stylish dark walls accented by colorful modern art create a sleek setting in which to sip a specialty martini made with some esoteric liquor. For nibbling, try the lemongrass clam chowder, the twice-cooked beef strips, or the "Koreadilla"— a quesadilla with spicy pork and goat cheese. ⊠ *Hotel Lucia, 400 S.W. Broadway, Downtown* ☎ *503/222–2688* ⊕ *www.borestobar.com* ⊟ *AE, DC, MC, V.*

$$ ✕**Carafe.** *French.* Straightforward French favorites and closeness to the Keller Auditorium make this quaint bistro a popular choice. Confit of albacore tuna niçoise served with heirloom tomatoes, haricots verts, and hard-boiled egg, as well as crispy duck leg confit with pickled apricots, squash ribbons, and balsamic, are a few of the dishes here. If you're in the mood for lighter fare, there are also plenty of pastas, sandwiches, and soups. Call ahead, especially if there's a show going on at the Keller. ⊠ *200 S.W. Market St.* ☎ *503/248–0004* ⊕ *www.carafebistro.com* ⊟ *AE, DC, MC, V* ⊘ *Closed Sun.*

$ ✕**Clyde Common.** *Continental.* If you want to experience "community," then this bustling, contemporary spot is for you. Visitors from all walks of life—politicians, quasi-celebrities, socialites, the hip and trendy, straight and gay— eat here. Big communal tables dominate the space, which means you'll never know who you'll end up sitting next to or what interesting conversations you may have. The open kitchen allows you to see what's going on from any vantage point. The edgy menu includes frogs' legs, chicken livers, and sardines, accompanied by a host of interesting ingredients such as horseradish, nettles, and refried peanuts. There's no shortage of invention on the drink menu, either: try the "Ace Gibson" with Medoyeff vodka and house pickled onion, or the "Anemic Mary" with serrano chili and sun-dried tomato vodka, celery juice, and sour mix. *Ace Hotel ⊠ 1014 S.W. Stark St., Downtown ☎ 503/228–3333 ⊕ www.clydecommon.com ⊟ AE, D, MC, V.*

$ ✕**Dan & Louis's Oyster Bar.** *Seafood.* Oysters at this Portland landmark near the river come fried, stewed, or on the half shell. The clam chowder is tasty, but the crab stew is a rare treat. Combination dinners let you mix your fried favorites. The collection of steins, plates, and marine art has grown since the restaurant opened in 1907 to fill beams, nooks, crannies, and nearly every inch of wall. ⊠ *208 S.W. Ankeny St., Downtown ☎ 503/227–5906 ⊕ www.danandlouis.com ⊟ AE, D, DC, MC, V.*

$–$$ ✕**Departure.** *Japanese.* If you want to sink into a swanky restaurant that could just as easily be in a much bigger city, then Departure is for you. The interior is over-the-top lush, and a scenic highlight for locals and visitors alike is the outdoor rooftop lounge, with gorgeous views of the city. The food is artfully prepared; most dishes, such as the Hamachi sashimi and calamari tempura come in smallish but flavorful portions. The fried ginger ice cream, for instance, is served with panko bread crumbs, sesame seeds, and powdered sugar. ⊠ *525 S.W. Morrison St., Downtown ☎ 503/802–5370 ⊕ www.departureportland.com ⊟ AE, MC, V ⊗ Closed Sun. and Mon. No lunch.*

★ **Fodor's**Choice ✕**El Gaucho.** *Steak.* Three dimly lit dining rooms
$$$$ with blue walls and striped upholstery are an inviting place for those with healthy wallets. The specialty here is 28-day, dry-aged, certified Angus beef, but chops, ribs, and chicken entrées are also cooked in the open kitchen. The chateaubriand for two is carved tableside. Seafood lovers might want to try the tomato fennel bouillabaisse. Service is impeccable at this Seattle transplant in the elegant Benson Hotel. Each night live Latin guitar music serenades the dinner guests. ⊠ *319 S.W. Broadway, Downtown ☎ 503/227–8794 ⊕ www.elgaucho.com ⊟ AE, DC, MC, V ⊗ No lunch.*

★ Fodor'sChoice ✕**Gracie's.** *American.* Stepping into this dining
$$$ room is like stepping into a prestigious 1940s supper club.
Dazzling chandeliers, beautifully rich floor-to-ceiling drap-
eries, velvet couches, and marble-topped tables exude class.
Dishes like grilled swordfish and stuffed pork loin are per-
fectly seasoned and served with seasonal vegetables. On
weekends, there's a brunch menu that includes fresh fruit,
waffles, and omelets. ⊠ *Hotel DeLuxe, 729 S.W. 15th Ave.,
Downtown* ☎ *503/222–2171* ⊕ *www.graciesdining.com*
⊟ *AE, D, MC, V.*

$$$ ✕**The Heathman.** *Continental.* Chef Philippe Boulot revels
in fresh ingredients of the Pacific Northwest. His menu
changes with the season and includes entrées made with
grilled and braised fish, fowl, veal, lamb, and beef. Among
the chef's Northwest specialties are a delightful Dungeness
crab, mango, and avocado salad and a paella made with
mussels, clams, shrimp, scallops, and chorizo. Equally
creative choices are available for breakfast and lunch. The
dining room, scented with wood smoke and adorned with
Andy Warhol prints, is a favorite for special occasions.
⊠ *Heathman Hotel, 1001 S.W. Broadway, Downtown*
☎ *503/790–7752* ⊟ *AE, D, DC, MC, V.*

$$$ ✕**Higgins.** *French.* Chef Greg Higgins, former executive chef
at the Heathman Hotel, focuses on ingredients from the
Pacific Northwest and on organically grown herbs and
produce while incorporating traditional French cooking
styles and other international influences into his menu.
Start with a salad of warm beets, asparagus, and artichokes
or the country-style terrine of venison, chicken, and pork
with dried sour cherries and a roasted-garlic mustard. Main
courses, which change seasonally, might include dishes
made with Alaskan spot prawns, halibut, duck, or pork
loin. Vegetarian items are available. A bistro menu is avail-
able in the adjoining bar, where comfortable leather booths
and tables provide an alternative to the main dining room.
⊠ *1239 S.W. Broadway, Downtown* ☎ *503/222–9070*
⊟ *AE, D, DC, MC, V* ☉ *No lunch weekends.*

$$$ ✕**Jake's Famous Crawfish.** *Seafood.* Diners have been enjoy-
ing fresh Pacific Northwest seafood in Jake's warren of
wood-paneled dining rooms for more than a century. The
back bar came around Cape Horn during the 1880s, and
the chandeliers hanging from the high ceilings date from
1881. The restaurant gained a national reputation in 1920
when crawfish was added to the menu. White-coat waiters
take your order from an almost endless sheet of daily seafood specials year-round, but try to come during crawfish

season (May–September), when you can sample the tasty crustacean in pie, cooked Creole style, or in a Cajun-style stew over rice. ✉ *401 S.W. 12th Ave., Downtown* ☎ *503/226–1419* ⊕ *www.mccormickandschmicks.com* ▭ *AE, D, DC, MC, V* ⊘ *No lunch Sun.*

$$$ ✕**Jake's Grill.** *American.* Not to be confused with the Jake's of seafood fame, although they do share the same owners, this eatery in the Governor Hotel has more turf than surf. Steaks and the Sunday brunch are popular draws. Private booths with green velvet curtains make for a cozy, intimate dinner. The bar is famous for its Bloody Marys. ✉ *611 S.W. 10th Ave., Downtown* ☎ *503/220–1850* ⊕ *www.mccormickandschmicks.com* ▭ *AE, D, DC, MC, V.*

$ ✕**Kells Irish Restaurant and Pub.** *Irish.* Step into cool, dark Kells for a pint of Guinness and such authentic pub fare as fish-and-chips, Guinness stew, shepherd's pie, and Irish soda bread. Burgers and vegetarian sandwiches round out the bar menu, and there's breakfast on weekends. Live Irish music performers play every night of the week. Be sure to ask the bartender how all those folded-up dollar bills got stuck to the ceiling. ✉ *112 S.W. 2nd Ave.* ☎ *503/227–4057* ⊕ *www.kellsirish.com* ▭ *AE, D, MC, V.*

$$$ ✕**Kincaid's.** *Steak.* Expensive cuts of steak and prime rib are the draw at this steak house in the Embassy Suites hotel. The menu includes wood-fired pizzas, pasta, and café meals. Surf lovers can choose the Hawaiian tuna, cioppino, or seafood linguine. The bar menu draws a loyal happy-hour crowd. ✉ *121 S.W. 3rd Ave., Downtown* ☎ *503/223–6200* ⊕ *www.kincaids.com* ▭ *AE, D, MC, V.*

$$$$ ✕**London Grill.** *Continental.* The plush, dimly lit dining room in the historic Benson Hotel serves classic dishes made with fresh, seasonal local ingredients. Try the cedar-smoked salmon with juniper-berry sauce. With one of the longest wine lists around and a good chance of live jazz guitar or piano music, this is a place to truly indulge. Breakfast is also available. Jackets are encouraged, but not required, for men. ✉ *309 S.W. Broadway* ☎ *503/295–4110* ▭ *AE, D, DC, MC, V.*

$ ✕**Mama Mia Trattoria.** *Italian.* Warmth and comfort are the specialties at Mama's, which is the place to come to if you're in the mood for old-school Italian-American favorites like spaghetti with meatballs, lasagna, or potato gnocchi. Don't let the sultry red interior, sparkly chandeliers, and starched tablecloths fool you. This mildly boisterous place allows you to be more casual than it is (just like mama), and the bar is open late into the night. ✉ *439 S.W. 2nd Ave.*

3

☎ 503/295–6464 ▭ AE, D, DC, MC, V ⊙ No lunch weekends. Open late.

$$ ✕ Mandarin Cove. *Chinese.* One of Portland's better Chinese
restaurants has Hunan- and Szechuan-style beef, chicken,
pork, seafood, and vegetarian dishes. There are almost two
dozen seafood choices. Try the sautéed scallops simmered
in spicy tomato sauce. ⊠ 111 S.W. Columbia St. ☎ 503/222–
0006 ▭ AE, DC, MC, V.

$ ✕ Mother's Bistro. *American.* The menu is loaded with home-
style favorites—macaroni and cheese with extra ingredients
of the day, soups, pierogi, matzo ball soup, pot roast, and
meat loaf. For vegetarians there's a couscous stew. The high
ceilings in the well-lit dining room lend an air of spacious-
ness, but the tables are a bit close together. The bar is open
late Friday and Saturday. ⊠ 212 S.W. Stark St., Downtown
☎ 503/464–1122 ⊕ www.mothersbistro.com ▭ AE, D,
MC, V ⊙ Closed Mon. No dinner Sun.

$$ ✕ Murata. *Japanese.* Slip off your shoes and step inside one
of the tatami rooms at Murata, Portland's best Japanese
restaurant. You can also pull up a chair at the corner sushi
bar. So ordinary looking it barely stands out among the
office towers near Keller Auditorium, the restaurant draws
a crowd of locals, celebrities, and Japanese businesspeople
who savor the sushi, sashimi, tempura, hamachi, and teri-
yaki. Grilled salmon cheeks stand out among many seafood
specialties. ⊠ 200 S.W. Market St. ☎ 503/227–0080 ▭ AE,
MC, V ⊙ Closed Sun. No lunch Sat.

$$ ✕ Newport Seafood Grill. *Seafood.* When it comes to river,
bridge, and city-skyline views, there's not a bad seat in this
circular glass dining room, which floats on the Willamette
River. The menu includes seafood and chicken salads, sea-
sonal specials, and creative seafood fare. Salmon, clams and
scallops are among the most popular menu items. Upstairs,
a comfortable lounge has a popular happy hour every day
in the late afternoon and before closing. ⊠ RiverPlace, 425
S.W. Montgomery St., Downtown ☎ 503/227–3474 ⊕ www.
newportseafoodgrill.com ▭ AE, D, DC, MC, V.

$$ ✕ Pazzo. *Italian.* The aromas of roasted garlic and wood
smoke greet patrons of the bustling, street-level dining
room of the Hotel Vintage Plaza. Pazzo's menu relies on
deceptively simple new Italian cuisine—creative pastas,
risottos, and grilled meats, fish, and poultry as well as
antipasti and appetizers. All the baked goods are made in
the Pazzoria Bakery & Cafe next door. The decor is a mix
of dark wood, terra-cotta, and dangling garlands of garlic.

Breakfast is served daily. ⊠ *627 S.W. Washington St., Downtown* ☎ *503/228–1515* ⊟ *AE, D, DC, MC, V.*

¢ ✕**Pizzicato.** *Pizza.* This local chain serves pies and slices topped by inventive combinations such as chanterelles, shiitakes, and portobellos; or andouille sausage, shrimp, and smoked mozzarella. The menu also includes large salads to share, antipasti, and panini. The restaurant interiors are clean, bright, and modern. Beer and wine are available. ⊠ *705 S.W. Alder St., Downtown* ☎ *503/226–1007* ⊠ *505 N.W. 23rd Ave., Nob Hill* ☎ *503/242–0023* ⊕ *www.pizzicatopizza.com* ⊟ *AE, D, DC, MC, V.*

$$$ ✕**Portland City Grill.** *American.* On the 30th floor of the US Bank Tower, Portland City Grill has one of the best views in town. You can sit at a windowside table and enjoy the Portland skyline while eating fine steak and seafood with an Asian flair; it's no wonder that this restaurant is a favorite hot spot. The adjoining bar and lounge has comfortable armchairs all along its windowed walls, which are the first to get snatched up during the extremely popular happy hour each day. ⊠ *111 S.W. 5th Ave., Downtown* ☎ *503/450–0030* ⊕ *www.portlandcitygrill.com* ⊟ *AE, D, MC, V* ⊘ *No lunch weekends.*

$$ ✕**Red Star Tavern & Roast House.** *American.* Cooked in a wood-burning oven, smoker, rotisserie, or grill, the cuisine at Red Star can best be described as American comfort food inspired by the bounty of the Pacific Northwest. Spit-roasted chicken, maple-fired baby-back ribs with a brown-ale glaze, charred salmon, and crayfish étouffée are some of the better entrées. The wine list includes regional and international vintages, and 10 microbrews are on tap. The spacious restaurant, in the 5th Avenue Suites Hotel, has tufted leather booths, murals, and copper accents. ⊠ *503 S.W. Alder St., Downtown* ☎ *503/222–0005* ⊕ *www.red-startavern.com* ⊟ *AE, D, DC, MC, V.*

$ ✕**Rock Bottom Brewing Co.** *American.* Some locals might balk at the idea of a corporate brewpub in a city that prides itself on its outstanding local microbrews, but this slightly upscale establishment manages to do just fine and serves some tasty dinner options, including burgers, pasta, and salads. With a full bar, pool upstairs, and rustic decor, there is plenty to please the after-work crowd. Brewery tours are available. ⊠ *210 S.W. Morrison St.* ☎ *503/796–2739* ⊕ *www.rockbottom.com* ⊟ *AE, D, MC, V.*

$ ✕**Saucebox.** *Asian.* Creative pan-Asian cuisine and many creative cocktails draw the crowds to this popular restaurant and nightspot near the big downtown hotels. Inside the long and narrow space with closely spaced tables draped with white cloths, Alexis Rockman's impressive and colorful 24-foot painting *Evolution* spans the wall over your head, and mirrored walls meet your gaze at eye level. The menu includes Korean baby-back ribs, Vietnamese pork tenderloin, and Indonesian roasted Javanese salmon. An excellent late-night menu is served after 10 PM. ⊠ *214 S.W. Broadway, Downtown* ☎ *503/241–3393* ⊕ *www.saucebox. com* ⊟ *AE, DC, MC, V* ⊘ *No lunch*.

$$ ✕ **Seres Restaurant.** *Chinese.* Tantalizing dishes of the east meet the stylistic panache of the west at this highly polished establishment. Beauty is in the details, from stainless steel chopsticks to delicate orchids; it's also present in the artful twists of traditional favorites, such as crispy prawns with honeyed walnuts or spicy sesame beef served with sweet sauce and topped with roasted sesame seeds. ⊠ *1105 N.W. Lovejoy St.* ☎ *971/222–7327* ⊕ *www.seresrestaurant.com* ⊟ *AE, MC, V.*

$$ ✕ **Southpark Seafood Grill & Wine Bar.** *Seafood.* Wood-fired seafood is served in this comfortable, art deco–tinged room with two bars. Chef Ronnie MacQuarrie's Mediterranean-influenced menu includes grilled grape-leaf-wrapped salmon with pomegranate and sherry glaze as well as tuna au poivre with mashed potatoes and red-wine demi-glace. There's a wide selection of fresh Pacific Northwest oysters and fine regional wines available by the glass. Some of the desserts are baked to order. ⊠ *901 S.W. Salmon St., Downtown* ☎ *503/326–1300* ⊕ *www.southparkseafood.com* ⊟ *AE, D, MC, V.*

$$ ✕ **Typhoon!** *Thai.* A Buddha statue with burning incense watches over diners at this popular restaurant in the Lucia Hotel. Come enjoy the excellent food in a large, modern dining room filled with colorful art and sleek red booths. The spicy chicken or shrimp with crispy basil, the curry and noodle dishes, and the vegetarian spring and salad rolls are standouts. As for tea, 145 varieties are available, from $2 a pot to $55 for some of the world's rarest. ⊠ *400 S.W. Broadway, Downtown* ☎ *503/224–8285* ⊕ *www. typhoonrestaurants.com* ⊟ *AE, D, DC, MC, V.*

$$ ✕ **Urban Farmer.** *American.* In the atrium of the upscale hotel the Nines, you'll discover why this restaurant calls itself a modern steakhouse. Making much use of organic and sustainable ingredients, the dishes here are presented with flair in glass canning jars and mini cast-iron skillets. The focus is understandably on its steaks (choose from corn-fed or grass-fed), but there are also interesting alternatives,

such as slow-braised lamb flavored with apricot, and roasted Alaskan halibut served with fried green tomatoes. Leave room for moonshine whiskey or the banana-cream pie served with coffee ice cream. ⊠ *525 S.W. Morrison St., Downtown* ☎ *503/222-4900* ⊕ *www.urbanfarmerrestaurant.com* ⊟ *AE, MC, V.*

$$$ ✕**Veritable Quandary.** *American.* There are so many delicious options at this long-standing local favorite: the tantalizing French toast and revered chocolate soufflé pair well with the beautiful outdoor patio, where you're surrounded by roses, fuchsias, and hanging begonia baskets. The menu emphasizes fresh, flavorful produce and seafood; prices are reasonable for the quality, and the wine list is one of the best in town. ⊠ *1220 S.W. 1st Ave., Downtown* ☎ *503/227–7342* ⊕ *www.veritablequandary.com* ⊟ *AE, D, DC, MC, V.*

PEARL DISTRICT AND OLD TOWN/ CHINATOWN

The Pearl District, once full of worn, empty warehouses, and little more than a reminder of Portland's industrial past, is now the city's most bustling destination for arts and dining. Many of the warehouses have been refurbished into hot spots to gather for drinks and food. On any given day or night, visitors can comb the scene for a perfectly selected glass of wine or a lush designer cocktail. Within this small area are global selections of Greek, French, Italian, Peruvian, Japanese, and more. Restaurants here tend to be slightly more upscale, though there are plenty of casual bakeries, coffee shops, and places to grab sandwiches. Keep in mind that the city's gallery walk event, held the first Thursday of every month, keeps restaurants jammed on that night.

$ ✕**Alexis.** *Greek.* The Mediterranean furnishings here consist only of white walls and basic furnishings, but the authentic Greek flavor keeps the crowds coming for *kalamarakia* (deep-fried squid served with *tzatziki,* a yogurt dip), *horiatiki* (a Greek salad with feta cheese and kalamata olives), and other traditional dishes. If you have trouble making up your mind, the gigantic Alexis platter includes a little of everything. ⊠ *215 W. Burnside St., Old Town* ☎ *503/224–8577* ⊟ *AE, D, MC, V* ☺ *Closed Sun.*

★ Fodor'sChoice ✕**Andina.** *Peruvian.* Portland's sleekest, trendi-
$$$ est, and most brightly colored restaurant gives an artful presentation to designer and traditional Peruvian cuisine.

Asian and Spanish flavors are the main influences here, and they're evident in an extensive seafood menu that includes five kinds of ceviche, grilled octopus, and pan-seared scallops with black quinoa. There are also entrées with poultry, beef, and lamb. A late-night bar is rife with sangria, small plates, and cocktails; downstairs, a shrinelike wine shop hosts private multicourse meals. ⊠ *1314 N.W. Glisan St., Pearl District* ☎ *503/228–9535* ⊕ *www.andinarestaurant. com* ⊟ *AE, D, MC, V* ⊗ *No lunch Sun.*

¢   ✕ **Backspace.** *Café.* Taking "eclectic" to a new level, Backspace is an internet café, online gaming site, art gallery, concert venue, vegan nosh stop and coffee shop all rolled in one. In between checking e-mail or marathon rounds of Halo, you can select a focused, freshly brewed cup of Stumptown coffee paired with a Voodoo donut. There are also lots of sandwiches, such as roasted red pepper hummus or the club vegan, with veggie turkey and ham, red onions and herbed faux mayonnaise. There's also a great selection of healthy soups, salads and entrees, including the soy tacos with grilled mushrooms, or a curry rice bowl. ⊠ *115 N.W. 5th Ave., Old Town* ☎ *503/248–2900* ⊕ *www. backspace.bz* ⊟ *AE, MC, V.*

$$$ ✕ **Blue Hour.** *Mediterranean.* At this vast, towering restaurant, the wait staff are as sophisticated as the white tablecloths and floor-to-ceiling curtains. The menu changes daily based on available ingredients and the chef's whims. Four-course prix fixe menus are available for lunch and dinner. Ongoing appetizers to try are the "20 greens" salad and sea scallops wrapped in applewood-smoked bacon with celery root puree. Top the meal off with a bittersweet chocolate chestnut torte with honey cream. ⊠ *250 N.W. 13th Ave., Pearl District* ☎ *503/226–3394* ⊕ *www.bluehouron-line.com* ⊟ *AE, D, MC, V.*

¢   ✕ **BridgePort BrewPub & Restaurant.** *American.* The hops- and ivy-covered, century-old industrial building seems out of place among its newer, posher fashion and furniture-focused neighbors, but once inside you'll be clear about the business here: frothy pints of BridgePort's ale, brewed on the premises. The India Pale Ale is a specialty, but a good option for the indecisive is the seven-glass sampler that might also include "Old Knucklehead," the brewery's barley wine–style ale. Seafood, chicken, steak, pasta, salads, and small plates are served for lunch and dinner, as well as pub favorites. In summer the flower-festooned loading dock is transformed into a beer garden. ⊠ *1313 N.W. Marshall St., Pearl*

District ☎ 503/241–3612 ⊕ *www.bridgeportbrew.com* ⊟ *MC, V.*

$$ ✕**Caffé Mingo.** *Italian.* Straightforward, flavorful, and fresh is what you'll find at this restaurant with some of the best pizza around. There are also fish and chicken entrées, as well as nightly soup and pasta specials. Don't miss out on the rich chocolate mousse with fresh berries and cream for dessert. ⊠ *807 N.W. 21st Ave.* ☎ *503/226–4646* ☺ *No lunch* ⊟ *AE, DC, MC, V.*

¢ ✕**Cha! Cha! Cha!** *Mexican.* Burritos and tacos are so tasty at this lively taqueria that if it weren't always shoehorned with customers, patrons would probably get up and dance. Part of a local chain, Cha! Cha! Cha! takes cuisine you'd expect to find on a taco truck in L.A. or southern Mexico and puts it on a plate in the Pearl. The extensive menu includes *machaca* (a burrito with shredded beef, sautéed vegetables, scrambled eggs, and Spanish rice) and fish tacos filled with fresh pollack. ⊠ *1208 N.W. Glisan St., Pearl District* ☎ *503/221–2111* ⊟ *AE, D, MC, V.*

$ ✕**Eleni's Philoxenia.** *Greek.* This upscale version of its sister restaurant in Sellwood offers an extensive menu of Mediterranean specialties. The chef's personal favorite is the *kalatsounia* (spinach, fresh dill, and green onions rolled inside phyllo dough). Other surprising standouts are the *lahano salata* (thinly sliced cabbage and shaved fennel, toasted almonds, and lemon paprika dressing) and the *makaronia me kima* (ground beef simmered with peppers, onion, tomatoes, zucchini, and garlic served over spaghetti). ⊠ *112 N.W. 9th Ave., Pearl District* ☎ *503/227–2158* ⊕ *www.elenisrestaurant.com* ⊟ *AE, D, MC, V* ☺ *Closed Sun. and Mon. No lunch.*

$$$ ✕**Fenouil.** *French.* The large stone fireplace, expansive bar bistro menu, and widely revered French onion soup are a few of the reasons patrons keep coming back to this warm and elegant two-story restaurant. Notable entrée choices vary by season, but two reliable crowd pleasers are the grilled Kobe sirloin and the wood-fired duck breast with Armagnac-soaked prunes. There's live music on Friday nights. At the end of each month the chef creates an all-inclusive "regional dinner" that explores foods from a unique culinary region. ⊠ *900 N.W. 11th Ave., Pearl District* ☎ *503/525–2225* ⊕ *www.fenouilinthepearl.com* ⊟ *AE, DC, MC, V.*

★ **Fodor's**Choice✕**50 Plates.** *American.* You wish you had more **$$** room to try everything here, where everything seems designed to put mom's tried-and-true favorites to the test. Evoking regional cuisine from all 50 states, the restaurant creates fresh culinary interpretations. The delightful "silver dollar sammies" include sweet and spicy Carolina pulled pork on a sweet potato roll and a smoked portobello rendition with butter lettuce, fried green tomatoes, and herbed goat cheese. There's also a crowd-pleasing succotash whose components vary depending upon the availability of locally harvested ingredients. The rich desserts include dark chocolate fudge cake, served with homemade brown-sugar ice cream, and bananas Foster. ✉ *333 N.W. 13th Ave., Pearl District* ☎ *503/228–5050* ⊕ *www.50plates.com* ▭ *AE, MC, V.*

¢ ✕**Fong Chong.** *Chinese.* Some people believe that this run-down restaurant serves the best dim sum in town, and that includes the dumplings filled with shrimp, pork, or vegetables, accompanied by plenty of different sauces. If you haven't eaten dim sum before, just take a seat: the food is brought to you on carts and you pick what you want as it comes by; your ticket will be stamped based on the cost of the individual dish (ask if you aren't sure how this works). ✉ *301 N.W. 4th Ave., Chinatown* ☎ *503/228–6868* ▭ *AE, MC, V.*

$$$ **The Gilt Club.** *Continental.* Cascading gold curtains, ornate showpiece chandeliers, and high-back booths complement a swanky rich-red dining room. The food is equally lush, with buttercup pumpkin gnocchi topped with an Oregon venison ragu, and a truffle, red quinoa, and goat cheese custard with roasted autumn baby vegetables. The drink menu is loaded with flavor-embellished drinks such as "Tracy's First Love," with vodka, cucumber, basil, and lime. ✉ *306 N.W. Broadway* ☎ *503/ 222–4458* ⊘ *Closed Sun.* ⊕ *www.giltclub.com* ▭ *AE, MC, V.*

¢ ✕**Hot Lips Pizza.** *Pizza.* A favorite of Portland's pizza-lovers, Hot Lips bakes organic and regional ingredients into creative pizzas, available whole or by the slice. Seasonal variations might feature apples, squash, wild mushrooms, and blue cheese. It also has soups, salads, and sandwiches. Beverages include house-made berry sodas, a large rack of wines, and microbrew six-packs. Dine inside the Ecotrust building, outside on the "eco-roof," or take it all across the street for an impromptu picnic in Jamison Square. ✉ *721 N.W. 9th Ave., Pearl District* ☎ *503/595–2342* ⊕ *www.hotlipspizza.com* ▭ *AE, D, MC, V.*

$$$ **Le Bouchon.** *French.* A warm, jovial waitstaff make Francophiles feel right at home at this bistro in the Pearl District, which serves classic examples of the cuisine for lunch and dinner. Duck confit, truffle chicken, bouillabaisse, and

escargot are all cooked with aplomb by chef Claude Mus-quin. And for dessert, chocolate mousse is a must-try. ⊠ *517 N.W. 14th Ave., Pearl District* ☎ *503/248–2193* ⊟ *AE, MC, V* ☺ *Closed Sun. and Mon.*

$ ✕**Le Happy.** *French.* This tiny crepe-dealer outside of the hubbub of the Pearl District can serve as a romantic dinner-date spot or just a cozy place to enjoy a drink and a snack. You can get sweet crepes with fruit, cheese, and cream or savory ones with meats and cheeses; in addition, the dinner menu is rounded out with steaks and salads. It's a classy joint, but not without a sense of humor: Le Trash Blanc is a bacon-and-cheddar crepe, served with a can of Pabst. ⊠ *1011 N.W. 16th Ave., Pearl District* ☎ *503/226–1258* ⊟ *MC, V* ☺ *Closed Sun. No lunch.*

$$$ ✕**Oba!** *Latin American.* Many come to Oba! for the upscale bar scene, but this Pearl District salsa hangout also serves excellent Latin American cuisine, including coconut prawns, roasted vegetable enchiladas and tamales, and other sea-food, chicken, pork, and duck dishes. The bar is open late Friday and Saturday. ⊠ *555 N.W. 12th Ave., Pearl District* ☎ *503/228–6161* ⊕ *www.obarestaurant.com* ⊟ *AE, D, DC, MC, V* ☺ *No lunch.*

¢ ✕**Pearl Bakery.** *Café.* A light breakfast or lunch can be had at this popular spot, which is known for its excellent fresh breads, and sandwiches. The cakes, cookies, croissants, and Danish are some of the best in the city. ⊠ *102 N.W. 9th Ave., Pearl District* ☎ *503/827–0910* ☺ *No dinner* ⊕ *www.pearlbakery.com* ⊟ *MC, V.*

$ ✕**Silk, by Pho Van.** *Vietnamese.* This spacious, minimalist restaurant is the newer and trendier of the two Pho Van locations in Portland—the less expensive twin is on the far east side, on 82nd Avenue. A big bowl of pho (noodle soup) is delicious, enough to fill you up, and costs only $8 or $9. The friendly waitstaff will help you work your way through the menu and can make suggestions to give you the best sampling of Vietnamese cuisine. ⊠ *1012 N.W. Glisan St., Pearl District* ☎ *503/248–2172* ⊕ *www.phovanrestaurant. com* ⊟ *AE, D, MC, V* ☺ *Closed Sun.* ⊠ *1919 S.E. 82nd Ave.* ☎ *503/788–5244.*

$$$ ✕**Ten01.** *American.* Soft light, endless ceilings, and clean architectural lines make for a very chic dining room at Ten01. Start with the sweet onion–cauliflower soup with spicy lamb sausage, almonds, golden raisins, and curry. Then indulge in practically plucked-off-the-farm jumbo quail wrapped in bacon, or a sautéed Alaskan halibut with maitake mushrooms, pancetta, and truffle-mushroom

sauce. Save room for the signature chocolate peanut butter bread pudding, which is dense with chunks of compressed devil's food chocolate cake and served with malted milk ice cream and peanut butter caramel. The wine list is among the city's best. ⊠ *1001 N.W. Couch St., Pearl District* ☎ *503/226–3463* ⊘ *Closed Sun.* ⊕ *www.ten-01.com* ▭ *AE, DC, MC, V.*

WEST OF DOWNTOWN

Beyond downtown to the west are a handful of restaurants worth visiting. Without parking to worry about, the 5- to 15-minute drive will reward you with some delicious dining surprises, including pancakes, pizza, and some of the best tapas in Portland. Several establishments are right alongside the Willamette River, so there are also lovely views to be had. During the summer months, many offer deck seating. These seats are in high demand, but watching the boats sail by on a warm summer night while indulging in a round of tasty appetizers is totally worth the wait.

$$ ✕**Aquariva.** *Italian.* Choose from a vast selection of innovative Italian tapas—such as the spinach gnocchi covered in tomato-basil fondue or Oregon mushroom risotto with white truffle oil—in one of the most prime dining locations in Portland. Gaze out the windows at the Willamette River while sipping on a glass of Italian Syrah chosen from an impressive wine list. There are plenty of cushy couches to lounge in for happy hour, but if the weather's nice, head for the deck. ⊠ *470 S.W. Hamilton Ct., South Waterfront* ☎ *503/802–5850* ⊕ *www.aquarivaportland.com* ▭ *AE, DC, MC, V.*

$$$ ✕**Chart House.** *American.* On a hill high above the Willamette River, the Chart House has a stunning view of the city and the surrounding mountains from almost all of its tables. Prime rib is a specialty, but the seafood dishes, including coconut-crunchy shrimp deep-fried in tempura batter and the Cajun-spiced yellowfin ahi, are just as tempting. ⊠ *5700 S.W. Terwilliger Blvd.* ☎ *503/246–6963* ⊕ *www. chart-house.com* ▭ *AE, D, DC, MC, V* ⊘ *No lunch weekends.*

☺ ✕**Old Spaghetti Factory.** *Italian.* An old trolley car, oversize
¢ velvet chairs, dark wood, and fun antiques fill this huge restaurant overlooking the Willamette River. With a lounge upstairs, room for 500 diners, and a great view of the river, the flagship location of this nationwide chain (it opened in

CLOSE UP

Eco Fruit of the Vine: Organic Wine

Portland has been globally recognized for the sustainability practices of its dining scene. Another trend putting this region in the spotlight is the production of organic wine. Although Oregon has only about 13,000 acres of wine grapes compared to California's 450,000-plus acres, it's estimated that nearly 50 percent of Oregon's vineyards are sustainable or organic compared to California's one percent. Twenty-three percent of its vineyards have met very stringent certification guidelines and are LIVE-certified sustainable or organic, or Demeter-certified biodynamic. (LIVE—Low Input Viticulture & Enology—is just one of two sustainable certification agencies in the United States, established in 1997, that recognizes farms and vineyards for sustainable agricultural practices. Demeter is an international certification body.)

The goals of organic wine production are to reduce reliance on synthetic chemicals and fertilizers with the purpose of protecting the farmer and the environment, and ensure land protection by maintaining natural, chemical-free soil fertility. Perhaps the biggest hindrance in producing organic wine is preserving the wine with a sulfite-free preservative. Wines require long periods of storage so standardized methods of preserving wines includes adding sulfites. Even though yeast naturally produces sulfites during fermentation, adding additional sulfites goes against certification standards.

People with allergies, including sulfite sensitivities, often seek out organic wines. The FDA requires warning labels for wines with sulfites more than 10 parts per million (ppm). Most red wines contain approximately 40 ppm sulfite. There's also the term "no detectable sulfite," which means that wine constitutes less than one milligram per liter. Many wineries create wine made from organic grapes and label it as such, so long as the detectable sulfite level remains below 100 ppm.

100% certified organic wine labels are still uncommon; the preservation and storage challenges still conflict with the strict certification requirements. However, many of the wineries in Portland's neighboring communities of Yamhill and Washington counties are turning new soil on what they believe are best practices for farming—and cultivating highly respected wine in the process.

3

1969) is a great place for families, with basic pasta dishes and a kids' menu. ✉ *715 S.W. Bancroft St.* ☎ *503/222–5375* ⊕ *www.osf.com* ♻ *Reservations not accepted* 🖃 *AE, D, DC, MC, V.*

¢ ✕**Original Pancake House.** *American.* The original of what's now a franchise with more than 100 branches, this pancake house is the real deal. Faithful customers have been coming for close to 50 years to wait for a table at this bustling, cabin-like local landmark, and you can expect to find a contented crowd of locals and tourists alike from the time the place opens at 7 AM until afternoon. With pancakes starting at $7.25, it's not the cheapest place to get a stack, but with 20 varieties and some of the best waffles and crepes around, it's worth the trip. ✉ *8601 S.W. 24th Ave., Portland* ☎ *503/246–9007* ⊕ *www.originalpancakehouse. com* ♻ *Reservations not accepted* 🖃 *No credit cards* ☉ *Closed Mon. and Tues. No dinner.*

$$ ✕**Three Square Grill.** *American.* Hidden within an old shop-
ⓒ ping plaza in the Hillsdale neighborhood you'll discover the best place in Portland to go on Tuesdays: that's fried chicken and waffle night. Indulge in large servings of comfort food, including Louisiana-style bouillabaisse with shrimp, crab, oysters and crawfish, as well as 21-day dry aged New York steak with truffle butter. Dishes focus on organic ingredients, some of which came from the chef's own garden, and everything from the bread to desserts is baked fresh daily. Weekend brunches and live music in the evenings are a big hit at this kid-friendly place. ✉ *6320 S.W. Capitol Hwy.* ☎ *503/244–4467* ⊕ *www.threesquare. com* 🖃 *MC, V* ☉ *Closed Mon.*

NOB HILL AND VICINITY

Head northwest to sample the broadest scope of this city's food scene. From the finest of the fine (Paley's Place, Wildwood, Papa Haydn, and Hoyt 23) to the come-as-you-are-casual (McMenamins Blue Moon, Pizza Schmizza, and Rose's Deli), there's something for everyone within a handful of blocks. Most restaurants in the Nob Hill area are open for lunch and dinner and on the weekends; reservations are recommended for the higher-end establishments. This neighborhood draws an eclectic crowd: progressives and conservatives, lifetime residents and recent transplants, wealthy as well as struggling students. There are numerous retail shops and galleries in the neighborhood to help you work up an appetite before or after your meal.

$$$ ✕**23 Hoyt.** *Contintental.* From the prominent antler chandelier to the owner's private collection of contemporary art on walls and in glass cases, an eclectic mix of fun in a chic, contemporary setting is what this place is about. The restaurant has received national accolades for its interpretation of Northwest cuisine. Items, which change seasonally, may include a mixed grill dish with juniper-rubbed quail, rabbit sausage, and smoky bacon; or a Moroccan couscous with Alaskan halibut, manila clams, squid, and sea scallops. If it's available, don't miss the strudel made with crispy phyllo layered with poached pears and caramel custard. In a savory twist, it's served with black pepper ice cream. ✉ *529 N.W. 23rd Ave.* ☎ *503/445–7400* ⊕*www.23hoyt.com* ⊟ *AE, MC, V* ⊙ *Closed Sun. and Mon. No lunch.*

$$$ ✕**Bastas.** *Italian.* In a converted Tastee-Freez, this arty bistro serves dishes from all over Italy. The walls are painted with Italian earth tones, and a small side garden provides alfresco dining in good weather. The menu includes scaloppine, grilled lamb, and creative seafood and pasta dishes. ✉ *410 N.W. 21st Ave., Nob Hill* ☎ *503/274–1572* ⊕*www.bastastrattoria.com* ⊟ *AE, MC, V* ⊙ *No lunch.*

$$ ✕**BeWon.** *Korean.* Named for the favorite secret garden of ancient Korean royalty, BeWon prepares a tasty Korean feast. An array of traditional Korean side dishes, presented in an elegant assembly of little white bowls, accompanies such entrées as stir-fried seafood, simmered meat and fish, rice and soup dishes, and kimchi (spicy fermented cabbage). To really experience the cuisine, there's *han jung shik,* a traditional seven-course prix-fixe dinner available with or without wine pairings. ✉ *1203 N.W. 23rd Ave.* ☎ *503/464– 9222* ⊕*www.bewonrestaurant.com* ⊟ *AE, D, MC, V* ⊙ *No lunch weekends.*

¢ ✕**Ken's Artisan Bakery.** *Café.* Golden crusts are the trademark of Ken's rustic breads, croissants, tarts, and puff pastries, good for breakfast, lunch, and light evening meals. Sandwiches, barbecue pulled pork, and croque monsieur are served on thick slabs of freshly baked bread, and local berries fill the flaky pastries. And if the dozen tables inside the vibrant blue bakery are crammed (they usually are), you can sit outside at one of the sidewalk tables. On Monday nights they serve pizza, and the bakery stays open to 9 PM. ✉ *338 N.W. 21st Ave.* ☎ *503/248–2202* ⊕*www.kensartisan.com* ⊟ *MC, V* ⊙ *No dinner Tues.–Sun.*

¢ ✕**Kornblatt's.** *American.* This kosher deli and bagel bakery evokes a 1950s diner. Thick sandwiches are made with fresh bread and lean fresh-cooked meats, and the tender home-smoked salmon and pickled herring are simply mouthwatering. For breakfast try the poached eggs with spicy corned-beef hash, blintzes, or potato latkes. ⊠ *628 N.W. 23rd Ave., Nob Hill* ☎ *503/242–0055* ⊕ *www.kornblattsdeli.com* ▭ *AE, MC, V.*

$$ ✕ Lucy's Table. *Contintental.* Amid this corner bistro's regal purple and gold interior, chef Michael Conklin creates Northwest cuisine with a mix of Italian and French accents. The seasonal menu includes lamb, steak, pork, and seafood dishes. For dessert try the *boca negra,* chocolate cake with Frangelico whipped cream and cherries poached with port and walnut Florentine. Valet parking is available Wednesday–Saturday. ⊠ *706 N.W. 21st Ave., Nob Hill* ☎ *503/226–6126* ⊕ *www.lucystable.com* ▭ *AE, DC, MC, V* ☉ *Closed Sun. No lunch.*

$ ✕ MacTarnahan's Taproom. *American.* The copper beer-making equipment at the door tips you off to the specialty of the house: beer. This restaurant in the Northwest industrial district is part of a 27,000-sq-ft brewery complex. Start with a tasting platter of seven different beers. The haystack baby back ribs with garlic-rosemary fries are popular, and the fish-and-chips use a batter made with Mac's signature ale. Asparagus-artichoke lasagna is a good vegetarian option. You can enjoy it all on the patio overlooking the landscaped grounds. ⊠ *2730 N.W. 31st Ave., off N.W. Yeon St.* ☎ *503/228–5269* ⊕ *www.macsbeer.com* ▭ *AE, DC, MC, V.*

$$$ ✕ Meriwether's. *Continental.* A fabulous garden patio adorns this quaint, higher-end—yet unpretentious—restaurant. The outdoor seating area is covered and heated so during cooler months you can still enjoy Tuscan seafood stew or celery root ravioli while basking in the garden, where something is always in bloom. Dishes are prepared with fruits and vegetables harvested from Meriwether's own farm, 20 minutes away. The always-changing dessert menu features tasty seasonal treats. ⊠ *2601 N.W. Vaughn* ☎ *503/228–1250* ⊕ *www.meriwethersnw.com* ▭ *AE, D, MC, V.*

$$$ ✕ Paley's Place. *French.* This charming bistro serves French cuisine Pacific Northwest–style. Among the entrées are halibut poached in olive oil and a grilled Laughing Stock Farm pork chop served with polenta. A vegetarian selection is also available. There are two dining rooms and a classy bar. In warmer months there's outdoor seating on the front porch and back patio. ⊠ *1204 N.W. 21st Ave., Nob Hill*

☎ *503/243–2403* ⊕ *www.paleysplace.net* ▭ *AE, MC, V*
⊗ *No lunch.*

$$ ✕**Papa Haydn/Jo Bar.** *American.* Many patrons come to this
bistro just for the luscious desserts or for the popular Sun-
day brunch (reservations essential). Favorite dinner items
include pan-seared scallops, dinner salads, and grilled flat-
iron steak. Wood-fired, rotisserie-cooked meat, fish, and
poultry dishes plus pasta and pizza are available next door
at the jazzy **Jo Bar.** ✉ *701 N.W. 23rd Ave., Nob Hill*
☎ *503/228–7317 Papa Haydn, 503/222–0048 Jo Bar*
⊕ *www.papahaydn.com* ▭ *AE, MC, V.*

¢   ✕**Pastini.** *Italian.* It's hard to go wrong with anything at
this classy Italian bistro, which has more than two dozen
pasta dishes under $10. Rigatoni *zuccati* comes in a light
cream sauce with butternut squash, wild mushrooms, and
spinach; *linguini misto mare* is a seafood linguine in white
wine. It also has panini, antipasti, and dinner salads. Open
for lunch and dinner, Pastini is part of a local chain. There's
often a crowd, but from this location you can browse the
shops while waiting for a table. ✉ *1506 N.W. 23rd Ave.*
☎ *503/595–1205* ⊕ *www.pastini.com* ⚎ *Reservations not
accepted* ▭ *AE, DC, MC, V* ⊗ *No lunch Sun.*

$$$$ ✕**Plainfield's Restaurant.** *Indian.* Portland's finest Indian food
is served in an elegant Victorian house. The tomato-coco-
nut soup with fried curry leaves and the vegetarian and
vegan dishes are highlights. Appetizers include the authen-
tic Bombay *bhel* salad with tamarind dressing and the *dahi
wadi* (crispy fried lentil savory donuts in a spicy yogurt
sauce). Meat and seafood specialties include lobster in
brown onion sauce and tandoori lamb. ✉ *852 S.W. 21st
Ave., one block south of Burnside, close to Nob Hill*
☎ *503/223–2995* ⊕ *www.plainfields.com* ▭ *AE, D, DC,
MC, V* ⊗ *No lunch.*

$$$ ✕**The Ringside.** *American.* This Portland institution has
been famous for its beef for more than 50 years. Dine in
cozy booths on rib eye, prime rib, and New York strip,
which come in regular- or king-size cuts. Seafood lovers
will find plenty of choices: a chilled seafood platter with
an 8-ounce lobster tail, Dungeness crab, oysters, jumbo
prawns, and Oregon bay shrimp. The onion rings, made
with the local Walla Walla sweets variety, are equally
renowned. ✉ *2165 N.W. Burnside St., close to Nob Hill*
☎ *503/223–1513* ⊕ *www.ringsidesteakhouse.com* ▭ *AE,
D, MC, V* ⊗ *No lunch.*

$ ✕**Serratto.** *Continental.* Good for a date night, business meeting or even a casual outing with a friend, this open, spacious dining room comes with warm service, a knowledgeable staff and a solid menu. Pasta is made from scratch and artfully prepared. Good options include the ravioli filled with butternut squash and goat cheese, served in a white wine-sage cream sauce with toasted hazelnuts, and the cavatelli with Dungeness crab, sunchokes, fennel, onions and kale in a lemon-tomato-fennel broth. Equally tantalizing entrees including lamb shank with mascarpone polenta and a tomato-fennel-rosemary ragout or grilled pork loin with roasted shallot apple sauce. Top off the meal with the bittersweet chocolate cobbler, served warm with vanilla bean gelato. ⊠ *2112 N.W. Kearney St., Nob Hill* ☎ *503/221–1195* ⊕ *www.serratto.com* ⊠ *AE, MC, V.*

¢   ✕**St. Honoré Boulangerie.** *Café.* Light meals and pastries are available at this authentic French bakery, named for the patron saint of bakers. Start the day off with a plain or chocolate croissant, or café au lait. For lunch and dinner there's quiche, savory puff pastries and tarts, croque monsieur, and a variety of fresh salads. Or simply unwind from shopping with a glass of wine and a luscious dessert at one of the sidewalk café tables. ⊠ *2335 N.W. Thurman St.* ☎ *503/445–4342* ⊕ *www.sainthonorebakery.com* ⊟ *MC, V.*

$$$ ✕**Wildwood.** *Continental.* The busy center bar, stainless-steel open kitchen, and blond-wood chairs set the tone at this restaurant serving fresh Pacific Northwest cuisine. Chef Dustin Clark's entrées include dishes made with lamb, pork loin, chicken, steak, and seafood. An obsession with sustainable, fresh ingredients means that that menu changes often and that there's always a broad vegetarian selection. Wildwood also has a family-style Sunday supper menu with selections for two or more people. ⊠ *1221 N.W. 21st Ave., Nob Hill* ☎ *503/248–9663* ⊕ *www.wildwoodrestaurant.com* ⊟ *AE, MC, V* ⊘ *No lunch Sun.*

EAST OF THE WILLAMETTE

A whole new food movement is sprouting up east of the river, just outside downtown Portland. As restaurants become more daring and inventive, they are also finding less predictable locations. One benefit of dining outside of downtown is that parking is less expensive and easier to find. Getting from place to place, though, takes more time as these establishments are not necessarily concentrated in any one area. But with some of Portland's most sought-after

CLOSE UP

A Chef's Paradise

The quest for the most eco-friendly, farm-supporting methods has become an obsession among chefs who flock from all over the world to take advantage of the area's local abundance. Portland is perfectly poised to take the cooking universe by storm. First, compared to major metropolitan cities like New York, Chicago, and Los Angeles, real estate is somewhat affordable, which makes setting up shop a more obtainable reality for aspiring chefs.

Second, because of the urban growth boundary, city sprawl is kept to a minimum. Farm land is within miles, and therefore everyday deliveries of a broad spectrum of fruits and vegetables are achievable. Most chefs in Portland try to adhere to delivery from a distributor within a 100-mi radius. Not only does this make the menu offerings exciting and ever-changing, it requires chefs to come up with creative new dishes based on what's available for that month, that week, or even that day. Many chefs indicate that it's the artistic challenge and constant change of ingredients that makes Portland seductive.

Also within the 100-mi proximity of Portland are lush forests and the Pacific Ocean, where regional specialty ingredients, such as chanterelle mushrooms and wild caught salmon, are in fresh supply. Walk into any one of Portland's most notable restaurants, and you'll find entire menus serving dishes exclusively made from regional ingredients. For desserts you're bound to discover the amazing selection of local fruits—Anjou pears, peaches, and blackberries—that turn up in pies, pastries, toppings, and cakes.

Exploration of creative cuisine infused by local ingredients isn't only reserved for fine dining. Scores of local bakeries (such as Ken's Artisan Bakery), pizzerias (Hot Lips Pizza) have built their businesses around locally harvested, organic-based menu items as well.

dining spots—such as Genoa, Pok Pok, Clark Lewis—on the east side, a little research will go a long way toward uncovering amazing new flavors.

$ ✕**Alameda Brewhouse.** *American.* The spacious room—with light wood, high ceilings, and lots of stainless steel—feels chic while still managing to remain friendly and casual. Many people come for the excellent microbrews made here, but the food's worth a look too; this is no boring pub grub. With creative pasta dishes such as mushroom-artichoke linguine, salmon gyros, tuna tacos, and delicious burgers,

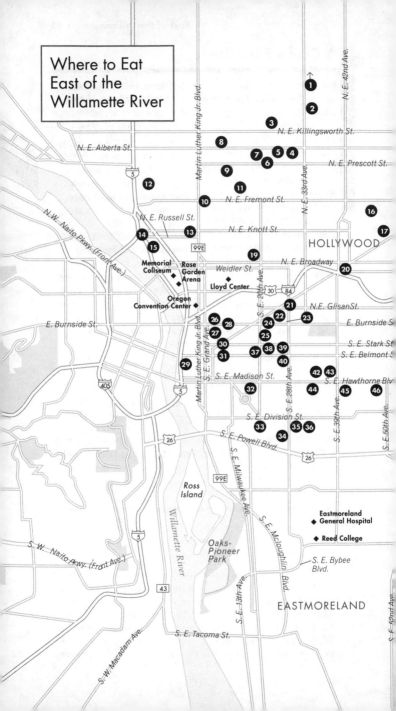

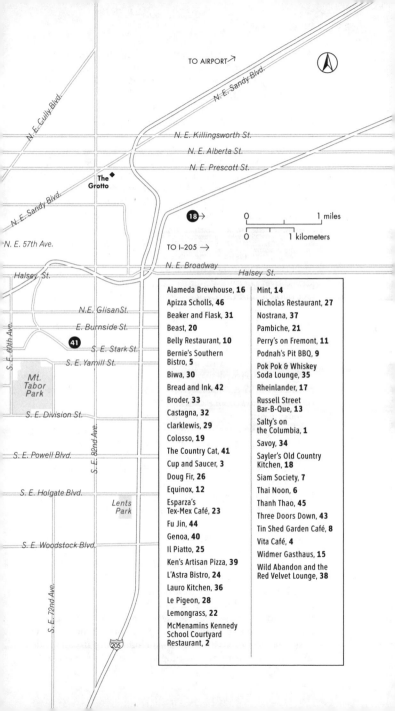

TO AIRPORT→

N. E. Sandy Blvd.

N. E. Cully Blvd.

N. E. Killingsworth St.

N. E. Alberta St.

N. E. Prescott St.

The Grotto

N. E. Sandy Blvd.

18 →

0   1 miles
0   1 kilometers

N. E. 57th Ave.

TO I-205 →

N. E. Broadway

Halsey St.   Halsey St.

N.E. Glisan St.

E. Burnside St.

41

S. E. Stark St.

S. E. Yamill St.

S. E. 60th Ave.

Mt. Tabor Park

S. E. Division St.

S. E. 82nd Ave.

S. E. Powell Blvd.

S. E. Holgate Blvd.

Lents Park

S. E. Woodstock Blvd.

S. E. 72nd Ave.

205

Alameda Brewhouse, **16**	Mint, **14**
Apizza Scholls, **46**	Nicholas Restaurant, **27**
Beaker and Flask, **31**	Nostrana, **37**
Beast, **20**	Pambiche, **21**
Belly Restaurant, **10**	Perry's on Fremont, **11**
Bernie's Southern Bistro, **5**	Podnah's Pit BBQ, **9**
Biwa, **30**	Pok Pok & Whiskey Soda Lounge, **35**
Bread and Ink, **42**	Rheinlander, **17**
Broder, **33**	Russell Street Bar-B-Que, **13**
Castagna, **32**	Salty's on the Columbia, **1**
clarklewis, **29**	Savoy, **34**
Colosso, **19**	Sayler's Old Country Kitchen, **18**
The Country Cat, **41**	Siam Society, **7**
Cup and Saucer, **3**	Thai Noon, **6**
Doug Fir, **26**	Thanh Thao, **45**
Equinox, **12**	Three Doors Down, **43**
Esparza's Tex-Mex Café, **23**	Tin Shed Garden Café, **8**
Fu Jin, **44**	Vita Café, **4**
Genoa, **40**	Widmer Gasthaus, **15**
Il Piatto, **25**	Wild Abandon and the Red Velvet Lounge, **38**
Ken's Artisan Pizza, **39**	
L'Astra Bistro, **24**	
Lauro Kitchen, **36**	
Le Pigeon, **28**	
Lemongrass, **22**	
McMenamins Kennedy School Courtyard Restaurant, **2**	

it's clear that this restaurant has as much thought going into its menu and ingredients as it does into its brewing. ✉ *4675 N.E. Fremont St., Alameda* ☎ *503/460–9025* ⊕ *www.alamedabrewhouse.com* ▤ *AE, DC, MC, V.*

$$$ ✕ **Apizza Scholls.** *Italian.* You will pay more for this pizza, but the crispy yet chewy crust—the end result of 24-hour fermentation—is worth it. Slow fermentation with a minimum of yeast produces acidity, which gives it a creamy, textured flavor. Dough is made daily then topped by whole fresh cheeses and a small amount of meats to spotlight the richness of the crust and sauce flavorings. ✉ *4741 S.E. Hawthorne Blvd.* ☎ *503/233–1286* ⊕ *www.apizzascholls. com* ▤ *MC, V* ⊘ *No lunch.*

$ ✕ **Beaker and Flask.** *Continental.* Inspired by *The Gentleman's Companion,* an influential cocktail manual published in 1946, the sassily named cocktails here are modern twists on classics. For instance, there's the rum-based Sal's Minion, served over coconut water ice cubes, or the Chimney Sweep, a concoction of ouzo, blended scotch, and Ramazzotti (an Italian bitters). Drink choices frequently change based on seasons and available ingredients. The food, equally chic and selectively prepared, often unites ingredients in unconventional ways, as in the macaroni and cheese with blood sausage, and a herb-thyme crust or the maple-braised pork belly accompanied by creamed kale, squash, and apple relish. ✉ *727 S.E. Washington St.* ☎ *503/235–8180* ⊕ *www. beakerandflask.com* ▤ *MC, V* ⊘ *Closed Sun.*

$$$$ ✕ **Beast.** *Continental.* This quintessential example of Portland's creative cuisine is inside a nondescript red building with no signage. Inside the seating is communal, at two large tables that seat 8 and 16. The frequently changing menus are prix-fixe, and you have the option of either three or five courses. The dishes that come from the open kitchen live up to the restaurant's name: there might be chicken and duck liver mousse, wine and truffle-braised beef, or steak tartare with quail egg toast. (Vegetarians may struggle to eat here.) There are two seatings per night; call ahead for times and the day's menus. ✉ *5425 N.E. 30th Ave.* ☎ *503/841–6968* ⊕ *www.beastpdx.com* ▤ *MC, V* ⊘ *Closed Sun.–Tues.*

$$ ✕ **Belly Restaurant.** *American.* In this neighborhood restaurant, people feel welcomed and can dine on an incredible meal made from sustainable ingredients. The name "Belly" is about showing up with an appetite big enough for the vast selection of small dishes—including potato and kale soup or pork meatballs—or the hearty three-course meals.

Sunday brunches are also a hit: there's banana-bread French toast and a chance to build your own biscuit sandwich stuffed with eggs, bacon, sausage and gravy. ⊠ *3500 N.E. Martin Luther King Jr. Blvd.* ☎ *503/249–9764* ⊕ *www. bellyrestaurant.com* ▭ *AE, D, DC, MC, V* ☉ *Sun. brunch only. Closed Mon.*

$$ ✕**Bernie's Southern Bistro.** *Southern.* You definitely won't find finer soul food in Portland. Made of fresh, organic ingredients, the healthy portions here are in a different realm from that of your garden-variety fried chicken. Other specialties include crisp fried green tomatoes, crawfish, and catfish, in addition to delectable collard greens and black-eyed peas. The inside of the restaurant is painted in warm orange, and the lush outdoor patio is a Portland favorite. ⊠ *2904 N.E. Alberta St.* ☎ *503/282–9864* ⊕ *www.bernies-bistro.com* ▭ *AE, D, MC, V* ☉ *Closed Mon. No lunch.*

$ ✕**Biwa.** *Japanese.* Taking ramen to whole new heights is what this bustling, industrial restaurant with an open kitchen does best. Homemade noodles are the focal point of aromatic, flavorful soups enriched by accompaniments such as sliced pork and grilled chicken. Also try the thicker udon noodles served in a soup made from dried fish and seaweed. A fitting sendoff for the filling, authentic meals here would be one of the many sakes. ⊠ *215 S.E. 9th Ave.* ☎ *503/239–8830* ⊕ *www.biwarestaurant.com* ▭ *MC, DC, V* ☉ *Closed Sun. No lunch.*

$ ✕**Bread and Ink.** *American.* The old-fashioned elegance will strike you as soon as you walk in; the dining room, done in cream and forest green and with high ceilings, is not trendy in any way. The look's impressive, but it's mainly the earnest dedication to quality food that's made Bread and Ink a neighborhood landmark. Breakfast, a specialty, might include brioche French toast, smoked fish, and blintzes (they're legendary). Lunch and dinner yield good choices, including burgers, poached salmon, and crab cakes. ⊠ *3610 S.E. Hawthorne Blvd., Hawthorne District* ☎ *503/239–4756* ⊕ *www.breadandinkcafe.com* ▭ *AE, D, MC, V.*

¢ ✕**Broder.** *Swedish.* Smells of freshly brewed coffee and wonderful breads greet you as you walk into this friendly Swedish restaurant. Broder is known for its excellent takes on breakfast: if you can't decide between the many tasty, home-cooked options on the menu, go with the Swedish Breakfast Bord. For only 10 bucks, you get the best of what's offered: depending on the day, that could include walnut toasts, smoked trout, ham, seasonal fruit, yogurt and honey, a soft-boiled egg, and some sort of brilliant cheese. The coffee cakes, pastries, and breads are delectable. Lunch includes a variety of sandwiches and salads—and yes, they serve meatballs. ⊠ *2508 S.E. Clinton St.* ☎ *503/736–3333* ⊕ *www.broderpdx. com* ⊟ *MC, V* ⊗ *No dinner.*

$$$ ✕ **Castagna.** *Continental.* Enjoy the bouillabaisse or one of the inventive Mediterranean seafood entrées at this tranquil Hawthorne restaurant. The pan-seared scallops with mushrooms are the signature dish. Next door is the more casual **Cafe Castagna** (☎ *503/231–9959*), a bistro and bar open nightly serving pizzas and other slightly less expensive, lighter fare. ⊠ *1752 S.E. Hawthorne Blvd., Hawthorne District* ☎ *503/231–7373* ⊕ *www.castagnarestaurant.com* ⊟ *AE, D, DC, MC, V* ⊗ *Closed Sun.–Tues. No lunch.*

$$$ ✕ **clarklewis.** *Continental.* This cutting-edge restaurant, aka "darklewis" for its murky lighting, is making big waves for inventive farm-fresh meals served inside a former warehouse loading dock. Regional vegetables, seafood, and meat from local suppliers appear on a daily changing menu of pastas, entrées, and sides. Diners can order small, large, and family-style sizes, or let the chef decide with the fixed-price meal. Although the food is great, the lack of signage or a reception area can make your first visit feel a little like arriving to a party uninvited. ⊠ *1001 S.E. Water Ave., Produce Row* ☎ *503/235–2294* ⊕ *www.clarklewispdx.com* ⊟ *AE, MC, V* ⊗ *Closed Sun. No lunch weekends.*

$ ✕ **Colosso.** *Spanish.* A dimly lit tapas bar and restaurant, this casual eatery is one of the most romantic places to dine in northeast Portland. The best way to get the full experience of the place is to order a pitcher of sangria and split a few of the small tapas plates between friends. In the evening the restaurant is usually crowded with folks drinking cocktails late into the night. ⊠ *1932 N.E. Broadway, Broadway District* ☎ *503/288–3333* ⊟ *D, MC, V* ⊗ *No lunch.*

$$$ ✕ **The Country Cat.** *American.* Bacon lovers beware: you've found hog heaven. Slow cooked, smoked country ham and samplers of pork shoulders, head, and belly, await you. Menu items entail a whole 'lotta South mixed in with a Northwest twist. Chowder potpie, hickory-smoked duck leg, and fried chicken coated with a Tabasco vinaigrette are favorites. There's also a bar; brunch is served on weekends. ⊠ *7937 S.E. Stark St.* ☎ *503/408–1414* ⊕ *www.the-countrycat.net* ⊟ *AE, MC, V.*

¢ ✕ **Cup and Saucer.** *Café.* This casual diner-style restaurant, extremely popular with hip young locals, is always packed on weekends, especially for breakfast and lunch. The long menu includes the all-day-breakfast, quiches, burgers, sandwiches, soups, and salads, with plenty of vegetarian and vegan options. ⊠ *3566 S.E. Hawthorne Blvd., Hawthorne District* ☎ *503/236–6001* ⊕ *www.cupandsaucercafe.com* ⊯ *Reservations not accepted* ⊟ *MC, V.*

¢ ✕ **Doug Fir.** *American.* In what resembles a futuristic lumberjack hangout, the surroundings make use of brick and glass, and the walls and ceilings are made from wood logs. Add a menu of hearty, homey dishes, and you've got a fun, eclectic restaurant. The morning shift can go for the banana-hazelnut pancakes or egg scrambles, and lunch crowds will appreciate big hearty sandwiches that include a signature hamburger. For dinner, grandma's meatloaf with gravy or Diego's marionberry chicken are both good. Downstairs is a concert venue open seven nights a week that attracts lots of wannabe rockers who come to hang out, drink, and socialize. ⊠ *830 E. Burnside St.* ☎ *503/231–9663* ⊕ *www.dougfirlounge.com* ⊟ *AE, MC, V.*

$ ✕ **Equinox.** *Continental.* Locally grown organic produce, free-range meats, wild seafood, and cage-free chickens all come to the table at this fusiony neighborhood restaurant on North Mississippi Street. Renovated-garage chic and a pleasant outdoor patio create a casual atmosphere for enjoying unusual combinations of ingredients. Spicy *togorashi* chicken is roasted with sesame seeds, chilies, and orange peel, and topped with a ginger demi-glace. Vegetarian entrées might include tofu, spinach, and coconut-tomato-basil curry. An almond flan dessert is served in a towering martini glass. ⊠ *830 N. Shaver St., at N. Mississippi St., Albina* ☎ *503/460–3333* ⊕ *www.equinoxrestaurantpdx.com* ⊟ *D, MC, V* ☉ *Closed Mon. No dinner Sun.*

$ ✕ **Esparza's Tex-Mex Cafe.** *Southwestern.* Be prepared for south-of-the-border craziness at this beloved local eatery. Wild West kitsch festoons the walls, but it isn't any wilder than some of the entrées that emerge from chef-owner Joe Esparza's kitchen. Look for such creations as lean smoked-sirloin tacos—Esparza's is renowned for its smoked meats—and, for the truly adventurous diner, ostrich enchiladas. ⊠ *2725 S.E. Ankeny St., at S.E. 28th Ave., near Laurelhurst* ☎ *503/234–7909* ⊯ *Reservations not accepted* ⊟ *AE, D, MC, V.*

¢ ✕ **Fu Jin.** *Chinese.* Although the place is a bit tattered, this family-run neighborhood restaurant consistently serves good wok-cooked favorites at reasonable prices. The fried tofu dishes and sesame-crusted shrimp are tasty. ⊠ *3549*

S.E. Hawthorne Blvd., Hawthorne District ☎ *503/231–3753* ▭ *D, MC, V* ⊗ *Closed Thurs.*

$$$$ ✕**Genoa.** *Italian.* Widely regarded as the finest restaurant in Portland, Genoa serves a five-course prix-fixe Italian menu that changes with the availability of ingredients and the season. Diners can chose from several entrées; the portions are hearty, thoughtfully crafted, and paired with some vibrant accompaniments such as sautéed brussels sprout leaves or roasted root vegetables. As for the dining room, its dark antique furnishings, long curtains, and dangling light fixtures all help make it feel sophisticated. Seating is limited to a under few dozen diners, so service is excellent. ✉ *2822 S.E. Belmont St., near Hawthorne District* ☎ *503/238–1464* ⌂ *Reservations essential* ⊕ *www.genoarestaurant.com* ▭ *AE, D, DC, MC, V* ⊗ *No lunch.*

$ ✕**Il Piatto.** *Italian.* On a quiet residential street, this laid-back trattoria and espresso house turns out inventive dishes and classic Italian favorites. A tasty sun-dried-tomato–pesto spread instead of butter accompanies the bread. Entrées include smoked salmon ravioli in a lemon cream sauce with capers and leeks. The vegetarian lasagna with grilled eggplant and zucchini, topped with pine nuts, is rich and satisfying. The extensive wine selection focuses on varieties from Tuscany. ✉ *2348 Ankeny St., near Laurelhurst* ☎ *503/236–4997* ⊕ *www.ilpiattopdx.com* ▭ *DC, MC, V* ⊗ *No lunch Sat.–Mon.*

¢ ✕**Ken's Artisan Pizza.** *Italian.* Old wine barrels and hungry crowds surround the pizza prep area and its glowing, 700-degree wood-fired oven. Ken, also of Ken's Artisan Bakery & Café, prides himself on the use of fresh, organic ingredients for the dough, sauces, and toppings. Fans rave about the margherita pizza with arugula. Another favorite is the handpressed sausage and onion. Although there are some fun appetizers and salads, pizza is the star. ✉ *304 S.E. 28th Ave.* ☎ *503/517–9951* ⊕ *www.kensartisan.com* ▭ *MC, V* ⊗ *Closed Sun. and Mon. No lunch.*

$ ✕**L'Astra Bistro.** *Continental.* Come as you are to this no-frills restaurant for a simple selection of Italian and French dishes: gnocchi with spinach, garlic sausage with lentils, and roasted duck are some unassuming favorites. Ice cream lovers will appreciate special flavors which change daily. Ask for them if they're not on the menu. ✉ *22 N.E. 7th Ave.* ☎ *503/236–3896* ⊕ *www.lastrabistro.com* ▭ *MC, V* ⊗ *Closed Sun. No lunch.*

$$ ✕**Lauro Kitchen.** *Mediterranean.* The wide, inviting space, large windows, and exposed wooden beams set the mood

for enjoying the action from an open kitchen, from which dishes like the seafood paella or the Greek-style braised pork shoulder emerge. Complete your meal with a glass of scotch or brandy, or warm cherry bread pudding with pistachio caramel sauce. Since this place is usually busy, expect to wait for a table. ⊠ *3377 S.E. Division St.* ☎ *503/239–7000* ⊕ *www.laurokitchen.com* ⊟ *AE, DC, MC, V.*

★ **Fodor's**Choice ✕**Lemongrass.** *Thai.* Set in an old house, this
$ lovely, intimate establishment consistently serves tantalizing pad Thai and a garlic basil chicken with sauce so delicious you wish you had a straw. Fresh flowers adorn the white linen tables. Dishes are cooked to order and just about everything is delectable, including the chicken chili paste and peanut curry. ⊠ *1705 N.E. Couch St.* ☎ *503/231– 5780* ⚖ *Reservations not accepted* ⊟ *No credit cards.*

$$$ ✕**Le Pigeon.** *French.* With exposed brick, bar seating, and an open kitchen, the atmosphere at this 42-seat restaurant is trendy, yet casual. And yes, pigeon, aka squab—cooked in red wine and served with liver crostini—is an entrée. Hardcore meat lovers might also appreciate the veal tongue appetizer. Aside from a changing menu, there are a few pasta and salad dishes as well. The wine menu is extensive, and they are open late. ⊠ *738 E. Burnside St.* ☎ *503/546– 8796* ⚖ *Reservations essential* ⊕ *www.lepigeon.com* ⊟ *MC, V* ⊗ *No lunch.*

$ ✕**McMenamins Kennedy School Courtyard Restaurant.** *American.* Whether you are coming to the Kennedy School to stay at the hotel, to watch a movie, or just to enjoy dinner and drinks, the Courtyard Restaurant can add to your evening. The food, with old reliables like burgers, salads, and pizzas, fish-and-chips, pasta, prime rib, and beef stew, can satisfy most any appetite. Several standard McMenamins microbrews are always available, in addition to seasonal specialty brews. ⊠ *5736 N.E. 33rd Ave., near Alberta District* ☎ *503/288–2192* ⊕ *www.kennedyschool.com* ⊟ *AE, D, MC, V.*

$$ ✕**Mint.** *Continental.* The owner of this cool, romantic restaurant also happens to be a top-notch bartender. Drinks made with maple syrup, nutmeg, and avocados are commonplace—and just as the beverages here are hard to categorize, so too are the menu items. Global flavors influence an evolving choice of interesting items like opah (a kind of fish) poached in coconut lemongrass sake, and sautéed rabbit loin with garlic mashed potatoes and wild boar bacon. When you're done, slip next door to 820, the sister

lounge to this suave establishment. ⊠ *816 N. Russell St.* ☎ *503/284–5518* ⊕ *www.mintrestaurant.com* ▭ *AE, MC, V* ⊙ *Closed Sun. No lunch.*

¢ ✕ **Nicholas Restaurant.** *Middle Eastern.* In a small streetfront along an unimpressive stretch of Grand Avenue, this hidden gem serves some of the best Lebanese food in Portland, for prices that can't be beat. Everything from the fresh homemade pita to the hummus, falafel, baba ghanoush, and kebabs is delicious and comes in enormous portions. No alcohol is served here. ⊠ *318 S.E. Grand Ave., near Burnside Bridge* ☎ *503/235–5123* ⊕ *www.nicholasrestaurant.com* ▭ *No credit cards.*

$ ✕ **Nostrana.** This well-liked restaurant delivers delicious pizzas and wood-grilled specialties (even desserts) from their signature oven. Between pies topped with roasted squash and smoked mozzarella to those sprinkled with radicchio and pancetta, the pizzas here would make mamma mia proud. Other tempting entrées are the fresh prawns and Satsuma oranges with white bean purée, and the Tuscan pork ribs with smashed celery root and spicy onion relish. ⊠ *1401 S.E. Morrison St.* ☎ *503/234–2427* ⊕ *www.nostrana.com* ▭ *MC, V.*

$ ✕ **Pambiche.** *Caribbean.* Locals know that you can drive by Pambiche any night of the week and find it packed. With traditional Cuban fare (plantains, roast pork, mojitos, and Cuban espresso), it is no surprise why. If you have some time to wait for a table, you should stop by and make an evening of it at this hopping neighborhood hot spot. Don't miss out on the incredible desserts here; it is the sole reason why some people make the trip. Try the La Selva Negra, a coconut chocolate cake filled with mango and other tropical fruit. ⊠ *2811 N.E. Glisan St., near Laurelhurst* ☎ *503/233–0511* ⊕ *www.pambiche.com* ⌕ *Reservations not accepted* ▭ *D, MC, V.*

$$ ✕ **Perry's on Fremont.** *American.* This diner, famous for burgers, chicken potpies, and fish-and-chips, has gone a bit more upscale with the addition of pricier menu items such as steak and salmon. Eat outside on the large patio among the flowers, and don't pass up one of the desserts. ⊠ *2401 N.E. Fremont St.* ☎ *503/287–3655* ⊕ *www.perrysonfremont.com* ▭ *AE, D, MC, V* ⊙ *Closed Sun. and Mon. No lunch weekdays.*

$ ✕ **Podnah's Pit BBQ.** *Southern.* This nondescript little storefront diner hardly even declares itself with outdoor signage—but don't be fooled—the Texas- and Carolina-style dishes at Podnah's are the stuff big boy barbecues are made of. Melt-in-your-mouth pulled pork, ribs, chicken, and lamb are all slow-smoked on hardwood and served up in a sassy vinegar-based sauce. ⊠ *1469 N.E. Prescott St.* ☎ *503/281–3700* ▭ *MC, V* ⊙ *Closed Mon.*

¢ ✕ **Pok Pok & Whiskey Soda Lounge.** *Asian.* There's no shortage of culinary adventure here. Food here resembles what street vendors in Thailand would make: charcoal-grilled game hen stuffed with lemongrass or shredded chicken and coconut milk (made in-house). Diners have options of sitting outside by heated lamps under tents, or down below in the dark, funky cave of the Whiskey Soda Lounge. Foods are unique blends of flavors and spices, such as the coconut and jackfruit ice cream served on a sweet bun with sticky rice, condensed milk, chocolate syrup, and peanuts. ⊠ *3226 S.E. Division St.* ☎ *503/232–1387* ⊕ *www.pokpokpdx.com* ▭ *MC, V.*

$$ ✕ **Rheinlander.** *German.* A strolling accordionist and singing servers entertain as patrons dine on authentic traditional German food, including sauerbraten, hasenpfeffer, schnitzel, sausage, and rotisserie chicken. **Gustav's,** the adjoining pub and grill, serves slightly less expensive entrées, including sausages, cabbage rolls, and German meatballs, in an equally festive and slightly more raucous environment. ⊠ *5035 N.E. Sandy Blvd.* ☎ *503/288–5503* ⊕ *www.rheinlander.com* ▭ *AE, MC, V.*

$ ✕ **Russell St. Bar-B-Que.** *Southern.* Pig bric-a-brac inside this redbrick building tips you off to the star specialty at this casual neighborhood joint, but there are also beef, poultry, seafood, and smoked tofu dishes available. A saucy pulled pork sandwich and collard greens pairs well with a strawberry soda. ⊠ *325 N.E. Russell St., off N.E. Martin Luther King Jr. Blvd.* ☎ *503/528–8224* ⊕ *www.russellstreetbbq.com* ▭ *AE, MC, V.*

$$$ ✕ **Salty's on the Columbia.** *Seafood.* Pacific Northwest salmon (choose blackened or grilled, a half or full pound) is what this comfortable restaurant overlooking the Columbia River is known for. Blackberry-barbecue-glazed salmon highlights local ingredients. Loaded with prawns, oysters, crab, mussels, and clams, the seafood platter offers plenty of variety. The menu also includes chicken and steak. There are both a heated, covered deck and an uncovered deck for open-air dining. ⊠ *3839 N.E. Marine Dr.* ☎ *503/288–4444* ⊕ *www.saltys.com* ▭ *AE, D, DC, MC, V.*

$ ✕ **Savoy.** *American.* Diners have their choice of sitting in either the dark and cozy tavern or the bright and open bistro. The macaroni and Wisconsin white cheddar cheese, buttery-rich garlic bread, and crispy roasted chicken are served without fanfare. Reasonably priced, seasonal menu items and a world-class tiramisu make this a solid choice for no-fuss dining. ⊠ *2500 S.E. Clinton* ☎ *503/808–9999* ⊕ *www.savoypdx.com* ⊟ *MC, V* ⊙ *No lunch.*

$$ ✕ **Sayler's Old Country Kitchen.** *Steak.* Home of the massive 72-ounce steak (free if you can eat it in an hour—and some do), Sayler's complements its steak-focused menu with a few seafood and chicken dinners. With no pretense of being trendy or hip, this large family-style restaurant and lounge near Gresham has been around since 1946 and relies today on the same old-fashioned menu and quality it did back then. ⊠ *10519 S.E. Stark St.* ☎ *503/252–4171* ⊕ *www.saylers.com* ⊟ *AE, D, MC, V* ⊙ *No lunch.*

$$ ✕ **Siam Society.** *Asian.* Oversize red shutter doors, a beautiful outdoor patio surrounded by full plants and flowers, and a lush upstairs lounge create an inviting atmosphere. Expect large portions of dishes such as char-grilled steak with a red wine reduction sauce and sweet potato fries lightly sprinkled with white truffle oil. The banana-roasted pork is made by slow-cooking pork shoulder for five days while wrapped in banana leaves; it's served with grilled pineapple. Drinks not to be missed include a ginger-lime cosmo and jalapeño-pear kamikaze. ⊠ *2703 N.E. Alberta St.* ☎ *503/922–3675* ⊕ *www.siamsociety.com* ⊟ *MC, V* ⊙ *Closed Mon.*

¢ ✕ **Thai Noon.** *Thai.* The excellent traditional dishes here, including red, green, and yellow curry; stir-fries; and noodle dishes, are served in a vibrant orange dining room with only about 12 tables. You can choose the spiciness of your meal, but beware that although "medium" may be milder than "hot," it's still spicy. Thai iced tea is also transformed into a boozy cocktail in the adjoining bar and lounge. Try the fried banana split or the mango ice cream for dessert. ⊠ *2635 N.E. Alberta St., Alberta District* ☎ *503/282–2021* ⊕ *www.thainoon.com* ⊟ *MC, V.*

¢ ✕ **Thanh Thao.** *Vietnamese.* This busy Asian diner in the heart of Portland's bohemian Hawthorne neighborhood has an extensive menu of Vietnamese stir-fries, noodles, soups, and Thai favorites. Be prepared to wait for *and* at your table: the place is often packed, and service is famously slow. But the food and generous portions are worth the wait. ⊠ *4005 S.E. Hawthorne Blvd., Hawthorne District* ☎ *503/238–6232* ⊟ *D, MC, V* ⊙ *Closed Tues.*

$$ ✕**Three Doors Down.** *Italian.* Down a side street, this small Italian restaurant is known for quality Italian food, with exquisite seafood dishes, skillful pasta concoctions, and rich desserts. The intimate restaurant's reputation brings people back again and again, even though they might have to wait on the sidewalk for close to an hour. ⊠ *1429 S.E. 37th Ave., Hawthorne District* ☎ *503/236–6886* ⊕ *www.3doorsdowncafe. com* ⊟ *AE, D, MC, V* ⊘ *Closed Mon. No lunch.*

¢ ✕**Tin Shed Garden Cafe.** *Café.* This small restaurant is a popular breakfast spot known for its shredded potato cakes, biscuits and gravy, sweet-potato cinnamon French toast, creative egg and tofu scrambles, and breakfast burritos. The lunch and dinner menu has creative items like a creamy artichoke sandwich, and a chicken sandwich with bacon, Gorgonzola, and apple, in addition to burgers, salads, and soups. A comfortable outdoor patio doubles as a beer garden on warm spring and summer evenings, and the adjacent community garden rounds off the property with a peaceful sitting area. ⊠ *1438 N.E. Alberta St., Alberta District* ☎ *503/288–6966* ⌾ *Reservations not accepted* ⊕ *www.tinshedgardencafe.com* ⊟ *MC, V*

¢ ✕**Vita Cafe.** *Vegetarian.* Vegan mac and cheese and vegetarian biscuits and gravy are just a few of the old favorites with a new, meatless spin. This hip restaurant along Alberta Street has a large menu with American, Mexican, Asian, and Middle Eastern–inspired entrées, and both herbivores and carnivores are sure to find something. There is also plenty of free-range, organic meat to go around. Finish off your meal with a piece of German chocolate cake or a peanut-butter fudge bar. ⊠ *3024 N.E. Alberta St., Alberta District* ☎ *503/335–8233* ⊕ *www.vita-cafe.com* ⊟ *MC, V.*

$$ ✕**Widmer Gasthaus.** *German.* This old world–style brewpub, part of the Widmer Brothers Brewery, is steps away from the MAX light rail station on North Interstate Avenue. Ale-dunked sausages, schnitzel, and sauerbraten go well with the signature hefeweizen and other German-style beers that come from the handsome hardwood-and-brass bar. Chicken potpie, steak, pasta, and burgers are also served, in addition to the Widmer brothers' beloved beer cheese soup. ⊠ *955 N. Russell St., at N. Interstate Ave., Albina* ☎ *503/281–3333* ⌾ *Reservations not accepted* ⊕ *www. widmer.com* ⊟ *AE, D, MC, V.*

$ ✕**Wild Abandon and the Red Velvet Lounge.** *Continental.* Inside this small, bohemian-looking building, where the dominant color is deep red and the light fixtures are multi-color glass, owner Michael Cox creates an inventive Mediterranean-influenced menu that includes fresh seafood, pork, beef, and pasta entrées. Vegetarian selections might be ziti, pan-fried tofu, or polenta lasagna made with roasted eggplant, squash, and spinach. The popular Sunday brunch includes omelets, Benedict dishes, breakfast burritos, and vegan French toast. ✉ *2411 S.E. Belmont St., near Hawthorne District* ☎ *503/232–4458* ⊕ *www.wildabansonrestaurant. com* ⊟ *AE, D, DC, MC, V* ⊘ *Closed Tues.*

Where to Stay

WORD OF MOUTH

"[T]he knock on the Hotel De Luxe is generally that their rooms are small-ish. Same is true of The Benson and The Heathman, both of which I think were built about the same time. Most often recommended Portland hotel is probably the Monaco. Many/most(?) of its rooms are suites."

—beachbum

Updated
by Janna
Mock-
Lopez

WHEN IT COMES TO LODGING, Portland covers the water-front: modern to historical, fancy to basic, innovative to conventional. Reputable, large chains are here, and so are luxury boutique hotels that emphasize service and splendor. Convenient options abound for destinations like the convention center and airport; and sprinkled throughout the city are one-of-a-kind bed-and-breakfasts that offer travelers a glimpse of authentic Portland living.

Aside from price, the main thing to consider is where in the city you want to be. Many of the elegant hotels near the city center and on the riverfront also have appeal because of their proximity to Portland's attractions. MAX light rail is within easy walking distance of most properties. The additional accommodations clustered near the Convention Center and the airport are almost all chain hotels that tend to be less expensive than those found downtown.

An alternative to the standard city hotel scene is to stay at one of the several beautiful B&Bs spread throughout residential neighborhoods in the northwest and northeast. These are usually lovely houses, with unique and luxurious guest rooms, deluxe home-cooked breakfasts, and friendly and knowledgeable innkeepers.

HOTEL PRICES

Portland's hotels will please visitors used to big-city lodging prices. Even most the more luxurious hotels can be booked for under $250 per night, and there are a lot of options for around $169 per night or less. If you are willing to stay outside of the downtown area (though this is the most convenient place to stay), you can easily find a room in a suburban chain hotel for well under $100 per night. Unlike in some cities, you will not see quite as many weekend discounts, although some of the top hotels for business travelers do offer these.

Before booking your stay, visit ⊕ *www.travelportland. com* to check out "Portland Perks," packages that usually include double-occupancy accommodation, free nightly parking, a Continental breakfast for two, and visitor vouchers for savings on dining, tax-free shopping, and more.

PORTLAND HOTEL BEST BETS

★ **Fodor's**Choice
Heathman Hotel, Hotel de-
luxe, Lion and the Rose

BEST FOR KIDS
Marriott Residence Inn Lloyd
Center, Shilo Inn Rose Garden,
Silver Cloud Inn

BEST B&BS
Lion and the Rose, Portland's
White House

BEST SERVICE
Benson Hotel, Heathman
Hotel

BEST LOCATION
The Nines, RiverPlace Hotel

BEST FOR ROMANCE
Hotel deLuxe, Paramount

PET-FRIENDLY
Aloft Portland Airport at Cascade Station

4

WHAT IT COSTS

¢	$	$$	$$$	$$$$
HOTELS				
under $60	$61–$100	$101–$140	$141–$180	over $180

Hotel prices are for a double room excluding room tax, which varies from 6%–9½% depending on location.

DOWNTOWN

Staying downtown ensures you'll have immediate access
to just about everything Portland offers, including events,
restaurants, cultural venues, shops, movie theaters, and
more. Transportation options are abundant thanks to the
MAX, bus lines, and taxis; in addition, many hotels offer
shuttle service. Portland has clean streets and, overall, is
considered relatively safe.

$$$–$$$$ ⊞ **Ace Hotel.** Designed to appeal to younger, budget-minded
travelers who crave quality, this funky, bohemian property
is in the center of downtown. Each room is uniquely
adorned by original hand-painted wall art; in a handful
you can find retro accessories like turntables (and record
collections) and bathrooms with cast-iron tubs. In case you
forgot your camera, there's even a photo booth in the lobby
to capture your stay. The great Clyde Common restaurant

TO AIRPORT

N.E. Siskiyou

43 - 46

47

49

41   42

N.E. Knott St.

N.E. Russell St.

48

N.E. Thompson St

N.E. Hancock St.

N.E. Schuyler St.

N.E. 2nd Ave.

N.E. 9th Ave.

S.E. Martin Luther King Jr. Blvd.

N.E. Broadway

LLOYD
DISTRICT

N.E. Weidler St.

31   32

N.E. Halsey St.

N.E. Wasco St.

Lloyd
Center ♦

N.E. Multnomah St.

35

36

33   **MAX LIGHT RAIL**

N.E. 1st Ave.

34   N.E. Holladay St.

♦
Oregon
Convention
Center

N.E. Lloyd Blvd.

N.E. Glisan St.

84

N.E. Everett St.

S.E. 11th Ave.

S.E. 12th Ave.

S.E. 14th Ave.

S.E. 15th Ave.

E. Burnside St.

37

S.W. Ankeny St.

S.E. Ash St.

5

99E

S.E. 1st Ave.

S.E. 2nd Ave.

S.E. Martin Luther King Jr. Blvd.

S.E. 7th Ave.

S.E. 8th Ave.

Sandy Blvd.

S.E. Stark St.

S.E. Washington St.

BUCKMAN
DISTRICT

TO HAWTHORNE
DISTRICT →

S.E. Belmont St.

38

S.E. Water Ave.

S.E. Main St.

S.E. 3rd Ave.

S.E. Grand Ave.

S.E. Madison St.

0   1/2 mile

0   1/2 kilometer

Ace Hotel, **15**

Aloft Portland Airport
at Cascade Station, **49**

Avalon Hotel & Spa, **29**

Benson Hotel, **10**

Courtyard Airport, **46**

Courtyard by Marriott-
Portland City Center, **12**

Crown Plaza Portland, **31**

Doubletree Hotel, **35**

Embassy Suites, **13**

Embassy Suites
Portland Airport, **44**

Georgian House, **48**

Governor Hotel, **18**

Heathman Hotel, **23**

Heron Haus, **4**

Hillsboro Courtyard
by Marriott, **6**

Hilton Garden Inn Beaverton, **25**

Hilton Portland &
Executive Tower, **24**

Holiday Inn Express, **1**

Hotel 50, **21**

Hotel Lucia, **11**

Hotel Modera, **26**

Hotel Monaco, **16**

Hotel Vintage Plaza, **14**

Inn at the Convention Center, **34**

Inn @ Northrup Station, **3**

The Jupiter Hotel, **37**

The Lion and the Rose, **47**

Mark Spencer, **9**

Marriott City Center, **17**

Marriott Residence Inn
Hillsboro, **7**

Marriott Residence Inn-
Lloyd Center, **36**

McMenamins
Kennedy School, **42**

Monticello Motel, **40**

The Nines, **20**

Palms Motel, **41**

Paramount, **22**

Park Lane Suites, **5**

Portland Marriott Downtown, **27**

Portland's White House, **43**

Quality Inn & Suites, **38**

Red Lion Hotel Convention
Center, **33**

Red Lion Hotel on the River, **39**

RiverPlace Hotel, **28**

Shilo Inn Rose Garden, **32**

Shilo Suites Airport, **45**

Silver Cloud Inn, **2**

Westin, **19**

is downstairs. **Pros:** unique lodging experience; original artwork in each room; city bicycles available for rent. **Cons:** poor water pressure; rooms are noisy. ✉ *1022 S.W. Stark St., Downtown* ☎ *503/228–2277* ⊕ *www.acehotel.com* ⤶ *79 rooms* ♿ *In-room: refrigerator, Wi-Fi. In-hotel: restaurant, laundry service, Wi-Fi hotspot, parking (fee), some pets allowed* ⊟ *AE, D, DC, MC, V.*

$$$$ 🏨 **Avalon Hotel & Spa.** On the edge of Portland's progressive South Waterfront District and just a few minutes from downtown, this tranquil boutique property is sheltered among trees along the meandering Willamette River. Rooms range widely in size (from about 340 up to 1,030 sq ft, and they are all tastefully decorated with simple yet warm furnishings; most have a balcony. There are a full service spa and extensive fitness facility on-site. Aquariva, an Italian restaurant and wine bar on the premises, serves wonderful tapas and drinks. **Pros:** great river views; trails nearby for walking and jogging; breakfast served on each hotel floor. **Cons:** not in the center of downtown, spa tubs in the fitness facility are not coed; steep overnight parking fee. ✉ *455 S.W. Hamilton Ct., Downtown* ☎ *503/802–5800 or 888/ 556–4402* ⊕ *www.avalonhotelandspa.com* ⤶ *99 rooms* ♿ *In-room: refrigerator (some), Wi-Fi. In-hotel: restaurant, room service, bar, gym, concierge, laundry service, Wi-Fi hotspot, parking (fee)* ⊟ *AE, MC, V* ⧖ *CP.*

$$$$ 🏨 **Benson Hotel.** Portland's grandest hotel was built in 1912. The hand-carved Circassian walnut paneling from Russia and the Italian white-marble staircase are among the noteworthy design touches in the public areas. In the guest rooms expect to find small crystal chandeliers and inlaid mahogany doors. Some even have the original ceilings. Extra touches include fully stocked private bars and bathrobes in every room. **Pros:** beautiful lobby; excellent location. **Cons:** hallways could use updating. ✉ *309 S.W. Broadway, Downtown* ☎ *503/228–2000 or 888/523–6766* ⊕ *www.bensonhotel.com* ⤶ *287 rooms* ♿ *In-room: refrigerator (some), dial-up, Wi-Fi. In-hotel: 2 restaurants, room service, bar, gym, concierge, laundry service, Wi-Fi hotspot, parking (fee)* ⊟ *AE, D, DC, MC, V.*

$$$ 🏨 **Courtyard by Marriott – Portland City Center.** Certified Gold LEED (Leadership in Energy and Design) for its energy efficiency, this 2009 hotel is one of just over a dozen U.S. hotels with this designation. The lobby, as welcoming as a living room, has individual kiosks rather than one big reception desk. The spacious rooms showcase local art and photography and the bathrooms offer bins for recycling,

and water-saving toilets. The Original restaurant serves upscale twists on traditional diner-style fare **Pros:** everything's new and environmentally conscious, great on-site restaurant. **Cons:** small gift shop; tubs available only in some rooms (on request). ⊠ *550 S.W. Oak St., Downtown* ☎ *503/505–5000* ⊕ *www.marriott.com* ⬥ *256 rooms* ⌂ *In-room: refrigerator, Wi-Fi. In-hotel: restaurant, room service, bar, gym, concierge, laundry service, Wi-Fi hotspot, parking (fee)* ▤ *AE, D, DC, MC, V.*

$$$–$$$$ ☒ **Embassy Suites.** The grand lobby welcomes you here, in the former Multnomah Hotel, built in 1912. The spacious, two-room suites have large windows, sofa beds, and wet bars. The indoor pool curves around the lower level of the hotel. A complimentary shuttle will take you anywhere within a 2-mi radius, based on availability. A cooked-to-order full breakfast and cocktail reception with light snacks are included in the rate. **Pros:** beautiful building; free shuttle service; excellent location. **Cons:** snack reception is popcorn and nachos; no in-and-out privileges in self-park garage across the street. ⊠ *319 S.W. Pine St., Downtown* ☎ *503/279–9000 or 800/643–7892* ⊕ *www.embassyportland.com* ⬥ *276 suites* ⌂ *In-room: refrigerator, Wi-Fi. In-hotel: restaurant, bar, pool, gym, spa, concierge, laundry service, Wi-Fi hotspot, parking (fee)* ▤ *AE, D, DC, MC, V* ⑩ *BP.*

$$$$ ☒ **Governor Hotel.** With mahogany walls and a mural of Pacific Northwest Indians fishing in Celilo Falls, the clubby lobby of the distinctive Governor helps set the 1920s Arts and Crafts style that's throughout the hotel. Painted in soothing earth tones, the tasteful guest rooms have large windows, honor bars, and bathrobes. Some have whirlpool tubs, fireplaces, and balconies. Jake's Grill is on the property, the streetcar runs right out front, and the hotel is one block from MAX. **Pros:** large rooms; beautiful 1920s property; excellent restaurant. **Cons:** some rooms in need of updates; no late-night room service. ⊠ *614 S.W. 10th Ave., Downtown* ☎ *503/224–3400 or 800/554–3456* ⊕ *www. govenorhotel.com* ⬥ *68 rooms, 32 suites* ⌂ *In-room: refrigerator, dial-up, Wi-Fi. In-hotel: restaurant, room service, bar, concierge, laundry service, Wi-Fi hotspot, parking (fee)* ▤ *AE, D, DC, MC, V.*

★ **Fodor's**Choice ☒ **Heathman Hotel.** The Heathman more than
$$$$ deserves its reputation for quality. From the teak-paneled lobby (hung with Warhol prints) to the rosewood elevators and marble fireplaces, this hotel exudes refinement. The guest rooms provide the latest in customized comfort: a

bed menu allows you to choose from orthopedic, European pillowtop, or European featherbed mattresses, and the bathrooms have plenty of marble and mirrors. The second-floor mezzanine—with a small art gallery (works change every few weeks) and a small library (primarily filled with the works of notable Heathman guests)—overlooks the high-ceiling Tea Court, a popular gathering spot in the evening. **Pros:** superior service; central location adjoining the Performing Arts Center; renowned on-site restaurant. **Cons:** small rooms; expensive parking. ⊠ *1001 S.W. Broadway, Downtown* ☎ *503/241–4100 or 800/551–0011* ⊕ *www.heathmanhotel.com* ⏎ *117 rooms, 33 suites* ⚏ *In-room: refrigerator, Internet, Wi-Fi. In-hotel: restaurant, room service, bar, gym, concierge, laundry service, Wi-Fi hotspot, parking (fee), some pets allowed* ⊟ *AE, D, DC, MC, V.*

$$$ ⊡ **Hilton Portland & Executive Tower.** Together, two buildings comprise a gargantuan complex of luxuriously contemporary bedrooms, meeting rooms, restaurants, and athletic facilities, including two indoor swimming pools. The property is within walking distance of the Performing Arts Center, Pioneer Courthouse Square, the Portland Art Museum, and MAX light rail. **Pros:** nice workout facilities and indoor pools; prime downtown location near attractions and restaurants. **Cons:** sporadic downtown construction could mean noise and traffic; not for those looking for homier lodging. ⊠ *921 S.W. 6th Ave., Downtown* ☎ *503/226–1611 or 800/445–8667* ⊕ *www.hilton.com* ⏎ *773 rooms, 9 suites* ⚏ *In-room: Internet. In-hotel: 2 restaurants, bars, pools, gym, Wi-Fi hotspot, parking (fee)* ⊟ *AE, D, DC, MC, V.*

★ **Fodor's**Choice ⊡ **Hotel deLuxe.** If you long to be transported
$$$–$$$$ back to the Hollywood glamour of the 1940s this place is perfect. The more than 400 black-and-white photographs on the corridor walls are cast into cinematic themes (Music Masters, Rebels, Exiles, and Immigrants). If the standard King James Bible in the drawer doesn't ignite your spiritual flame, than choose from a selection of other texts, including Buddhist, Taoist, Catholic, and even Scientologist offerings. **Pros:** "pillow menu" and other extra touches lend an air of luxury; artistic vibe. **Cons:** older windows in building can be drafty at night; cold bathroom floors. ⊠ *729 S.W. 15th Ave., Downtown* ☎ *503/219–2094 or 866/895–2094* ⊕ *www.hoteldeluxeportland.com* ⏎ *130 rooms* ⚏ *In-room: refrigerator, Wi-Fi. In-hotel: restaurant, room service, bar,*

Wi-Fi hotspot, parking (fee), some pets allowed ▭AE, D, DC, MC, V ⊚CP.

$$–$$$ ⊡ **Hotel 50.** This reasonable boutique property recently underwent a major renovation and the final results are pleasing. Décor is modern and clean, with glass, stone, and marble floor accents in the lobby. In the guest rooms, decorated with chocolate browns, deep purples, and oak highlights, there are 42" wall-mounted plasma HDTVs, ample work space, top-of-the-line memory-foam beds, and oversized walk-in showers. Another star attraction is the riverfront location. **Pros:** comfortable beds, river locations. **Cons:** no gift shop; no on-site fitness facility. ✉ *50 S.W. Morrison St., Downtown* ☎ *503/221-0711 or 877/237-6775* ⊕ *503/484-1417* ⊕ *www.hotelfifty.com* ⇌ *140 rooms 1 suite* ⊼ *In-room: refrigerator, Wi-Fi. In-hotel: restaurant, room service, bar, laundry service, Wi-Fi hotspot, parking (paid), some pets allowed* ▭ *AE, D, DC, MC, V.*

$$$–$$$$ ⊡ **Hotel Lucia.** Modern track lighting, black-and-white David Hue Kennerly celebrity photos, and comfy leather chairs adorn this eight-story boutique hotel in the heart of downtown—within walking distance of Nordstrom, Powell's, and the MAX line. The hotel's goal to "deliver calm" is accomplished in part through seven choices in pillows, stored customer profiles (so you automatically receive that same pillow next time), and Aveda soaps and lotions. The Pet Package comes with a special bed, set of dishes, treats, and Fiji water. **Pros:** prime location; luxurious amenities; consistently good service. **Cons:** small rooms; limited shelf and storage space in the bathrooms; those with allergies should request a pet-free room. ✉ *400 S.W. Broadway St., Downtown* ☎ *503/225–1717 or 877/225–1717* ⊕ *www. hotellucia.com* ⇌ *127 rooms, 33 suites* ⊼ *In-room: Wi-Fi. In-hotel: restaurant, room service, gym, concierge, laundry service, parking (fee), some pets allowed* ▭AE, D, DC, MC, V.

$$–$$$ ⊡ **Hotel Modera.** This boutique property, with contemporary furnishings and local artwork, is accessibly sophisticated. The well-appointed rooms are equipped with a flat-screen TV, wireless phone, an iPod docking station, and a do-not-disturb switch that lights up a sign outside your room. The most distinguishing feature are the outdoor firepits in the courtyard, where guests gather for warmth, cocktails, and conversation. **Pros:** large massage showerheads; noiseless ice makers located in every hall. **Cons:** rooms on the small side; located in the business district and far from restaurants and nightlife. ✉ *515 S.W. Clay St., Downtown* ☎ *503/484–1084 or 877/484–1084* ⊕ *www.hotelmodera.com* ↪ *168 rooms, 6 suites* ♿ *In-room: refrigerator, Wi-Fi. In-hotel: restaurant, laundry service, Wi-Fi hotspot, parking (fee)* ⊟ *AE, D, DC, MC, V.*

$$$–$$$$ ⊞ **Hotel Monaco.** Constructed in 1912, this building originally served as Lipman Wolfe, an upscale downtown department store. In 1996 the historic building reopened as a 221-suite luxury boutique hotel, and in 2007 the new owners, the Kimpton Group, completed a major upgrade. A tall vestibule with a marble mosaic floor leads to the art-filled lobby, where guests gather by the fireplace for an early-evening glass of wine or a morning cup of coffee. Upholstered chairs, fringed ottomans, lots of patterns, and other appointments in the sitting areas will make you feel right at home (or wish you had one like this). Downstairs in the lobby is the Dosha Spa. **Pros:** bathrooms stocked with lots of amenities; historic building; free Starbucks coffee in the morning. **Cons:** can get chilly at night because of drafty windows; rooms on lower floors tend to be noisier. ✉ *506 S.W. Washington St., Downtown* ☎ *503/222–0001 or 888/207–2201* ⊕ *www.portland-monaco.com* ↪ *82 rooms, 137 suites* ♿ *In-room: refrigerator, Wi-Fi. In-hotel: restaurant, room service, gym, laundry service, Wi-Fi hotspot, parking (fee), some pets allowed* ⊟ *AE, D, DC, MC, V.*

$$$–$$$$ ⊞ **Hotel Vintage Plaza.** This historic landmark takes its theme from the area's vineyards. Guests can fall asleep counting stars in top-floor rooms, where skylights and wall-to-wall conservatory-style windows are some of the special details. Hospitality suites have extra-large rooms with a full living area, and the deluxe rooms have a bar. All are appointed in warm colors and have cherrywood furnishings; some rooms have hot tubs. Complimentary wine is served in the evening, and an extensive collection of Oregon vintages is displayed in the tasting room. Two-story town house suites are named after local wineries. **Pros:** beautiful decor; nice complimentary wine selections; pet-friendly. **Cons:** those with allergies should ask for pet-free rooms; some street noise on the lower levels on the Washington side of the hotel. ✉ *422 S.W. Broadway, Downtown* ☎ *503/228–1212 or 800/243–0555* ⊕ *www.vintageplaza.com* ↪ *107 rooms, 21 suites* ♿ *In-room: refrigerator, Wi-Fi. In-hotel: restaurant, room service, bar, gym, concierge, Wi-Fi hotspot, parking (fee), some pets allowed* ⊟ *AE, D, DC, MC, V.*

$$-$$$ ⬚**Mark Spencer.** The Mark Spencer, near Portland's gay-bar district and Powell's City of Books, is one of the best values in town. The rooms are clean and comfortable, and all have full kitchens. The hotel, a major supporter of local arts, offers special packages that include theater tickets to performances by the Artists Repertory Theatre, Portland Opera, and Center Stage. **Pros:** afternoon tea and cookies is included; rooftop garden deck open to all guests. **Cons:** some rooms could use updating; those with allergies should request a pet-free room. ⊠ *409 S.W. 11th Ave., Downtown,* ☎ *503/224–3293 or 800/548–3934* ⊕ *www.markspencer. com* ⏍ *102 rooms* ⟁ *In-room: kitchen, Wi-Fi. In-hotel: laundry facilities, laundry service, Wi-Fi hotspot, pets allowed* ⊟ *AE, D, DC, MC, V* ⦿*CP.*

$$$ ⬚**Marriott City Center.** Close to many restaurants and arts organizations, this 20-story stone-and-brick property has a grand staircase, maple paneling, and marble floors inside. The "plus" rooms have voice mail, large work desks, and coffeemakers. The MAX light rail is two blocks away. **Pros:** work-friendly rooms; great location. **Cons:** refrigerators available upon request only. ⊠ *520 S.W. Broadway, Downtown* ☎ *503/226–6300 or 800/228–9290* ⊕ *www.marriott. com* ⏍ *249 rooms, 10 suites* ⟁ *In-room: refrigerator, Wi-Fi. In-hotel: restaurant, room service, bar, gym, concierge, laundry service, Wi-Fi hotspot, parking (fee)* ⊟ *AE, D, DC, MC, V.*

$$$$ ⬚**The Nines.** If you're looking for a little of the cosmopolitan flair of New York or Chicago, or if you want to spot celebrities passing through town, then this is the place for you. The decor is very swanky in this former landmark department store, with abstract art in the lobby and hallways, and furnishings in deep, rich tones of cream, turquoise, brown and burgundy. Rooms are spacious and well-appointed with iPod docking stations, 42", flat-screen TVs and DVD players. **Pros:** spacious bathrooms; excellent gym. **Cons:** rooms facing the atrium and overlooking the hotel's bar and restaurant can be noisy. ⊠ *525 S.W. Morrison St., Downtown* ☎ *503/222–9996 or 877/229–9995* ⊕ *www. thenines.com* ⏍ *331 rooms, 13 suites* ⟁ *In-room: refrigerator, DVD, Wi-Fi. In-hotel: 2 restaurants, room service, bar, gym, laundry service, Wi-Fi hotspot, parking (fee), some pets allowed* ⊟ *AE, D, DC, MC, V.*

$$$ ⬚**Paramount.** This pale-stone, 15-story hotel is two blocks from Pioneer Square, MAX, and the Portland Art Museum. The cozy rooms are adorned with earth tones, plush dark-wood furnishings, and dried flowers, and some have outdoor balconies and whirlpool tubs. The grand suites also have wet bars and gas fireplaces. Dragonfish, an excellent Pan-Asian restaurant, is on the premises. **Pros:** beautiful granite bathrooms; in-room honor bars. **Cons:** small fitness facilities; near ongoing downtown construction. ⊠ *808 S.W. Taylor St., Downtown* ☎ *503/223–9900* ⊕ *www.portland-paramount.com* ✎ *154 rooms* ⚠ *In-room: refrigerator, Wi-Fi. In-hotel: restaurant, room service, gym, concierge, laundry service, parking (fee)* ☐ *AE, D, DC, MC, V.*

\$\$–\$\$\$ ⚟ Park Lane Suites. Located a few blocks from Washington Park, Nob Hill, and downtown, this all-suites property is in a prime location. Rooms come with spacious, work-friendly living areas, and the kitchens come stocked with decent dishware, lots of cabinet space, and a full-size refrigerator, stovetop, microwave, and dishwasher. **Pros:** proximity to several of Portland's most prominent neighborhoods; expanded kitchen capacity. **Cons:** parking is free but limited; not enough soundproofing. ⊠ *809 S.W. King Ave., Downtown* ☎ *503/226–6288* ⊕ *www.parklanesuites.com* ✎ *44 rooms* ⚠ *In-room: kitchen, refrigerator, Internet, Wi-Fi. In-hotel: laundry facilities, laundry service, some pets allowed* ☐ *AE, D, DC, MC, V.*

\$\$\$–\$\$\$\$ ⚟ Portland Marriott Downtown. The large rooms at this 16-floor, corporate-focused Marriott are decorated in off-whites; the best ones face east, with a view of the Willamette and the Cascades. All rooms have work desks, high-speed Internet access, and voice mail. Champions Lounge, filled with sports memorabilia, is a singles' hot spot on weekends. **Pros:** excellent waterfront location; six blocks from MAX light rail. **Cons:** no refrigerators or minibars; can get crowded. ⊠ *1401 S.W. Naito Pkwy., Downtown* ☎ *503/226–7600 or 800/228–9290* ⊕ *www.marriott.com* ✎ *503 rooms, 6 suites* ⚠ *In-room: dial-up, Wi-Fi. In-hotel: restaurant, room service, bar, pool, gym, concierge, laundry facilities, laundry service, airport shuttle (fee), parking (fee)* ☐ *AE, D, DC, MC, V.*

\$\$\$–\$\$\$\$ ⚟ RiverPlace Hotel. All the guest rooms here have muted color schemes, Craftsman-style desks, and ergonomic chairs, and over a quarter of them have amazing views of the river, marina, and skyline, as well as a landscaped courtyard. Extras include bathrobes, afternoon tea and cookies, and rooms stocked with Starbucks coffee and Tazo tea. **Pros:** great location; wide selection of room options; great beds. **Cons:** no pool. ⊠ *1510 S.W. Harbor Way, Downtown* ☎ *503/228–3233 or 800/227–1333* ⊕ *www.riverplace-*

hotel.com ☞ *39 rooms, 45 suites* ☖ *In-room: DVD, Wi-Fi. In-hotel: restaurant, room service, concierge, parking (fee)* ▭ *AE, D, DC, MC, V.*

$$–$$$ ☷ **Silver Cloud Inn.** Staying at the Silver Cloud, adjacent to lively Northwest 23rd Avenue, is a great alternative to being right downtown. There's a broad selection of spacious, contemporary rooms—kings, suites, and Jacuzzi suites—with 42" HDTVs. During the week, local-area shuttle service is available. **Pros:** free parking; spacious rooms. **Cons:** no pool. ✉ *2426 N.W. Vaughn St., Downtown* ☎ *503/242–2400 or 800/205–6939* ⊕ *www.silvercloud.com* ☞ *82 rooms* ☖ *In-room: refrigerator, kitchen, Wi-Fi. In-hotel: laundry facilities, laundry service* ▭ *AE, D, DC, MC, V* ⚏ *CP.*

$$$–$$$$ ☷ **Westin.** This pale-stone European-style hotel combines luxury with convenience. Rooms here include entertainment-center armoires, work desks, plush beds covered with layers of down, and granite bathrooms with separate showers and tubs. Pioneer Square and MAX are two blocks away. The Daily Grill serves traditional American fare in upscale surroundings. **Pros:** prime downtown location; comfortable beds; well-equipped fitness center. **Cons:** no spa or sauna; limited room service menu. ✉ *750 S.W. Alder St., Downtown* ☎ *503/294–9000 or 888/625–5144* ⊕ *www.westin.com* ☞ *205 rooms* ☖ *In-room: safe, refrigerator, Internet, Wi-Fi. In-hotel: restaurant, room service, bar, gym, concierge, laundry service, parking (fee)* ▭ *AE, D, DC, MC, V.*

EAST OF THE WILLAMETTE

The area east of the Willamette is not nearly as condensed as downtown Portland, which means fewer interesting buildings. It's also a little harder to get around, though because of MAX and excellent bus service it's still doable. Properties tend to be older, with lower prices than downtown, and with more rooms free. The majority of chain hotels are clustered around the convention center; nearby is Lloyd Center Mall, which has an ice-skating rink, movie theaters, and several levels of shops and restaurants. There are also a number of B&Bs on this side of town, tucked away in historical neighborhoods like Irvington.

$$–$$$ ☷ **Crowne Plaza Portland.** This sleek, modern hotel is close to the Rose Quarter, the Coliseum, and the convention center, and is within easy walking distance of Lloyd Center,

TOP 5 PORTLAND LODGING TIPS

■ Vintage glamour meets the future at the Hotel deLuxe, where 1940s decor and black-and-white photographs coexist with flat-screen HDTVs and iPod docking stations in each room.

■ Make yourself at home at the Lion and the Rose, a 1906 Queen Anne–style mansion that's the city's only Victorian B&B.

■ Experience the funky, eclectic flair of the McMenamins Kennedy School, a renovated elementary school where guests can sleep in former classrooms and hang out at the Honor Bar or the Detention Bar.

■ See the city without having to leave your room: take in gorgeous river, marina, and skyline views at the River-Place Hotel.

■ Some hotels offer a pillow menu; the Heathman Hotel offers a bed menu—and plenty of refinement to spare.

the MAX line, and the Broadway Bridge leading to downtown. Given its attractive rooms and ample facilities, it's a reliable and convenient option for both business travelers and tourists. **Pros:** indoor pool; good selection of accommodations and room sizes. **Cons:** location near the Rose Quarter means traffic congestion during basketball games and concerts. ⊠ *1441 N.E. 2nd Ave., Lloyd District/Convention Center* ☎ *503/233–2401 or 877/777–2704* ⊕ *www.cpportland.com* ◆ *241 rooms* ♿ *In-room: refrigerator (some), Wi-Fi. In-hotel: restaurant, bar, pool, gym* ▤ *AE, D, DC, MC, V.*

$$–$$$ 🖪 **Doubletree Hotel.** This bustling, business hotel maintains a huge traffic in meetings and special events. The public areas are a tasteful mix of marble, rose-and-green carpet, and antique-style furnishings. The large rooms, many with balconies, have views of the mountains or the city center. Lloyd Center and the MAX light-rail line are across the street; the Oregon Convention Center is a five-minute walk away. **Pros:** convenient location; nice views, access to shops. **Cons:** pool is outdoors; can be crowded. ⊠ *1000 N.E. Multnomah St., Lloyd District* ☎ *503/281–6111 or 800/222–8733* ⊕ *www.doubletree.com* ◆ *476 rooms* ♿ *In-room: Ethernet, Wi-Fi. In-hotel: 2 restaurants, room service, bar, pool, gym, concierge, laundry service, Wi-Fi hotspot, parking (fee)* ▤ *AE, D, DC, MC, V.*

$–$$ 🖪 **Georgian House.** This redbrick Georgian Colonial with neoclassical columns is on a quiet, tree-lined street in a historic neighborhood. The gardens in back can be enjoyed from one of the guest verandas or from the gazebo. The largest and sunniest of the guest rooms is the Lovejoy Suite, with a tile fireplace and brass canopy bed. **Pros:** warm hospitality; intimate environment. **Cons:** residential neighborhood; some rooms have shared bathrooms; no elevator. ⊠ *1828 N.E. Siskiyou St., Irvington* ☎ *503/281–2250 or 888/282–2250* ⊕ *www.thegeorgianhouse.com* ◇ *2 rooms with shared bath, 2 suites* ☖ *In-room: no phone, no TV (some)* ⊟ *MC, V* ⦿ *BP.*

$$ ⊡ **Holiday Inn Express.** Spacious, updated rooms are at this hotel that's on the edge of Portland's trendy N.W. 23rd Avenue neighborhood. On-site is an indoor pool, and a generous continental breakfast buffet is included for guests. **Pros:** indoor pool; friendly service. **Cons:** close to a highway. ⊠ *2333 N.W. Vaughn Ave., N.W. 23rd Ave.* ☎ *503/484–1100 or 800/464–5329* ⊕ *www.hiexpress.com* ◇ *90 rooms* ☖ *In-room: refrigerator, Internet, Wi-Fi. In-hotel: laundry facilities, laundry service* ⊟ *AE, D, DC, MC, V* ⦿ *CP.*

$ ⊡ **Inn at the Convention Center.** Convenience is the big plus of this no-frills, independently run six-story hotel: it's directly across the street from the convention center, four blocks from Lloyd Center, and right along the MAX line. Rooms are simple and comfortable. **Pros:** right next to convention center; walking distance to Lloyd Center Mall. **Cons:** not wheelchair-friendly; could use updates. ⊠ *420 N.E. Holladay St., Lloyd District/Convention Center* ☎ *503/233–6331* ⊕ *www.innatcc.com* ◇ *97 rooms* ☖ *In-room: refrigerator (some), Wi-Fi. In-hotel: laundry facilities, laundry service, Wi-Fi hotspot, parking (no fee)* ⊟ *AE, D, DC, MC, V.*

$–$$ ⊡ **The Jupiter Hotel.** The hip and adventurous, looking for a place to crash for the night, flock to this contemporary hotel, which provides easy access to downtown. Rooms come with iPod docking stations, modern furniture, down comforters and colorful shag pillows, and chalkboard doors you can write on. Also on-site are a hair salon, a tattoo parlor, a clothing and gift boutique, and the Doug Fir rock club. **Pros:** easy access to downtown; funky lodging; built-in nightlife. **Cons:** not to everyone's taste; not immediately near a lot of shops or restaurants; near a loud hot spot. ⊠ *800 E. Burnside, Near Downtown* ☎ *503/230–9200 or 877/800–0004* ⊕ *www.jupiterhotel.com* ◇ *78 rooms, 1 suite* ☖ *In-room: Wi-Fi. In-hotel: restaurant, room service, bar, spa, Wi-Fi hotspot, parking (fee), some pets allowed* ⊟ *AE, D, DC, MC, V.*

4

★ Fodor's Choice 🏨 **Lion and the Rose.** Oak and mahogany floors,
$$$–$$$$ original light fixtures, antique silver, and a coffered dining-
room ceiling set a tone of formal elegance here, while the
wonderfully friendly, accommodating, and knowledgeable
innkeepers make sure that you feel perfectly at home. A
two-course breakfast and evening snacks are served daily.
In a beautiful residential neighborhood, you're a block from
the shops and restaurants that fill northeast Broadway and
within an easy walk of a free MAX ride downtown. Good
last-minute rates are sometimes available; check the Web
site. **Pros:** gorgeous house; top-notch service; afternoon tea
available upon request. **Cons:** kids under 10 not allowed;
no elevator; fills up quickly (particularly in summer). ✉ *1810
N.E. 15th Ave., Irvington* ☎ *503/287–9245 or 800/955–1647*
⊕ *www.lionrose.com* ⇌ *8 rooms* ♿ *In-room: Wi-Fi. In-hotel:
no kids under 10* ▤ *AE, D, DC, MC, V.*

$$$–$$$$ 🏨 **Marriott Residence Inn—Lloyd Center.** With large, fully
equipped suites and a short walk both to the Lloyd Center
and a MAX stop within the "fareless square," this three-
level apartment-style complex is perfect for extended-stay
visitors or for tourists. Rooms come equipped with full
kitchens and ample seating space, and many have wood-
burning fireplaces. There's a large complimentary breakfast
buffet each morning, and an hors d'oeuvres reception on
weekday evenings. **Pros:** full kitchens; accessible location.
Cons: pool is outdoors and closed during winter. ✉ *1710
N.E. Multnomah St., Lloyd District* ☎ *503/288–1400 or
800/331–3131* ⊕ *www.residenceinn.com* ⇌ *168 rooms*
♿ *In-room: kitchen, Wi-Fi. In-hotel: bar, pool, gym, laun-
dry facilities, Wi-Fi hotspot, parking (no fee), some pets
allowed* ⭐ *BP.*

$$ 🏨 **McMenamins Kennedy School.** In a renovated elementary
school in northeast Portland, the Kennedy School may well
be one of the most unusual hotels you'll ever encounter.
With all of the guest rooms occupying former classrooms,
complete with the original chalkboards and cloakrooms,
the McMenamin brothers have created a multi-use facility
that is both luxurious and fantastical. Go to the Detention
Bar for cigars and one of the only two TVs on-site; visit
the Honors Bar for classical music and cocktails. **Pros:**
funky and authentic Portland experience; room rates
include movie admission and use of the outdoor soaking
pool. **Cons:** no bathtubs (shower stalls only) in bathrooms;
no TVs in rooms; no elevator. ✉ *5736 N.E. 33rd Ave., near
Alberta District* ☎ *503/249–3983* ⊕ *www.kennedyschool.
com* ⇌ *35 rooms* ♿ *In-room: no TV, Wi-Fi. In-hotel: res-*

taurant, bars, Wi-Fi hotspot, parking (no fee) ▤ *AE, D, DC, MC, V* ⏀ *BP.*

$ ⚏ **Monticello Motel.** This is a smaller property with several accommodation options. One- and two-bedroom kitchen suites have cooking ranges with an oven, refrigerator, and microwave oven. Decor is standard motel fare with floral bedspreads and dark wood tables and chairs. It's close to freeway access, the MAX line, and buses. **Pros:** kitchen suites are well equipped. **Cons:** not immediately near shops and restaurants; little character; no elevator. ✉ *4801 N. Interstate Ave., North Interstate* ☎ *503/285–6641* ⊕ *www. monticellomotel.com* ⇝ *9 rooms* ☖ *In-room: refrigerator. In-hotel: Wi-Fi hotspot.*

¢ ⚏ **Palms Motel.** Clean, simple, and accessible to downtown, this property offers an affordable alternative to some of the larger chains. It's close to freeway access, the MAX line, and buses. The rooms, renovated 2008–09, are equipped with free Wi-Fi, microwaves, and refrigerators. **Pros:** affordable; friendly and eager staff. **Cons:** no frills; not immediately near shops and restaurants. ✉ *3801 N. Interstate Ave., North Interstate* ☎ *503/287–5788 or 800/620–9652* ⊕ *www.palms-motel.com* ⇝ *55 rooms* ☖ *In-room: refrigerator, Wi-Fi. In-hotel: Wi-Fi hotspot, parking (fee).*

$$$–$$$$ ⚏ **Portland's White House.** Hardwood floors with oriental rugs, chandeliers, antiques, and fountains create a warm and romantic mood at this elegant B&B in the historic Irvington District. The Greek Revival mansion was built in 1911 and is on the National Register of Historic Landmarks. Rooms have private baths, flat-screen TVs, and mahogany canopy or four-poster queen- and king-size beds. A full breakfast is included in the room rate, and the owners offer vegetarian or vegan options. Smoking and pets are not allowed, and there's no elevator. **Pros:** romantic; authentic historical Portland experience; excellent service. **Cons:** located in residential neighborhood; shops and restaurants several blocks away. ✉ *1914 N.E. 22nd Ave., Irvington* ☎ *503/287–7131 or 800/272–7131* ⊕ *www.port-landswhitehouse.com* ⇝ *8 suites* ☖ *In-room: dial-up, Wi-Fi. In-hotel: parking (free)* ▤ *AE, D, MC, V* ⏀ *BP.*

$$ ⚏ **Red Lion Hotel Convention Center.** Across the street from the convention Center and adjacent to the MAX, this hotel is convenient for both business travelers and tourists. It provides a few more on-site amenities than some of the other hotels right by the convention center, which is reflected in its slightly higher rates. They do accept pets, so be sure to ask for a no-pet room if you're allergic. **Pros:** right next to

convention center; walking distance to Lloyd Center Mall; pet-friendly. **Cons:** pet-friendly; can be crowded. ✉ *1021 N.E. Grand Ave., Lloyd District/Convention Center* ☎ *503/235–2100 or 800/343–1822* ⊕ *www.redlion.com* ✏ *174 rooms* ⚹ *In-room: refrigerator, Wi-Fi. In-hotel: restaurant, room service, bar, gym, Wi-Fi hotspot, parking (fee), some pets allowed* ⊟ *AE, D, MC, V.*

$$–$$$ ☒ **Shilo Inn Rose Garden.** This family-friendly hotel provides ♻ respectable accommodations and great service. Some rooms have sofas, and all the furnishings and amenities are up-to-date. It's a five-minute walk to the MAX transit center, which has direct service to the airport. **Pros:** recently remodeled property; spa and sauna on-site. **Cons:** no shuttle service; off the beaten path from shops and restaurants. ✉ *1506 N.E. 2nd Ave., Lloyd District* ☎ *503/736–6300 or 800/222–2244* ⊕ *www.shiloinns.com* ✏ *44 rooms* ⚹ *In-room: refrigerator, Wi-Fi. In-hotel: spa, no elevator, laundry service, Wi-Fi hotspot, parking (paid), some pets allowed* ⊟ *AE, D, DC, MC, V* ⊚ *CP.*

WEST OF DOWNTOWN

Once you start heading west, beyond Nob Hill and the West Hills, Portland begins to blur into the suburbs of Beaverton and Hillsboro. Several larger companies, including Nike and Intel, are headquartered here, so there are lots of lodging options, mostly larger chains. Weekdays tend to be busier, with lower rates on weekends.

Getting to and from the city from these outlying areas requires a drive on Highway 26, which is heavily congested during commute times. A great alternative to driving is taking the MAX. There are numerous stations throughout Hillsboro and Beaverton, and travel time is less than 30 minutes to downtown by MAX.

$$$–$$$$ ☒ **Heron Haus.** This lovely, bright B&B is inside a stately, 100-year-old three-floor Tudor-style mansion near Forest Park. Special features include a tulip-shaped bathtub in one room and a tiled, seven-head antique shower in another. You can enjoy a relaxing afternoon in the secluded sitting garden. All rooms have phones, work desks, and fireplaces. **Pros:** modern amenities; fancy continental breakfast included; plenty of room to roam on huge property. **Cons:** in a residential neighborhood; not immediately near public transportation. ✉ *2545 N.W. Westover Rd., Nob Hill* ☎ *503/274–1846* ⊕ *www.heronhaus.com* ✏ *6 rooms* ⚹ *In-*

room: Wi-Fi. In-hotel: no elevator, Wi-Fi hotspot, parking (no fee) ⊟*MC, V* ⊧⊙⊧*CP.*

$$–$$$ ⊡**Hillsboro Courtyard by Marriott.** This hotel provides easy access to shopping and restaurants in Hillsboro, as well as access onto U.S. 26 toward Portland. With large, comfortable rooms, it's perfect for business travelers, or for tourists who don't mind being several miles from downtown Portland. **Pros:** nice indoor pool; free shuttle service to downtown Portland (roughly 20 minutes without traffic). **Cons:** about 10 mi from downtown. ⊠*3050 N.W. Stucki Pl., Hillsboro* ☎*503/690–1800 or 800/321–2211* ⊕*www.marriott.com* ↪*149 rooms, 6 suites* ⟁*In-room: Wi-Fi. In-hotel: restaurant, room service, bar, pool, gym, laundry facilities, laundry service, Wi-Fi hotspot* ⊟*AE, D, DC, MC, V.*

$–$$ ⊡**Hilton Garden Inn Beaverton.** This four-level Hilton in suburban Beaverton brings a much-needed lodging option to Portland's west side. The property offers bright rooms with plush carpeting, work desks, and microwaves. It's right off U.S. 26. **Pros:** good value for money, nice indoor pool and whirlpool. **Cons:** not immediately near public transportation; far from shopping and restaurants. ⊠*15520 N.W. Gateway Ct., Beaverton* ☎*503/439–1717 or 800/445–8667* ⊕*www.hilton.com* ↪*150 rooms* ⟁*In-room: refrigerator, Wi-Fi. In-hotel: restaurant, room service, bar, pool, Wi-Fi hotspot, parking (no fee)* ⊟*AE, D, DC, MC, V.*

$$–$$$ ⊡**Inn @ Northrup Station.** Bright colors, original artwork, retro designs, and extremely luxurious suites fill this hotel in Nob Hill—it looks like a stylish apartment building from the outside, with patios or balconies adjoining most of the suites, and a garden terrace for all guests to use. The striking colors and bold patterns found on bedspreads, armchairs, pillows, and throughout the halls and lobby manage to be charming, elegant, and fun, never falling into the kitsch that plagues many places that strive for "retro" decor. All rooms have full kitchens, two TVs, three phones, and large sitting areas. **Pros:** roomy suites feel like home; great location that's close to the shopping and dining on Northwest 21st Avenue. **Cons:** past guests have commented on the lack of noise insulation. ⊠*2025 N.W. Northrup St., Nob Hill* ☎*503/224–0543 or 800/224–1180* ⊕*www.northrupstation.com* ↪*70 suites* ⟁*In-room: kitchen. In-hotel: Wi-Fi hotspot, parking (no fee)* ⊟*AE, D, DC, MC, V* ⊧⊙⊧*CP.*

$$–$$$ ⊡**Marriott Residence Inn Hillsboro.** Near the west side's many high-tech offices and factories, this all-suites hotel is popular with people relocating to Portland and perfect for

extended stays. It's within walking distance of several restaurants, a shopping center, and a multiplex theater. The
homey suites, some with fireplaces, have full kitchens. **Pros:**
full kitchens; free Wi-Fi; on-site market open 24 hours.
Cons: a distance from downtown Portland. ✉ *18855 N.W.
Tanasbourne Dr., Hillsboro* ☎ *503/531–3200 or 800/331–
3131* ⊕ *www.marriott.com* ⤳ *122 suites* ⚖ *In-room: VCR
(some), kitchen, Wi-Fi. In-hotel: tennis court, pool, gym,
no elevator, laundry facilities, laundry service, Wi-Fi
hotspot, parking (no fee), some pets allowed* ▭ *AE, D, DC,
MC, V* ⧀ *BP.*

PORTLAND INTERNATIONAL AIRPORT AREA

If you're flying in and out for a quick business trip, then
staying by the airport may be a good idea. The lodging
options here are only the larger chains. The airport is
about a 20- to 25-minute drive away from downtown
Portland.

Generally speaking, there's not much here in terms of noteworthy beauty, culture, restaurants, shops, or attractions—
with the possible exception of Cascade Station, a newer
mixed-use development for retail, lodging, and commercial
office space. Cascade Station offers the convenience of several restaurants and larger chain stores, including IKEA and
Best Buy. For all other attractions and nightlife, you'll have
to travel into the city or to a neighboring town.

$$–$$$ ▦ **Aloft Portland Airport At Cascade Station.** High-end vibrant
design, sophisticated amenities and fresh new concepts in
a hotel experience make the first Aloft in Oregon a standout
amid airport travel mediocrity. The ceilings are nine feet
high, windows are oversized and even the bathroom offers
natural light with full-length frosted glass panels surrounding walk-in showers. Other features include touchscreen
kiosks for choosing your room, getting your key, and print-
ing your departing flight's boarding pass. Dogs are not only
welcomed, they're treated like royalty by receiving their
own bed, toys, treats, and food bowl. Make time to relax
in the re:mix lounge, which flows into the WXYZ bar,
where there's a pool table and four-panel LCD TV "screen-
wall" for watching sports. **Pros:** lots of high-tech amenities;
welcoming social areas; unique, spacious rooms. **Cons:**
airport location; no sit-down restaurant. ✉ *9920 N.E. Cas-*

cades Pkwy., Airport ☎ *503/200–5678 or 866/672–7139*
⊕ *www.starwoodhotels.com/alofthotels* ⇨ *136 rooms* ◊ *In-room: refrigerator, Wi-Fi. In-hotel: bar, pool, gym, laundry facilities, laundry service, Wi-Fi hotspot, parking (free), some pets allowed* ▭ *AE, D, DC, MC, V.*

$–$$ ⊡ **Courtyard Airport.** This six-story Marriott inn is designed for business travelers. Rooms are brightly decorated in royal blue and gold tones with sitting areas and work desks. It's ¾ mi east of I–205 and 3 mi east of the airport. **Pros:** reliable service and amenities; work-friendly. **Cons:** airport location. ✉ *11550 N.E. Airport Way, Airport* ☎ *503/252–3200 or 800/321–2211* ⊕ *www.courtyard.com* ⇨ *150 rooms, 10 suites* ◊ *In-room: Wi-Fi. In-hotel: restaurant, room service, bar, pool, gym, laundry facilities, laundry service, Wi-Fi hotspot, parking (no fee)* ▭ *AE, D, DC, MC, V.*

$$–$$$ ⊡ **Embassy Suites Portland Airport.** Suites in this eight-story atrium hotel have beige walls and blond-wood furnishings. The lobby has a waterfall and koi pond. All suites come with separate bedrooms and living areas with sleeper sofas. It's on the MAX airport light-rail line. **Pros:** spacious suites; full breakfast included; free cocktails at happy hour. **Cons:** airport location. ✉ *7900 N.E. 82nd Ave., Airport* ☎ *503/ 460–3000* ⊕ *www.portlandairport.embassysuites.com* ⇨ *251 suites* ◊ *In-room: refrigerator. In-hotel: restaurant, room service, pool, gym, concierge, laundry service, airport shuttle, Wi-Fi hotspot, parking (no fee)* ▭ *AE, D, DC, MC, V* ⊚ *BP.*

$$–$$$ ⊡ **Red Lion Hotel on the River.** The rooms in this four-story hotel, on the Columbia River, have balconies and good views of the river and Vancouver, Washington. Public areas glitter with brass and bright lights that accentuate the greenery and the burgundy, green, and rose color scheme. **Pros:** river location; views from room balconies; close to the Jantzen Beach shopping center. **Cons:** pool is outdoors. ✉ *909 N. Hayden Island Dr., east of I–5's Jantzen Beach exit, Jantzen Beach* ☎ *503/283–4466 or 800/733–5466* ⊕ *www.redlion.com* ⇨ *320 rooms* ◊ *In-room: Wi-Fi. In-hotel: 2 restaurants, room service, bar, tennis court, pool, gym, laundry facilities, laundry service, Wi-Fi hotspot, parking (no fee)* ▭ *AE, D, DC, MC, V.*

$–$$ ⊡ **Quality Inn and Suites.** Although it's in Gresham, this hotel's proximity to I–205 makes for easy access to downtown, and it's just a short ride from the airport. Rooms are spacious and comfortable, and much of the hotel's interior has a woodsy flair that distinguishes it from many other chain hotels. **Pros:** suites include kitchenettes; hot breakfast buffet available every morning; value for money. **Cons:** a distance from downtown Portland. ✉ *2323 N.E. 181st Ave., Gresham* ☎ *503/492–4000 or 877/424–6423* ⊕ *www.choicehotels.com/hotel/or160* ⤳ *70 rooms, 23 suites* ⅜ *In-room: kitchen (some), dial-up, Wi-Fi. In-hotel: pool, gym, laundry facilities, Wi-Fi hotspot, parking (no fee), some pets allowed* ⊟ *AE, D, DC, MC, V* ⓧ *BP.*

$$$ ⊞ **Shilo Suites Airport.** Each room in this large, four-level all-suites inn is bright, with floral-print bedspreads and drapes, and has a microwave, wet bar, and two oversize beds. The indoor pool and hot tub are open 24 hours. **Pros:** large indoor pool; spacious rooms; free local calls. **Cons:** airport location. ✉ *11707 N.E. Airport Way, Airport* ☎ *503/252–7500 or 800/222–2244* ⊕ *www.shiloinns.com* ⤳ *200 rooms* ⅜ *In-room: refrigerator. In-hotel: restaurant, room service, bar, pool, gym, laundry facilities, laundry service, airport shuttle, Wi-Fi hotspot, parking (no fee)* ⊟ *AE, D, DC, MC, V* ⓧ *CP.*

Nightlife and the Arts

WORD OF MOUTH

"There are SO many good breweries here. One place right in downtown Portland has over 100 beers on tap, and that is Henry's 12th Street Tavern. . . . Other places we like are Pyramid, Widmer's, Bridgeport, Laurelwood, and Deschutes."

—mms

Updated
by Janna
Mock-
Lopez

PORTLAND IS QUITE THE CREATIVE TOWN. Every night performances from top-ranked dance, theater, and musical talent take the stage somewhere in the city. Expect to find never-ending choices for things to do, from taking in true independent films, performance art, and plays, to checking out some of the northwest's (and the country's) hottest musical groups at one of the city's many nightclubs.

As for the fine art scene, galleries abound in all four corners of Portland, and if you take the time and do a little research, you'll discover extraordinarily creative blends of artistic techniques. Painted, recycled, photographed, fired, fused, welded, or collaged—the scope and selection of art is one of the most notable attributes of what makes this city so metropolitan and alive.

PUBLICATIONS

"A&E, The Arts and Entertainment Guide," published each Friday in the *Oregonian* (⊕ *www.oregonlive.com),* contains listings of performers, productions, events, and club entertainment. *Willamette Week* (⊕ *wweek.com*), published free each Wednesday and widely available throughout the metropolitan area, contains similar, but hipper, listings. *Portland Family Magazine* (⊕ *www.portlandfamily.com*) is a free monthly publication that has an excellent calendar of events for recreational and educational opportunities for families. The *Portland Mercury* (⊕ *www.portlandmercury. com*) is another free entertainment publication distributed each Wednesday. *Just Out* (⊕ *www.justout.com),* the city's gay and lesbian newspaper, is published bimonthly.

NIGHTLIFE

Portland has become something of a base for young rock bands, which perform in dance clubs scattered throughout the metropolitan area. Good jazz groups perform nightly in clubs and bars. Top-name musicians and performers in every genre regularly appear at the city's larger venues.

BARS AND LOUNGES

From chic to cheap, cool to cultish, Portland's diverse bars and lounges blanket the town. The best way to experience some of the city's hottest spots is to check out the happy hour menus found at almost all of Portland's bars; they offer excellent deals on both food and drinks.

PORTLAND TOP 5 NIGHTLIFE TIPS

■ Become immersed in an Oregon Symphony classical or pops concert at the Arlene Schnitzer Concert Hall; enjoy a post-symphony glass of wine at a nearby restaurant bar afterward.

■ Spend a day strolling around the galleries at the Portland Art Museum and exploring the contemporary and Native American exhibits.

■ Catch an internationally known jazz band or discover a new blues group at one of Portland's many live music venues.

■ Go to a First Thursday event in the Pearl District or a Last Thursday showing in Alberta and soak up the local visual arts scene.

■ Sip a designer cocktail made with fresh ingredients—from run-of-the-mill juices and mixers to chilies, nutmeg, and even rhubarb—at any one of the trendy downtown bars.

DOWNTOWN

Many of the best bars and lounges in Portland are found in its restaurants.

At the elegant **Heathman Hotel** (⊠ *1001 S.W. Broadway* ☎ *503/241–4100*) you can sit in the marble bar or the wood-paneled Tea Court.

Huber's Cafe (⊠ *411 S.W. 3rd Ave.* ☎ *503/228–5686*), the city's oldest restaurant, is notable for its Spanish coffee and old-fashioned feel.

The young and eclectic crowd at the **Lotus Cardroom and Cafe** (⊠ *932 S.W. 3rd Ave.* ☎ *503/227–6185*) comes to drink and play pool or foosball.

The **Rialto** (⊠ *529 S.W. 4th Ave.* ☎ *503/228–7605*) is a large, dark bar with several pool tables and enthusiastic players as well as some of the best Bloody Marys in town.

Saucebox (⊠ *214 S.W. Broadway* ☎ *503/241–3393*) attracts a sophisticated crowd that enjoys colorful cocktails and trendy DJ music Wednesday–Saturday evenings.

With more than 120 choices, **Southpark** (⊠ *901 S.W. Salmon St.* ☎ *503/326–1300*) is a perfect spot for a post-symphony glass of wine.

At **Veritable Quandary** (⊠ *1220 S.W. 1st Ave.* ☎ *503/227–7342*), along the river, you can sit on the cozy, tree-filled outdoor patio or in the glass atrium.

CLOSE UP

Classic Cocktails

Classic cocktails are back with a vengeance chic enough to make James Bond proud, and they have a new twist: being infused with anything flavorful that grows under the sun. Throughout the northwest, emphasis on freshness and sustainability has spilled over into the mixers, shakers, and blenders of creative mixologists. Avocados, cucumbers, chilies, green peppers, cilantro, nutmeg, rhubarb, and beets are some of the luminaries infusing tangy hints and boldness into rums, vodkas, and whiskeys. Regionally, drink swankiness and sophistication have reached soaring heights. The book *Hip Sips,* by Portland Mint/820 bartender and restaurateur Lucy Brennan is dedicated to this intoxicating topic, with more than 60 imaginative recipes to choose from.

NORTHWEST

The modern bar at **Bluehour** (⊠*250 N.W. 13th Ave., Pearl District* ☎*503/226–3394*) draws a chic crowd for specialty cocktails such as the Bluehour Breeze (house-infused grapefruit vodka with a splash of cranberry).

Boisterous **Gypsy** (⊠*625 N.W. 21st Ave., Nob Hill* ☎*503/796–1859*) has 1950s-like furnishings.

Henry's 12th Street Tavern (⊠*10 N.W. 12th Ave., Pearl District* ☎*503/227–5320*) has 100 beers and hard ciders on draft, plasma-screen TVs, and a billiards room in a building that was once Henry Weinhard's brewery.

Young hipsters pack **Muu-Muus** (⊠*612 N.W. 21st Ave., Nob Hill* ☎*503/223–8169*) on weekend nights.

At **Oba!** (⊠*555 N.W. 12th Ave., Pearl District* ☎*503/228–6161*), plush tans and reds with lime-green backlit walls set a backdrop for South American salsa.

21st Avenue Bar & Grill (⊠*721 N.W. 21st Ave., Nob Hill* ☎*503/222–4121*) open until 2:30 AM, has a patio and outdoor bar.

An upscale martini-loving crowd chills at **Wildwood** (⊠*1221 N.W. 21st Ave., Nob Hill* ☎*503/248–9663*).

EAST PORTLAND

Artsy, hip east-siders, not to be mistaken for the jet-setters downtown, hangs and drinks martinis and wine at the minimalist **Aalto Lounge** (⊠*3356 S.E. Belmont St.* ☎*503/235–6041*).

One of the few bars on northeast Alberta Street, **Bink's** (⊠*2715 N.E. Alberta St.* ☎*503/493–4430*) is a small, friendly neighborhood spot with cozy seats around a fireplace, a pool table, and a good jukebox. It serves only beer and wine.

Swift Lounge (⊠*1932 N.E. Broadway* ☎*503/288–3333*), a popular tapas bar, draws a cocktail-sipping crowd of hipsters at night.

Green lanterns glow on the curvy bar as hip patrons sip Mojitos or other mixed drinks at the no-smoking hot spot **820** (⊠*820 N. Russell St.* ☎*503/284–5518*).

A laid-back beer-drinking crowd fills the **Horse Brass Pub** (⊠*4534 S.E. Belmont St.* ☎*503/232–2202*), as good an English-style pub as you will find this side of the Atlantic, with more than 50 beers on tap.

The open, airy **Imbibe** (⊠*2229 S.E. Hawthorne Blvd.* ☎*503/239–4002*) serves up creative cocktails, such as its namesake, the Imbibe Infusion—a thyme-and-ginger-infused vodka and strawberry martini with a touch of lemon.

Noble Rot (⊠*1111 E. Burnside St., 4th fl.* ☎*503/233–1999*) is a chic east-side wine bar with excellent food and red leather booths.

BREWPUBS, BREW THEATERS, AND MICROBREWERIES

Dozens of small breweries operating in the metropolitan area produce pale ales, bitters, bocks, barley wines, and stouts. Some have attached pub operations, where you can sample a foaming pint of house ale. "Brew theaters," former neighborhood movie houses where patrons enjoy food, suds, and recent theatrical releases, are part of the microbrewery phenomenon. Many are branches of McMenamins, a locally owned chain of bars, restaurants, nightclubs, and hotels, and some of these pubs can be found in restored historic buildings.

The **Bagdad Theatre and Pub** (⊠*3702 S.E. Hawthorne Blvd., Hawthorne District* ☎*503/236–9234*) screens second-run

Hollywood films and serves McMenamins ales and Pizzacato Pizza.

The first McMenamins brewpub, the **Barley Mill Pub** (✉ *1629 S.E. Hawthorne Blvd., Hawthorne District* ☎ *503/231–1492*), is filled with Grateful Dead memorabilia and concert posters. It's a fun place for families.

BridgePort BrewPub & Restaurant (✉ *1313 N.W. Marshall St., Pearl District* ☎ *503/241–7179*), Portland's oldest microbrewery, prepares hand-tossed pizza *(⇨ Where to Eat)* to accompany its ales.

Inside an old warehouse with high ceilings and rustic wood tables, the **Lucky Labrador Brew Pub** (✉ *915 S.E. Hawthorne Blvd.* ☎ *503/236–3555*) serves handcrafted ales and pub food both in the brewery and on the patio, where your four-legged friends are welcome to join you.

First opened in 1987, the **Mission Theatre** (✉ *1624 N.W. Glisan St., Nob Hill* ☎ *503/223–4527*) was the first McMenamins brew theater. It shows recent Hollywood offerings.

Ringlers (✉ *1332 W. Burnside St., Downtown* ☎ *503/225–0627*) occupies the first floor of the building that houses the famous Crystal Ballroom *(⇨ Dancing)*.

Ringlers Annex (✉ *1223 S.W. Stark St., Downtown* ☎ *503/525–0520*), one block away from Ringlers, is a pie-shaped corner pub where you can puff a cigar while drinking beer, port, or a single-malt scotch.

In a former church, the **St. John's Pub** (✉ *8203 N. Ivanhoe, St. John's* ☎ *503/283–8520*) includes a beer garden and a movie theater.

Tugboat Brewery (✉ *711 S.W. Ankeny St., Downtown* ☎ *503/226–2508*) is a small, cozy brewpub with books and games, picnic tables, and experimental jazz several nights a week.

Widmer Brewing and Gasthaus (✉ *955 N. Russell St., North Portland, near Fremont Bridge* ☎ *503/281–3333*) brews German-style beers and has a full menu; you can tour the adjacent brewery Friday and Saturday.

COFFEEHOUSES AND TEAHOUSES

Coffee is to Portland as tea is to England. For Portlanders, sipping a cup of coffee is a right, a ritual, and a pastime that occurs no matter the time of day or night. There's no shortage of cafés to park and read, reflect, or rejuvenate for the long day or night of exploration ahead.

DOWNTOWN

Serving quite possibly the best coffee around, **Stumptown Coffee Roasters** (✉ 128 S.W. 3rd Ave., Downtown ☎ 503/295–6144) has three local cafés, where its beans are roasted daily on vintage cast-iron equipment for a consistent, fresh flavor.

NOB HILL AND VICINITY

Anna Bannanas (✉ 1214 N.W. 21st Ave., Nob Hill ☎ 503/274–2559) serves great espresso and coffee, veggie sandwiches, soup, and smoothies. There's outdoor seating out front.

One of the more highly trafficked locales in the Portland coffee scene, **World Cup Coffee and Tea** (✉ 1740 N.W. Glisan St. ☎ 503/228–4152), sells excellent organic coffee and espresso in Nob Hill, as well as at its store in the Pearl District at the Ecotrust building and at Powell's City of Books on Burnside.

EAST PORTLAND

Common Grounds (✉ 4321 S.E. Hawthorne Blvd., East Portland ☎ 503/236–4835) has plush couches and serves desserts plus sandwiches and soup.

Palio Coffee and Dessert House (✉ 1996 S.E. Ladd St., Ladd's Addition, near Hawthorne District ☎ 503/232–9412), in the middle of peaceful residential Ladd's Addition, has delicious desserts and espresso, and is open later than many coffee shops in the area.

Post-collegiate sippers lounge on sofas and overstuffed chairs at **Pied Cow** (✉ 3244 S.E. Belmont St., East Portland ☎ 503/230–4866), a laid-back alternative to the more yuppified establishments.

Rimsky Korsakoffee House (✉ 707 S.E. 12th Ave., East Portland ☎ 503/232–2640), one of the city's first coffeehouses, is still one of the best, especially when it comes to desserts.

Stumptown Coffee Roasters (✉ 4525 S.E. Division St. ☎ 503/230–7702 ✉ 3356 S.E. Belmont St. ☎ 503/232–8889) has two cafés on the East Side. At the original site, organic beans are still roasted daily. At the Stumptown Annex, the newer branch next door, patrons can participate in "cup-pings" (tastings) daily at 3 PM.

With soft music and the sound of running water in the background, the **Tao of Tea** (✉ *3430 S.E. Belmont St., East Portland* ☎ *503/736–0119*) serves vegetarian snacks and sweets as well as more than 80 loose-leaf teas.

DANCING

A couple of cocktails and some good music are all that's needed to shake your groove thing at Portland's hot spots for dancing. Clubs feature both live bands and DJs spinning the latest in dance floor favorites.

Part 1950s diner, part log cabin, the **Doug Fir** (✉ *830 E. Burnside St., Downtown* ☎ *503/231–9663*) hosts DJs and live rock shows from up-and-coming bands seven nights a week.

Tuesday through Saturday, the **Fez Ballroom** (✉ *316 S.W. 11th St., Downtown* ☎ *503/221–7262*) draws a dancing crowd at this funky, Moroccan-style space.

McMenamins Crystal Ballroom (✉ *1332 W. Burnside St., Downtown* ☎ *503/225–0047*) is a famous Portland dance hall that dates from 1914. Rudolph Valentino danced the tango here in 1923, and you may feel like doing the same once you step out onto the 7,500-sq-ft "elastic" floor (it's built on ball bearings) and feel it bouncing beneath your feet. Bands perform everything from swing to hillbilly rock nightly except Monday.

GAY AND LESBIAN CLUBS

Portland's gay community has a decent selection of places to mingle, dance, and drink; several of these night spots are open into the wee hours, until 4 AM or so.

Part of the same disco-bar-restaurant complex as the Fez Ballroom, **Boxxes** (✉ *1035 S.W. Stark St., Downtown* ☎ *503/226–4171*) has multiple video screens that display everything from music to messages from would-be dates.

Attracting mostly gay men, **C.C. Slaughters** (✉ *219 N.W. Davis Ave., Old Town* ☎ *503/248–9135*) bar has a restaurant and a dance floor that's crowded on weekend nights; weeknights yield karaoke and country dancing.

Egyptian Room (✉ *3701 S.E. Division St., south of Hawthorne District* ☎ *503/236–8689*), Portland's lesbian bar-disco, has pool tables, video poker, and a medium-size dance floor.

Open till 4 AM, **Embers** (✉ *11 N.W. Broadway Ave., Old Town* ☎ *503/222–3082*) is a popular after-hours place to dance; the club hosts occasional drag shows and theme nights.

Fox and Hounds (✉ *217 N.W. 2nd Ave., Old Town* ☎ *503/243–5530*) is popular with both gay men and lesbians. A full menu is served in the evenings, and the place is packed for Sunday brunch.

Scandals (✉ *1125 S.W. Stark St., Downtown* ☎ *503/227–5887*) has plate-glass windows with a view of Stark Street and the city's streetcars. At this low-key place there's a small dance floor, video poker, and a pool table, and the bar serves light food noon to close.

LIVE MUSIC

Perhaps one of Portland's greatest attributes is the quality selection of live music—especially jazz and blues—that's available seven nights a week. Clubs are full most nights with faithful followers who go to see and hear some of the most talented musicians take the stage and command the crowds with awesome performances.

MUSIC FESTIVALS

The **Bite of Oregon** (✉ *Waterfront Park, Downtown* ☎ *503/248–0600* ⊕ *www.biteoforegon.com*) festival, held in early August and a benefit for Special Olympics Oregon, features the best in the local food and wine scene with eclectic choices in live entertainment.

Since 1982 the **Mt. Hood Jazz Festival** (✉ *26000 S.E. Stark St., Gresham* ☎ *503/661–2700* ⊕ *www.mthoodjazz.com*), held for three days in August, has drawn big names as well as new talent. Past years have seen appearances by Ella Fitzgerald, Sarah Vaughan, and George Benson. The festival is held on the campus of Mount Hood Community College in suburban Gresham. Take MAX light rail to Gresham Transit Center and transfer to Bus 26.

The second largest blues festival in the country, the four-day **Waterfront Blues Festival** (☎ *503/973–3378* ⊕ *www.waterfrontbluesfest.com*), has been drawing big names in blues and big crowds over the July 4 weekend since 1987. Past performers include Keb' Mo', Susan Tedeschi, Johnny Winter, and Sharon Jones & the Dap-Kings.

BLUES, FOLK, AND ROCK

The **Aladdin Theater** (⊠ *3017 S.E. Milwaukie Ave.* ☎ *503/234–9694*), in an old movie theater, is one of the best music venues in town. It serves microbrews and pizza.

Berbati's Pan (⊠ *10 S.W. 3rd Ave., Old Town* ☎ *503/226–2122*), on the edge of Old Town, has dancing and live music, everything from big band and swing to acid jazz, rock, and R&B.

Candlelight Room (⊠ *2032 S.W. 5th Ave., Downtown* ☎ *503/222–3378*) presents blues nightly.

Dublin Pub (⊠ *6821 S.W. Beaverton–Hillsdale Hwy., Beaverton* ☎ *503/297–2889*), on the west side, pours more than 50 beers on tap and hosts Irish bands and rock groups.

Kell's Irish Restaurant & Pub (⊠ *112 S.W. 2nd Ave., Old Town* ☎ *503/227–4057*) serves terrific Irish food and presents Celtic music nightly.

Locals crowd the **Laurelthirst Public House** (⊠ *2958 N.E. Glisan St., Laurelhurst* ☎ *503/232–1504*) to eat tasty food, sit in cozy red booths, and listen to folk, jazz, country, or bluegrass music on its tiny stage. There are pool tables in an adjoining room.

The down-to-earth **Produce Row Cafe** (⊠ *204 S.E. Oak St., east side, near Burnside Bridge and I–5* ☎ *503/232–8355*) has a huge beer list, a great beer garden, and live bluegrass, folk, and acoustic music most nights of the week.

COUNTRY AND WESTERN

Duke's (⊠ *14601 S.E. Division St.* ☎ *503/760–1400*) books occasional country and country-rock performers and hosts nightly DJ dancing to country music.

Not your ordinary truck stop, the Ponderosa Lounge at **Jubitz Truck Stop** (⊠ *10350 N. Vancouver Way* ☎ *503/345–0300*) presents live country music and dancing Thursday through Saturday.

JAZZ

Upstairs at the **Blue Monk** (⊠ *3341 S.E. Belmont St., East Portland* ☎ *503/595–0575*) local artists' works are on display and patrons nosh on large plates of pasta and salads; the live-jazz venue downstairs displays jazz memorabilia and photos.

Dubbed one of the world's "top 100 places to hear jazz" by *DownBeat*, **Jimmy Mak's** (✉ *300 S.W. 10th, Pearl District* ☎ *503/295–6542*) also serves Greek and Middle Eastern dishes and has a basement lounge outfitted with two pool tables and an Internet jukebox.

THE ARTS

The conundrum of delving into Portland's art scene won't be *if* you can find something to do—it will be *what* to do when you discover there's almost too much to choose from. For a city of this size, there is truly an impressive—and accessible—scope of talent from visual artists, performance artists, and musicians. The arts are alive, with outdoor sculptural works strewn around the city, ongoing festivals, and premieres of traveling Broadway shows. Top-named international acts, such as Bruce Springsteen, Rolling Stones, Paul McCartney, and Billy Joel, regularly include Portland in their worldwide stops.

TICKETS

Most Portland-based performing arts groups have their own box-office numbers; *see individual listings.*

For tickets to most events, call **Ticketmaster** (☎ *800/745–3000* ⊕ *www.ticketmaster.com*).

TicketsWest (☎ *503/224–8499* ⊕ *www.ticketswest.com*).

During the summer half-price tickets for almost any event are available the day of the show at Ticket Central in the **Visitor Information and Services Center** (✉ *Pioneer Courthouse Sq., Downtown* ☎ *503/275–8358 after 10* AM), open Monday–Saturday 9–4:30. This is an outlet for tickets from Ticketmaster and TicketsWest. Credit cards are accepted, but you must buy tickets in person.

PERFORMANCE VENUES

The **Agnes Flanagan Chapel at Lewis & Clark College** (✉ *615 S.W. Palatine Hill Rd., Southwest Portland*) hosts some smaller concerts.

The 2,776-seat **Arlene Schnitzer Concert Hall** (✉ *Portland Center for the Performing Arts, S.W. Broadway and Main St., Downtown* ☎ *503/274–6560*), built in 1928 in an Italian rococo revival style, hosts rock stars, choral groups, lectures, and concerts by the Oregon Symphony and others.

Downtown, the **First Baptist Church** (✉ *1425 S.W. 20th Ave., Downtown*) occasionally hosts more intimate concerts and performances.

With 3,000 seats and outstanding acoustics, **Keller Auditorium** (✉ *222 S.W. Clay St., Downtown* ☎ *503/274–6560*) hosts performances by the Portland Opera and Portland Ballet as well as country and rock concerts and touring shows.

Memorial Coliseum (✉ *1 Center Ct., Rose Quarter, Lloyd Center District* ☎ *503/235–8771* ⊕ *www.rosequarter.com*), a 12,000-seat venue on the MAX light-rail line, books rock groups, touring shows, the Ringling Brothers circus, ice-skating extravaganzas, and sporting events.

PGE Park (✉ *1844 S.W. Morrison St., Downtown/Nob Hill* ☎ *503/553–5400* ⊕ *www.pgepark.com*) is home to the Portland Beavers Triple-A baseball team and the Portland Timbers soccer team. The 20,000-seat stadium also hosts concerts and other sporting events. No parking is available at the park; MAX light rail is the most convenient option. Your game ticket entitles you to a free round-trip.

Portland Center for the Performing Arts (✉ *1111 S.W. Broadway, Downtown* ☎ *503/274–6560* ⊕ *www.pcpa.com*) hosts opera, ballet, rock shows, symphony performances, lectures, and Broadway musicals in its three venues *(⇨ Downtown in Exploring Portland)*.

Reed College's Kaul Auditorium (✉ *3203 S.E. Woodstock Blvd., Reed/Woodstock*) hosts the Portland Baroque Orchestra, among others.

The 21,000-seat **Rose Garden** (✉ *1 Center Ct., Broadway and N. Interstate Ave., Lloyd Center District* ☎ *503/235–8771* ⊕ *www.rosequarter.com*) is home to the Portland Trail Blazers basketball team and the site of other sporting events and rock concerts. The arena is on the MAX light-rail line.

The **Roseland Theater** (✉ *8 N.W. 6th Ave., Old Town/Chinatown* ☎ *503/224–2038*), which holds 1,400 people, primarily stages rock and blues shows.

CLASSICAL MUSIC

The Oregon Symphony, established in 1896, is Portland's largest classical group—and one of the largest orchestras in the country. Its season officially starts in September and ends in May, but throughout the summer the orchestra and its smaller ensembles can be seen at Waterfront Park and Washington Park for special outdoor summer performances.

CHAMBER MUSIC

Chamber Music Northwest (✉ *522 S.W. 5th Ave., Suite 725, Downtown* ☏ *503/294–6400* ⊕ *www.cmnw.org*) presents some of the most sought-after soloists, chamber musicians, and recording artists from the Portland area and abroad for a five-week summer concert series; performances take place at Reed College and Catlin Gabel School.

OPERA

Portland Opera (✉ *222 S.W. Clay St.* ☏ *503/241–1802 or 866/739–6737* ⊕ *www.portlandopera.org*) and its orchestra and chorus stage five productions annually at the Keller Auditorium.

ORCHESTRAS

The **Oregon Symphony** (✉ *923 S.W. Washington* ☏ *503/228–1353 or 800/228–7343* ⊕ *www.orsymphony.org*) presents more than 40 classical, pop, children's, and family concerts each year at the Arlene Schnitzer Concert Hall.

☾ The **Metropolitan Youth Symphony** (✉ *4800 S.W. Macadam St., Suite 105* ☏ *503/239–4566* ⊕ *www.playmys.org*) perform family-friendly concerts throughout the year at various Portland venues, including the Arlene Schnitzer Concert Hall.

The **Portland Baroque Orchestra** (☏ *503/222–6000* ⊕ *www.pbo.org*) performs works on period instruments in a season that runs October–April. Performances are held at various venues, including Reed College's Kaul Auditorium, the Agnes Flanagan Chapel at Lewis & Clark College, and the First Baptist Church.

DANCE

Portland has a wonderful variety of both progressive and traditional dance companies. As part of their productions, many of these companies bring in international talent for choreography and guest performances.

Body Vox (☏ *503/229–0627* ⊕ *www.bodyvox.com*) performs energetic contemporary dance–theater works at several locations in Portland.

Do Jump! Extremely Physical Theatre (✉ *1515 S.E. 37th Ave.* ☏ *503/231–1232* ⊕ *www.dojump.org*) showcases its creative acrobatic work at the Echo Theatre near Hawthorne.

Oregon Ballet Theatre (⊠ *818 S.E. 6th Ave.* ☎ *503/222–5538 or 888/922–5538* ⊕ *www.obt.org*) produces five classical and contemporary works a year, including a much-loved holiday *Nutcracker.* Most performances are at Keller Auditorium.

Since its founding in 1997, **White Bird Dance** (⊠ *5620 S.W. Edgemont Pl.* ☎ *503/245–1600* ⊕ *www.whitebird.org*) has been dedicated to bringing exciting dance performances to Portland from around the world.

FILM

If you're a film buff, be sure to check out the Northwest Film Center's calendar of events for special screenings and film festivals, with themes that include international, gay, and animation. These occur throughout the year.

Cinema 21 (⊠ *616 N.W. 21st Ave., Nob Hill* ☎ *503/223–4515*) an art-movie house in Nob Hill, hosts the annual gay and lesbian film festival.

Cinemagic (⊠ *2021 S.E. Hawthorne Blvd., Hawthorne District* ☎ *503/231–7919*) shows progressive and cult films.

An over-80-year-old landmark, and another host of the annual gay and lesbian film festival, the **Hollywood Theatre** (⊠ *4122 N.E. Sandy Blvd., Hollywood District* ☎ *503/281–4215*) shows everything from obscure foreign art films to old American classics and second-run Hollywood hits and hosts an annual Academy Awards viewing party.

The **Laurelhurst Theatre** (⊠ *2735 E. Burnside* ☎ *503/232–5511*) is a beautiful theater and pub showing excellent second-run features and cult classics for only $3.

Not-to-be-missed Portland landmarks when it comes to movie-viewing, the **McMenamins theaters and brewpubs** offer beer, pizza, and inexpensive tickets to second-run block-busters in uniquely renovated buildings that avoid any hint of corporate streamlining. The **Bagdad Theatre** (⊠ *3702 S.E. Hawthorne Blvd.* ☎ *503/236–9234*) is a local favorite. The **Kennedy School** (⊠ *5736 N.E. 33rd St.* ☎ *503/249–3983*) theater, in a renovated elementary school that also contains a bed-and-breakfast and a restaurant. The **Mission Theatre** (⊠ *1624 N.W. Glisan* ☎ *503/223–4527*) has a popular "Burger, Beer and a Movie" night.

The **Northwest Film Center** (⊠ *1219 S.W. Park Ave., Downtown* ☎ *503/221–1156* ⊕ *www.nwfilm.org*), a branch of the Portland Art Museum, screens art films, documentaries, and independent features and presents the three-week Portland International Film Festival in February and March. Films are shown at the Whitsell Auditorium, next to the museum.

THEATER

From the largest of productions to the smallest of venues, theater comes to life in Portland year-round. Comedy, puppetry, tragedy, and artistry can be found at any of these theater company performances.

Artists Repertory Theatre (⊠ *1516 S.W. Alder St., Downtown* ☎ *503/241–1278* ⊕ *www.artistsrep.org*) stages seven productions a year—regional premieres, occasional commissioned works, and classics.

Imago Theatre (⊠ *17 S.E. 8th Ave.* ☎ *503/231–9581* ⊕ *www. imagotheatre.com*)considered by some to be Portland's most outstanding innovative theater company, specializes in movement-based work for both young and old.

ᶜ **Oregon Children's Theatre** (☎ *503/228–9571* ⊕ *www.octc.org*) puts on three or four shows a year at major venues throughout the city for school groups and families.

Portland Center Stage (⊠ *Gerding Theater at the Armory, 128 N.W. 1st Ave., Downtown* ☎ *503/445–3700* ⊕ *www.pcs. org*) produces contemporary and classical works between October and April.

ᶜ **Tears of Joy Puppet Theater** (☎ *503/248–0557* ⊕ *www.tojt. org*) stages five children's productions a year at different locations in town.

5

Sports and the Outdoors

WORD OF MOUTH

"You can rent bikes in [Portland], Fat [Tire Farm] is good. There is Forest Park, a huge forest right in the middle of the city of Portland [with] trails and views, [offering] great hiking for any age or ability."

—Scarlett

6

Updated
by Janna
Mock-
Lopez

PORTLANDERS DEFINITELY GRAVITATE TO THE OUTDOORS
and they're well acclimated to the elements year-round—
including winter's wind, rain, and cold. Once the sun starts
to shine in spring and into summer, the city fills with hikers, joggers, and mountain bikers, who flock to Portland's
hundreds of miles of parks, paths, and trails. The Willamette and Columbia rivers are used for boating and water
sports—though it's not easy to rent any kind of boat for
casual use. Locals also have access to a playground for
fishing, camping, skiing, and snowboarding all the way
through June, thanks to the proximity of Mt. Hood.

As for competitive sports, Portland is home to several minor
league teams, including the Winterhawks (hockey), Beavers (baseball), and Timbers (soccer). Big-sports fervor is
reserved for Trail Blazers basketball games, held at the Rose
Quarter arena on the east side of the river. The Portland
Visitors' association, known as Travel Portland, *(⇨ Visitor
Information in Portland Essentials)* provides information
on sports events and outdoor activities in the city.

PARTICIPANT SPORTS

If there's something recreational to be done outdoors, Portlanders will find a way to do it. Because of the many parks,
rivers, streams, mountains, and beaches within reach of the
city, this region is a playground.

BICYCLING

Bicycling is a cultural phenomenon in Portland—possibly
the most beloved mode of transportation in the city. *Bicycling* magazine has named Portland the number one cycling
city in the United States. Aside from the sheer numbers of
cyclists you see on every road and pathway, notable bike-
friendly aspects of this city include well-marked bike lanes
on many major streets, bike paths meandering through
parks and along the shoreline of the Willamette River, street
signs reminding motorists to yield to cyclists at many inter-
sections, and bike racks on the front of Tri-Met buses.

Despite the occasionally daunting hills and frequent winter-
time rain, cycling remains one of the best ways to see what
Portland offers. Bike paths on both the east and west sides of
the Willamette River continue south of downtown, and you
can easily make a several-mile loop by crossing bridges to
get from one side to the other. (Most bridges, including the

PORTLAND TOP 5 OUTDOOR TIPS

■ Cheer on the Portland Trail Blazers when they're home playing a basketball game at the Rose Garden.

■ Ski down a Mt. Hood Meadows slope on a crisp, clear, early spring morning—less than an hour's drive away from the city.

■ Rent a bicycle and pedal down Portland's many bike-friendly roads and pathways, or on the Esplanade along-side the Willamette River, in what has been called the number one cycling city in the U.S.

■ Hike up and around Mt. Tabor and be rewarded with an awesome view of downtown Portland.

■ Hang out at PGE Park on a warm summer night, hot dog and beer in hand, and watch a Portland Beavers baseball game.

Broadway Bridge, the Steel Bridge, the Hawthorne Bridge, and the Sellwood Bridge, are accessible to cyclists.)

Forest Park's Leif Erikson Drive is an 11-mi ride through Northwest Portland's Forest Park, accessible from the west end of Northwest Thurman Street. Parts of this ride and other Forest Park trails are recommended only for mountain bikes. Bicycling on Sauvie Island is a rare treat, with a 12-mi loop around the island with plenty of spots for exploring. To get to Sauvie Island from Portland, you can brave the 10-mi ride in the bike lane of U.S. 30, or you can shuttle your bike there via Tri-Met Bus 17. The Springwater Corridor, when combined with the Esplanade ride on the east side of the Willamette, can take you all the way from downtown to the far reaches of southeast Portland along a former railroad line. The trail heads east beginning near Sellwood, close to Johnson Creek Boulevard.

For more information on bike routes and resources in and around Portland, visit the **Department of Transportation** (⊕ *www.portlandonline.com/transportation*) Web page. Here you can download maps, or order "Bike There," a glossy detailed bicycle map of the metropolitan area. Bikes can be rented at several places in the city. Rentals typically run from $20 to $50 per day with cheaper weekly rates from $75 to $150. Bike helmets are generally included in the cost of rental.

Good hybrid bikes for city riding are available at **CityBikes Workers Cooperative** (✉ *734 S.E. Ankeny St., near Burnside* *and Martin Luther King Blvd.* ☎*503/239–6951*) on the east side. For treks in Forest Park, mountain bikes can be rented at **Fat Tire Farm** (✉*2714 N.W. Thurman St., near Forest Park* ☎*503/222–3276*). For jaunts along the Willamette, try **Waterfront Bicycle Rentals** (✉*315 S.W. Montgomery St., Suite 3, Downtown* ☎*503/227–1719*).

FISHING

The Columbia and Willamette rivers are major sportfishing streams with opportunities for angling virtually year-round. Though salmon can still be caught here, runs have been greatly reduced in both rivers in recent years, and the Willamette River is still plagued by pollution. Nevertheless, the Willamette still offers prime fishing for bass, channel catfish, sturgeon, crappies, perch, panfish, and crayfish. It's also a good stream for winter steelhead. June is the top shad month, with some of the best fishing occurring below Willamette Falls at Oregon City. The Columbia River is known for its salmon, sturgeon, walleye, and smelt. The Sandy and Clackamas rivers, near Mt. Hood, are smaller waterways popular with local anglers.

OUTFITTERS

Outfitters throughout Portland operate guide services. Few outfitters rent equipment, though, so bring your own or be prepared to buy. **Northwest Flyfishing Outfitters** (✉*10910 N.E. Halsey St.* ☎*503/252–1529 or 888/292–1137*) specializes in all things fly-fishing, including tackle, rentals, and guided outings.

You can find a broad selection of fishing gear, including rods, reels, and fishing licenses, at **Stewart Fly Shop** (✉*23830 N.E. Halsey St., Near Troutdale* ☎*503/666–2471*).

REGULATIONS

Local sport shops are the best sources of information on current fishing hot spots, which change from year to year. Detailed fishing regulations are available from the **Oregon Department of Fish and Wildlife** (✉*17330 S.E. Evelyn St., Clackamas* ☎*503/947–6000* ⊕*www.dfw.state.or.us*).

GOLF

There are several public and top-class golf courses within Portland and just outside the city where you can practice your putt or test your swing. Even in the wet months, Portlanders still golf—and you can bet the first clear day after a wet spell will mean courses fill up with those who have so faithfully waited for the sun. Depending upon the time of year, it's not a bad idea to call ahead and verify wait times.

Broadmoor Golf Course (⊠ *3509 N.E. Columbia Blvd., near airport* ☎ *503/281–1337*) is an 18-hole, par-72 course where the green fee runs $24 and an optional cart costs $14 per rider.

At the 18-hole, par-72 **Colwood National Golf Club** (⊠ *7313 N.E. Columbia Blvd., near Airport* ☎ *503/254–5515*), the green fee is $29–$33, plus $26 for an optional cart.

Eastmoreland Golf Course (⊠ *2425 S.E. Bybee Blvd., Sellwood* ☎ *503/775–2900*) has a highly regarded 18-hole, 72-par course close to the Rhododendron Gardens, Crystal Springs Lake, and Reed College. The green fee is $15–$37 plus $28 for an optional cart.

Glendoveer Golf Course (⊠ *14015 N.E. Glisan St., near Gresham* ☎ *503/253–7507*) has two 18-hole courses, one par-71 and one par-73, and a covered driving range. The green fee runs $18–$34; carts are $13 for 9 holes, $26 for 18 holes.

Heron Lakes Golf Course (⊠ *3500 N. Victory Blvd., west of airport, off N. Marine Dr.* ☎ *503/289–1818*) consists of two 18-hole, par-72 courses: the Great Blue, generally acknowledged to be the most difficult links in the greater Portland area; and the Greenback. The green fee at the Green, as it's locally known, is $26–$37, while the fee at the Blue runs $30–$42. An optional cart at either course costs $26.

Pumpkin Ridge Golf Club (⊠ *12930 N.W. Old Pumpkin Ridge Rd., North Plains* ☎ *503/647–4747 or 888/594–4653* ⊕ *www.pumpkinridge.com*) has 36 holes, with the 18-hole Ghost Creek par-71 course open to the public. According to *Golf Digest,* Ghost Creek is one of the best public courses in the nation. Pumpkin Ridge hosted the U.S. Women's Open in 1997 and in 2003. The green fee is $150; the cart fee is $16.

Rose City Golf Course (⊠ *2200 N.E. 71st Ave., east of Hollywood District* ☎ *503/253–4744*) has one 18-hole, par-72 course. Green fees are $28–$35; carts are $26 for 18 holes.

ICE-SKATING

Ice-skating is the recreational activity of choice for Port-landers in good health and of all ages. Lloyd Center has a large rink right in the middle of the mall, which rents skates and other needed equipment by the hour; lessons are available as well.

Ice Chalet at Lloyd Center (✉ *Multnomah St. and N.E. 9th Ave., Lloyd District* ☎ *503/288–6073*) has open skating and skate rentals ($9 admission includes skate rental). The indoor rinks are open year-round.

SKIING

With fairly easy access to decent skiing nearly eight months out of the year, it's no wonder that skiers love Portland. There are several ski resorts on Mt. Hood, less than an hour's drive away, including Ski Bowl, Mt. Hood Meadows, and Timberline Lodge.

Mountain Shop (✉ *628 N.E. Broadway, Lloyd District/Irving-ton* ☎ *503/288–6768*) rents skis and equipment. **REI** (✉ *1405 N.W. Johnson St., Pearl District* ☎ *503/221–1938*) can fill all your ski-equipment rental needs.

SWIMMING AND SUNBATHING

Swimming and sunbathing season in Portland is brief: in summer temperatures are never too hot for too long, while most of the waters—including lakes, rivers, and the Pacific Ocean—remain cold. On those few hot and sunny days, though, locals and visitors flock to these watering holes to cool off and splash around.

Blue Lake Regional Park (✉ *20500 N.E. Marine Dr., Troutdale* ☎ *503/797–1850*) has a swimming beach that's packed on hot summer days. You can also fish and rent small boats here. This is a great place for a hike on the surrounding trails or for a picnic.

If you feel like tanning au naturel, drive about a half hour northwest of downtown to **Sauvie Island,** a wildlife ref-uge with a secluded beachfront that's popular with (and legal for) nude sunbathers. If the sky is clear, you'll get a spectacular view from the riverbank of three Cascade mountains—Hood, St. Helens, and Adams. Huge oceango-ing vessels cruise by on their way to and from the Port of Portland. To get here, take U.S. 30 north to Sauvie Island bridge, turn right, and follow Reeder Road until you hit gravel. Look for the Collins Beach signs. There's plenty of parking, but a permit is required. You can buy it ($3.50 for a one-day permit, $11 for an annual permit) at the Cracker Barrel country store just over the bridge on the left side of the road.

TENNIS

If tennis is your racquet, then you'll have the opportunity to try your hand at it on both indoor and outdoor courts. The Portland Parks and Recreation Department (⊕ *www. portlandonline.com/parks*) is an excellent resource for discovering where the nearest courts are located. **Lake Oswego Indoor Tennis Center** (✉ *2900 S.W. Diane Dr., Lake Oswego* ☎ *503/635–5550*) has four indoor tennis courts.

Portland Parks and Recreation (☎ *503/823–7529*) operates more than 100 outdoor tennis courts (many with night lighting) at Washington Park, Grant Park, and many other locations. The courts are open on a first-come, first-served basis year-round, but you can reserve one, starting in March, for play May–September.

The **Portland Tennis Center** (✉ *324 N.E. 12th Ave., just south of I–84* ☎ *503/823–3189*) operates four indoor courts and eight lighted outdoor courts.

The **St. John's Racquet Center** (✉ *7519 N. Burlington Ave., St. John's* ☎ *503/823–3629*) has three indoor courts.

SPECTATOR SPORTS

Since Portland isn't home to a large national football or baseball team, fans tend to show a lot of support for their city's only true professional team, the NBA's Portland Trail Blazers. Fans are also loyal in cheering on their minor league teams: hockey, auto racing, baseball, and soccer events are well-attended by excited crowds.

AUTO RACING

Portland International Raceway (✉ *West Delta Park, 1940 N. Victory Blvd., west of I–5, along Columbia Slough* ☎ *503/823–7223*) presents bicycle and drag racing and motocross on weeknights and sports-car, motorcycle, and go-kart racing on weekends April–September.

BASEBALL

The **Portland Beavers** (✉ *PGE Park, 1844 S.W. Morrison St., Downtown* ☎ *503/553–5555 for Beavers, 503/553–5400 for PGE Park*), Portland's Triple-A team, play at the downtown PGE Park from April through September.

BASKETBALL

The **Portland Trail Blazers** (✉ *Rose Garden, 1 Center Ct., Rose Quarter* ☎ *503/797–9617*) of the National Basketball Association play in the Rose Garden.

HORSE RACING

Thoroughbred and quarter horses race, rain or shine October–May, at **Portland Meadows** (✉ *1001 N. Schmeer Rd., between I–5 and Martin Luther King Blvd., along Columbia Slough* ☎ *503/285–9144 or 800/944–3127*).

ICE HOCKEY

The **Portland Winter Hawks** (✉ *Memorial Coliseum, 300 N. Winning Way, Rose Quarter* ☎ *503/236–4295*) of the Western Hockey League play home games September–March at Memorial Colisium and sometimes at the Rose Garden (⇨ *Portland Trail Blazers, above*).

SOCCER

The **Portland Timbers** (✉ *PGE Park, 1844 S.W. Morrison St., Downtown* ☎ *503/553–5400 for Portland Timbers office, 503/553–5400 for PGE Park*), Portland's United Soccer League First Division team, play at the downtown PGE Park from April through September.

Shopping

7

WORD OF MOUTH

"If it's an Outlet Mall you're looking for, [the] best nearest Portland is Woodburn Outlets, about 30 minutes south. Otherwise, popular shopping districts in the city are NW 21st & 23rd Streets, the Pearl District, and Hawthorne Blvd."

—beachbum

Updated
by Janna
Mock-
Lopez

ONE OF PORTLAND'S GREATEST ATTRIBUTES IS its neighborhoods' dynamic spectrum of retail and specialty shops. The Pearl District is known for chic interior design and high-end clothing boutiques. Trek over to the Hawthorne area and you'll discover wonderful stores for handmade jewelry, clothing, and books. The Northwest has some funky shops for housewares, clothing, and jewelry, while in the Northeast there are fabulous galleries and crafts. Downtown has a blend of it all as well as bigger options, including the Pioneer Place mall and department stores such as Nordstrom's and Macy's.

No Portland shopping experience would be complete without a visit to the nation's largest open-air market, Saturday Market, where an array of talented artists converge to peddle handcrafted wares beyond your wildest do-it-yourself dreams. It's also open Sunday.

Portland merchants are generally open Monday–Saturday between 9 or 10 AM and 6 PM, and on Sunday noon–6. Most shops in downtown's Pioneer Place, the east side's Lloyd Center, and the outlying malls are open until 9 PM Monday–Saturday and until 6 PM on Sunday.

SHOPPING AREAS

Portland's main shopping area is **downtown**, between Southwest 2nd and 10th avenues and between Southwest Stark and Morrison streets. The major department stores are scattered over several blocks near Pioneer Courthouse Square. Northeast **Broadway** between 10th and 21st avenues is lined with boutiques and specialty shops. **Nob Hill**, north of downtown along Northwest 21st and 23rd avenues, has eclectic clothing, gift, book, and food shops. Most of the city's fine-art galleries are concentrated in the booming **Pearl District**, north from Burnside Street to Marshall Street between Northwest 8th and 15th avenues, along with furniture and design stores. **Sellwood**, 5 mi from the city center, south on Naito Parkway and east across the Sellwood Bridge, has more than 50 antiques and collectibles shops along southeast 13th Avenue, plus specialty shops and outlet stores for sporting goods. You can find the larger antiques stores near the intersection of Milwaukie Avenue and Bybee. **Hawthorne Boulevard** between 30th and 42nd avenues has a selection of alternative bookstores, coffeehouses, antiques stores, and boutiques.

PORTLAND TOP 5 SHOPPING TIPS

■ Munch on a fresh-out-of-the-fryer elephant ear pastry while perusing aisles of handmade wares at Portland's Saturday Market.

■ Scout for something totally fun and funky at one of Northwest 23rd Avenue's boutique gift shops.

■ Leisurely rifle through racks of clothes at some of Portland's more notable second-hand stores, such as Buffalo Exchange downtown and Red Light in Hawthorne.

■ Visit Columbia Sportswear downtown to see just how surprisingly fashionable clothing options for every type of outdoor condition can be.

■ Saunter through Powell's City of Books and see what treasures are in its rare-books section.

FLEA MARKETS

★ Fodor's Choice The open-air **Portland Saturday Market** (✉ *Burnside Bridge, underneath west end, Old Town* ☎ *503/222–6072* ⊕ *www.saturdaymarket.org*), open on weekends (including Sunday, despite the name), is a favorite place to experience the people of Portland and also find one-of-a-kind, unique handcrafted home, garden, and gift items. (⇨ *Old Town/Chinatown in Exploring Portland.*)

MALLS AND DEPARTMENT STORES

DOWNTOWN/CITY CENTER

Shopping downtown is not only fun, it's also easy, thanks to easy transportation access and its proximity to many of Portland's hotels. Locally based favorites Nike and Columbia Sportswear both have major stores downtown; REI has one in the Pearl District (⇨ *Outdoor Sports, below*)

Macy's at Meier & Frank Square (✉ *621 S.W. 5th Ave., Downtown* ☎ *503/223–0512*), until 2005 the main location of the local Meier & Frank chain, has five floors of general merchandise.

Seattle-based **Nordstrom** (✉ *701 S.W. Broadway, Downtown* ☎ *503/224–6666*) sells fine-quality apparel and accessories and has a large footwear department. Bargain lovers should head for the **Nordstrom Rack** (✉ *245 S.W. Mor-*

rison St., Downtown ☎ *503/299–1815*) outlet across from Pioneer Place mall.

Pioneer Place (⊠ *700 S.W. 5th Ave., Downtown* ☎ *503/228–5800*) has more than 80 upscale specialty shops (including April Cornell, Coach, J. Crew, Godiva, and Fossil) in a three-story, glass-roof atrium setting. You can find good, inexpensive ethnic foods from more than a dozen vendors in the Cascades Food Court in the basement. Paradise Bakery is known for fresh home-baked breads and delicious chocolate chip cookies; Suki Hana has some yummy soups and noodle dishes.

Saks Fifth Avenue (⊠ *850 S.W. 5th Ave., Downtown* ☎ *503/226–3200*) has two floors of men's and women's clothing, jewelry, and other merchandise.

BEYOND DOWNTOWN

Once you venture outside of downtown, you can find several major malls and outlets to shop 'til you drop. Both Woodburn (30 mi south of Portland) and Troutdale (20 mi east) have outlet malls with dozens of discount name-brand clothing stores.

NORTHEAST PORTLAND

Lloyd Center (⊠ *N.E. Multnomah St. at N.E. 9th Ave., Northeast Portland* ☎ *503/282–2511*), on the MAX light-rail line, has more than 170 shops (including Nordstrom, Sears, and Macy's), an international food court, a multiscreen cinema, and an ice-skating pavilion. The mall is within walking distance of Northeast Broadway, which has many specialty shops, boutiques, and restaurants.

SOUTHEAST PORTLAND

Clackamas Town Center (⊠ *Sunnyside Rd. at I–205 Exit 14, Southeast Portland* ☎ *503/653–6913*) has four major department stores, including Nordstrom and Macy's, as well as more than 180 shops. Discount stores are nearby.

SOUTHWEST PORTLAND

Bridgeport Village (⊠ *S.W. Boones Ferry Rd., at S.W. Lower Boones Ferry rd., off I–5 Exit 290 Tigard* ☎ *503/968–8940*), an outdoor mall, has tall buckets full of handheld yellow umbrellas on hand throughout the property in case it rains. Visit the movie theater complex, eat at one of over a dozen restaurants such as P.F. Chang's or Zao Noodle bar, or visit major shops that include Tommy Bahama and Crate & Barrel.

South of Portland, the **Streets of Tanasbourne** (✉ *N.W. 194th at Cornell Rd., off U.S. 26, Hillsboro* ☎ *503/533–0561*) has 52 choices of high-end specialty shops, including Clogs 'n' More, Abercrombie & Fitch, and White House/Black Market.

Washington Square (✉ *9585 S.W. Washington Sq. Rd., at S.W. Hall Blvd. and Hwy. 217, Tigard* ☎ *503/639–8860*) contains five major department stores, including Macy's and Sears; a food court; and more than 140 specialty shops. Discount and electronics stores are nearby.

The **Water Tower** (✉ *5331 S.W. MacAdam Ave., Southwest Portland*), in the John's Landing neighborhood on the Willamette River, is a pleasant mall, with Pier 1 Imports and several restaurants.

SPECIALTY STORES

Portland's specialty stores are as varied and authentic as the city itself. Residents applaud and encourage locally made quirky goods, so stores offering these creative wares are abundant. Discover all the innovative approaches to household items, art, jewelry, and clothing for a fun afternoon.

7

ANTIQUES

Moreland House (✉ *826 N.W. 23rd Ave., Nob Hill* ☎ *503/222–0197*) has eclectic antiques and gifts, with a notable selection of dog collectibles, old printing-press type, and fresco tiles.

Shogun's Gallery (✉ *1111 N.W. 23rd Ave., Nob Hill* ☎ *503/224–0328*) specializes in Japanese and Chinese furniture, especially the lightweight wooden Japanese cabinets known as *tansu*. Also here are chairs, tea tables, altar tables, armoires, ikebana baskets (originally for flower arrangements), and Chinese wooden picnic boxes, most at least 100 years old and at reasonable prices.

Stars Antique Mall (✉ *7027 S.E. Milwaukie Ave., Sellwood-Moreland* ☎ *503/235–5990* ⊕ *starsantique.com*), Portland's largest antiques mall, has two stores across the street from each other in the Sellwood-Moreland neighborhood. Since it rents its space to about 300 antiques dealers; you might find anything from low-end 1950s kitsch to high-end treasures.

ART DEALERS AND GALLERIES

Portland's art galleries, once concentrated downtown, are spreading throughout the city to Northeast and Southeast Portland.

EVENTS

First Thursday (☎ *503/295–4979* ⊕ *www.firstthursdayport-land.com*) gives art appreciators a chance to check out new exhibits while enjoying music and wine. Typically, the galleries are open in the evening but hours vary depending on the gallery. Find out what galleries are participating in First Thursday.

The Alberta Arts District hosts a **Last Thursday Arts Walk** (☎ *503/972–2206* ⊕ *www.artonalberta.org*) each month.

Many galleries in the **Pearl District** (⊕ *www.firstthursday.org*) host First Thursday events.

Butters Gallery, Ltd. (✉ *520 N.W. Davis, Pearl District* ☎ *503/248–9378*) has monthly exhibits of the works of nationally known and local artists in its Pearl District space.

Exit 21 Gallery (✉ *1502 S.E. 21st, Hawthorne* ☎ *503/867–8495*) has wall-mounted and floor-standing sculptures made from reclaimed materials as well as hand-knitted apparel. They are recognized for supporting local artists and showcasing an eclectic blend of works, with a wide range of price.

The **Laura Russo Gallery** (✉ *805 N.W. 21st Ave., Nob Hill* ☎ *503/226–2754*) displays contemporary Northwest work of all styles, including landscapes and abstract expressionism.

Emphasizing sustainable and fair trade practices, the **Onda Gallery** (✉ *2215 N.E. Alberta St., Alberta* ☎ *503/493–1909*) is a collective of Northwestern and Latin American artists. Gift items are also for sale.

Pulliam/Deffenbaugh Gallery (✉ *929 N.W. Flanders St., Pearl District* ☎ *503/228–6665*) generally shows contemporary abstract and expressionistic works by Pacific Northwest artists.

Quintana's Galleries of Native American Art (✉ *120 N.W. 9th Ave., Pearl District* ☎ *503/223–1729 or 800/321–1729*) focuses on Pacific Northwest coast, Navajo, and Hopi art and jewelry, along with photogravures by Edward Curtis.

Talisman Gallery (✉ *1476 N.E. Alberta St., Alberta District* ☎ *503/284–8800* ⊕ *talismangallery.com*) showcases two artists each month—they may include local painters and sculptors.

Twist (✉ *30 N.W. 23rd Pl., Nob Hill* ☎ *503/224–0334* ✉ *Pioneer Pl.* ☎ *503/222–3137*) has a huge space in Nob Hill and a smaller shop downtown. In Nob Hill are contemporary American ceramics, glass, furniture, sculpture, and hand-crafted jewelry; downtown carries an assortment of objects, often with a pop, whimsical touch.

BOOKS

Annie Bloom's (✉ *7834 S.W. Capital Hwy., Multnomah Village* ☎ *503/246–0053* ⊕ *www.anniebloooms.com*), a local favorite, has a friendly, knowledgeable staff and great selections of children's books, remainders, Judaica, and fun greeting cards.

Broadway Books (✉ *1714 N.E. Broadway, Broadway District* ☎ *503/284–1726* ⊕ *www.broadwaybooks.net*) is a fabulous independent bookstore with books on all subjects, including the Pacific Northwest and Judaica.

In Other Words (✉ *3734 S.E. Hawthorne Blvd., Hawthorne District* ☎ *503/232–6003*) is a nonprofit bookstore that carries feminist literature and hosts feminist events and readings.

New Renaissance Bookshop (✉ *1338 N.W. 23rd Ave., Nob Hill* ☎ *503/224–4929*), between Overton and Pettygrove, is dedicated to new-age and metaphysical books and tapes.

★ **Powell's City of Books** (✉ *1005 W. Burnside St., Downtown* ☎ *503/228–4651* ⊕ *www.powells.com*), the largest retail store of used and new books in the world (with more than 1.5 million volumes), covers an entire city block on the edge of the Pearl District. It also carries rare and collectible books. There are also three branches in the Portland International Airport.

Powell's for Cooks and Gardeners (✉ *3747 Hawthorne Blvd., Hawthorne District* ☎ *503/235–3802*), on the east side, has a small adjoining grocery.

CLOTHING

Clogs 'n' More (✉ *717 S.W. Alder St., Downtown* ☎ *503/279–9358* ✉ *3439 S.E. Hawthorne, Hawthorne District* ☎ *503/232–7007*), with locations on the west and east sides of the city, carries quality clogs and other shoes.

Eight Women (✉ *3614 S.E. Hawthorne Blvd., Hawthorne District* ☎ *503/236–8878*) is a tiny boutique "for mother and child," with baby clothes, women's nightgowns, jewelry, and handbags.

Hanna Andersson sells high-quality, comfortable clothing for children and families from their **retail store** (✉ *327 N.W. 10th Ave.* ☎ *503/321–5275*) , next to the company's corporate office, as well as through their **outlet store** (✉ *7 Monroe Pkwy., Lake Oswego* ☎ *503/697–1953*) in Oswego Towne Square, south of Portland.

Imelda's Designer Shoes (✉ *3426 S.E. Hawthorne Blvd., Hawthorne District* ☎ *503/233–7476*) is an upscale boutique with funky, fun shoes for women with flair.

Magpie (✉ *520 S.W. 9th St., Downtown* ☎ *503/220–0920*) sells funky retro garb that dates from the '50s through the '80s. Lots of jewelry, shoes, dresses, coats, and even rhinestone tiaras can be found here.

Portland's best store for fine men's and women's clothing, **Mario's** (✉ *833 S.W. Morrison St., Downtown* ☎ *503/227–3477*) carries designer lines by Prada, Dolce & Gabbana, Etro, and Loro Piana—among others.

Niketown (✉ *930 S.W. 6th Ave., Downtown* ☎ *503/221–6453*), Nike's flagship retail store, has the latest and greatest in "swoosh"-adorned products. The high-tech setting has athlete profiles, photos, and interactive displays.

Portland Nike Factory Store (✉ *2650 N.E. Martin Luther King Jr. Blvd., Northeast Portland* ☎ *503/281–5901*) sells products that have been on the market six months or more.

Portland Outdoor Store (✉ *304 S.W. 3rd Ave., Downtown* ☎ *503/222–1051*) stubbornly resists all that is trendy, both in clothes and decor, but if you want authentic Western gear—saddles, Stetsons, boots, or cowboy shirts—head here.

Portland Pendleton Shop (✉ *S.W. 4th Ave. and Salmon St., Downtown* ☎ *503/242–0037*) stocks clothing by the famous local apparel maker.

Tumbleweed (✉ *1804 N.E. Alberta St., Alberta District* ☎ *503/335–3100*) carries fun and stylish designer clothing you might describe as "country chic," for the woman who likes to wear flirty feminine dresses with cowboy boots. There's also unique baby and toddler clothing in their children's shop next door.

Zelda's Shoe Bar (✉ *633 N.W. 23rd Ave., Nob Hill* ☎ *503/226–0363*), two connected boutiques in Nob Hill, carry a sophisticated, highly eclectic line of women's clothes, accessories, and shoes.

GIFTS

Babik's (✉ *738 N.W. 23rd Ave., Nob Hill* ☎ *503/248–1771*) carries an enormous selection of handwoven rugs from Turkey, all made from handspun wool and all-natural dyes.

The **Backyard Bird Shop** (✉ *8960 S.E. Sunnyside Rd., Clackamas* ☎ *503/496–0908*) has everything for the bird lover: bird feeders, birdhouses, a huge supply of bird seed, and quality bird-theme gifts ranging from wind chimes to stuffed animals.

Christmas at the Zoo (✉ *118 N.W. 23rd Ave., Nob Hill* ☎ *503/223–4048 or 800/223–5886*) is crammed year-round with decorated trees and has Portland's best selection of European hand-blown glass ornaments and plush animals.

In addition to offering the best eat-in or take-out soups, salads and desserts, **Elephants Delicatessen** (✉ *111 N.W. 22nd Ave., Nob Hill* ☎ *503/299–6304*) also has a vast gourmet food, cooking utensils, and household section.

La Bottega de Mamma Ro (✉ *940 N.W. 23rd Ave., Nob Hill* ☎ *503/241–4960*) carries Italian tabletop and home accessories, including a colorful line of dishes and cloth for tablecloths and napkins.

Made in Oregon (☎ *866/257–0938*), which sells books, smoked salmon, local wines, Pendleton woolen goods, carvings made of myrtle wood, and other products made in the state, has shops at Portland International Airport, the Lloyd Center, the Galleria, Washington Square, and Clackamas Town Center.

Even without getting a nod from Oprah in her magazine, **Moonstruck** (✉ *526 N.W. 23rd Ave., Nob Hill* ☎ *503/542–3400*), would still be known as a chocolatier extraordinaire. Just a couple of the rich confections might sustain you if you're nibbling—water is available for palate cleansing in between treats—but whether you're just grazing or boxing some up for the road, try the Ocumarian Truffle, chocolate laced with chili pepper; the unusual kick of sweetness and warmth is worth experiencing.

Pastaworks (⊠*3735 S.E. Hawthorne Blvd., Southeast Portland* ☎*503/232–1010*) sells cookware, fancy deli food, organic produce, beer, wine, and pasta.

At **Stella's on 21st** (⊠*1108 N.W. 21st Ave., Nob Hill* ☎*503/ 295–5930*), there are eccentric, colorful, and artsy items for the home, including lamps, candles, and decorations, as well as jewelry.

JEWELRY

Carl Greve (⊠*731 S.W. Morrison St., Downtown* ☎*503/223– 7121*), in business since 1922, carries exclusive designer lines of fine jewelry, such as Mikimoto pearls, and has the state's only Tiffany boutique. The second floor is reserved for china, stemware, and housewares.

Maloy's Jewelry Workshop (⊠*717 S.W. 10th Ave., Downtown* ☎*503/223–4720*), specializes in fine antique pieces, including some from the 18th century. Rare and vintage designs fill the sparkling glass cases.

Real Mother Goose (⊠*901 S.W. Yamhill St., Downtown* ☎*503/223–9510*), sells mostly handcrafted, unique artistic pieces. On patron favorite: dangling earrings that incorporate copper wire wrapped around brilliant, colored glass.

MUSIC

Artichoke Music (⊠*3130 S.E. Hawthorne Blvd., Hawthorne District* ☎*503/232–8845*) is a friendly family-owned business that sells guitars, banjos, mandolins, and other instruments that might come in handy for a bluegrass band. Music lessons are given in two soundproof practice rooms, and music performances and song circles are held in the café in the back.

Classical Millennium (⊠*3144 E. Burnside St., Laurelhurst* ☎*503/231–8909*) has the best selection of classical CDs in Oregon.

Music Millennium Northwest (⊠*3158 E. Burnside St., Laurelhurst* ☎*503/231–8926*) stocks a huge selection of music in every possible category, including local punk groups.

OUTDOOR SUPPLIES

Andy and Bax (✉ *324 S.E. Grand Ave., Near Morrison Bridge* ☎ *503/234–7538*) is an army-navy/outdoors store that has good prices on camo gear, rafting supplies, and just about everything else.

Columbia Sportswear (✉ *911 S.W. Broadway, Downtown* ☎ *503/226–6800* ⊕ *www.columbia.com*), a local legend and global force in recreational outdoor wear, is especially strong in fashionable jackets, pants, and durable shoes.

Next Adventure Sports (✉ *426 S.E. Grand Ave., Near Morrison Bridge* ☎ *503/233–0706*) carries new and used sporting goods, including camping gear, snowboards, kayaks, and mountaineering supplies.

REI (✉ *1405 N.W. Johnson St., Pearl District* ☎ *503/221–1938* ⊕ *www.rei.com*) carries clothes and accessories for hiking, biking, camping, fishing, bicycling, or just about any other outdoor activity you can possibly imagine.

PERFUME

Aveda Lifestyle Store and Spa (✉ *500 S.W. 5th Ave., Downtown* ☎ *503/248–0615*) sells the flower- and herb-based Aveda line of scents and skin-care products.

Perfume House (✉ *3328 S.E. Hawthorne Blvd., Hawthorne District* ☎ *503/234–5375*) carries hundreds of brand-name fragrances for women and men.

TOYS

Finnegan's Toys and Gifts (✉ *922 S.W. Yamhill St., Downtown* ☎ *503/221–0306*), downtown Portland's largest toy store, stocks artistic, creative, educational, and other types of toys.

Kids at Heart (✉ *3445 S.E. Hawthorne Blvd., Hawthorne District* ☎ *503/231–2954*) is a small, colorful toy store on Hawthorne with toys, models, and stuffed animals for kids of all ages.

Thinker Toys (✉ *7784 S.W. Capitol Hwy., Multnomah Village* ☎ *503/245–3936*), which bills itself as Portland's "most hands-on store," offers puppets, games, educational toys, and a large wooden play house that kids can hang out in.

Easy Side Trips from Portland

WORD OF MOUTH

"I would definitely plan a daytrip west to coast. It's only about an hour's drive to the ocean, and if you head to Tillamook the ice cream at the Cheese Factory can't be beat."

—bluzmama

8

FOR ALL THE BEAUTY AND DIVERSITY THAT PORTLAND offers, so, too, do the outlying areas nearby. Expanding beyond the city bridges is when the scenery gets exciting, and there are endless side trips to enhance the Portland experience.

One of Oregon's biggest tourist destinations, Multnomah Falls is 30 mi east of Portland, in the scenic Columbia Gorge. Multnomah Falls drops down 620 feet and is the second-tallest year-round waterfall in the nation. There are accessible hiking trails that meander up and around the falls area. On the Oregon side of the Columbia Gorge (Washington is across the river) there are nearly 80 waterfalls. Along the Gorge, 80 mi in length, are cliffs that are up to 4,000 feet high. Wayward winds take advantage of the Cascades' only range break and whip through this steep canyon crevasse. Taking advantage of these prime conditions, world-class windsurfers and kite-boarders head to Gorge hotspots like Hood River and the Dalles.

Beyond the Gorge to the east is Mt. Hood National Forest. With more than 60 mi of lakes, streams, and fir-carpeted mountains, the forest includes over a million acres (1,667 sq mi). Visitors can enjoy Mt. Hood year-round. In summer there's camping, fishing, and hiking; in fall people hunt and mushroom pick; in winter it's a popular place for skiing and snowboarding; and in spring visitors collect wildflowers.

Traveling down from the hills to the valleys, just southwest of Portland are Washington and Yamhill counties—sometimes called the "Napa of the Northwest." Thanks to the mild climate and soil, air, water, and temperature conditions comparable to the Burgundy region of France, this region produces primo pinot noir. More than 100 wineries cultivate grapes here, and many of them offer behind-the-scenes tours and have quaint wine-tasting rooms where sampling the merchandise is encouraged.

If you're looking to find a fabulous seafood dish to pair with your favorite wine, then travel 1½ hours west of Portland: you'll end up at the shores of the breathtaking Oregon Coast. There are endless beaches where pounding surf collides against dramatic cliffs, and hikes into dense forest only footsteps away. Because of their proximity to Portland, the most frequented destinations are Astoria, Seaside, and Cannon Beach. Though only within a 20-minute drive of one another, each community has its own unique charm and personality.

People love the Oregon Coast because of its tremendous beauty, wonderful selection of seafood restaurants, bountiful art galleries, and access to unspoiled terrain for picnics, hikes, and camping. Long, secluded walks along the shore can be had as easily as a more-social evening of small theater performances.

Tourism grows every year, as visitors from all over the world discover the scenic and recreational treasures that have already being thrilling Oregonians themselves. A sophisticated hospitality industry has appeared, making Oregon more accessible than ever before. You'll feel more than welcome here, but when you visit, expect a little ribbing if locals catch you mispronouncing the state's name: it's "Ore-ey-gun" not "Ore-uh-gone."

THE OREGON COAST

Updated by Janna Mock-Lopez

Oregon has 300 mi of white-sand beaches, not a grain of which is privately owned. U.S. 101, called Highway 101 by most Oregonians, parallels the coast along the length of the state. It winds past sea-tortured rocks, brooding headlands, hidden beaches, historic lighthouses, and tiny ports, with the gleaming gun-metal-gray Pacific Ocean always in view. With its seaside hamlets, outstanding seafood restaurants, and small hotels and resorts, the Oregon Coast epitomizes the finest in Pacific Northwest living.

8

Points of interest can be found on the Northwest Oregon map.

GETTING HERE AND AROUND

U.S. 101 runs the length of the coast, sometimes turning inland for a few miles. The highway enters coastal Oregon from Washington State at Astoria and from California near Brookings. U.S. 30 heads west from Portland to Astoria. U.S. 20 travels west from Corvallis to Newport. Highway 126 winds west to the coast from Eugene. Highway 42 leads west from Roseburg toward Coos Bay.

VISITOR INFORMATION

Contacts **Astoria–Warrenton Area Chamber of Commerce** (✉ *111 W. Marine Dr., Astoria* ☎ *503/325–6311 or 800/875–6807* ⊕ *www.oldoregon.com*). **Cannon Beach Chamber of Commerce** (✉ *207 N. Spruce St.* ☎ *503/436–2623* ⊕ *www.cannonbeach.org*).

Seaside Visitors Bureau (⊠ 7 N. Roosevelt Ave. ☎ 503/738–3097 or 888/306–2326 ⊕ www.seasideor.com). **Tillamook Chamber of Commerce** (⊠ 3705 U.S. 101 N ☎ 503/842–7525 ⊕ www.tillamook-chamber.org).

ASTORIA

96 mi northwest of Portland on U.S. 30.

The mighty Columbia River meets the Pacific at Astoria, the oldest city west of the Rockies. Named for John Jacob Astor, who had a major fur-trading post here, the settlement was a placid amalgamation of small town and hardworking port city in its early days. Settlers built sprawling Victorian houses on the flanks of **Coxcomb Hill.** Many of the homes have since been restored and are no less splendid as bed-and-breakfast inns. In recent years, the city itself has perked up, with a greater variety of trendy restaurants and hotels, staking its claim as a destination resort town.

★ The **Columbia River Maritime Museum,** on the downtown
☼ waterfront, explores the maritime history of the Pacific Northwest and is one of the two most interesting man-made

tourist attractions on the Oregon coast (Newport's aquarium is the other). Beguiling exhibits include the personal belongings of some of the ill-fated passengers of the 2,000 ships that have sunk here since 1811. Also here are a bridge from the World War II destroyer USS *Knapp* (which can be viewed from the inside), the fully operational U.S. Coast Guard Lightship *Columbia,* and a 44-foot Coast Guard motor lifeboat. ✉ *1792 Marine Dr., at 17th St.* ☎ *503/325–2323* ⊕ *www.crmm.org* ▧ *$10* ◷ *Daily 9:30–5.*

The **Astoria Column,** a 125-foot monolith atop Coxcomb Hill that was patterned after Trajan's Column in Rome, rewards your 164-step, spiral-stair climb with views over Astoria, the Columbia River, the Coast Range, and the Pacific. Or if you don't want to climb, the column's artwork, depicting important Pacific Northwest historical milestones, is stunning. ✉ *From U.S. 30 downtown take 16th St. south 1 mi to top of Coxcomb Hill* ▧ *Free* ◷ *Daily 9–dusk.*

The prim **Flavel House** was built between 1884 and 1886. Its Victorian-era furnishings, including six handcrafted fireplace mantels carved from hardwoods and accented with tiles imported from Asia and Europe, yield insight into the lifestyle of a wealthy 19th-century shipping tycoon. Visits start in the Carriage House interpretive center. ✉ *441 8th St., at Duane St.* ☎ *503/325–2203* ⊕ *www.oldoregon.com/ visitor-info/flavel-house-museum* ▧ *$5* ◷ *May–Sept., daily 10–5; Oct.–Apr., daily 11–4.*

☺ Starting in December 1805, the explorers Lewis and Clark
★ camped for several months on a spit of land south of present-day Astoria. "Ocean in view! O! The joy!" Clark wrote. **Fort Clatsop National Memorial** is a faithful replica of the log stockade depicted in his journal. Park rangers, who dress in period garb in summer and perform such early-19th-century tasks as making fire with flint and steel, lend an air of authenticity, as does the damp and lonely feel of the fort itself. ✉ *Fort Clatsop Loop Rd. 5 mi south of Astoria; from U.S. 101 cross Youngs Bay Bridge, turn east on Alt. U.S. 101, and follow signs* ☎ *503/861–2471* ⊕ *www.nps. gov/focl* ▧ *$3* ◷ *Daily 9–5.*

☺ The earthworks of 37-acre **Fort Stevens,** at Oregon's northwestern tip, were mounded up during the Civil War to guard the Columbia against a Confederate attack. No such event occurred, but during World War II, Japanese submarines shelled the fort, making it the only mainland U.S. military installation to come under enemy fire since the

War of 1812. The fort's abandoned gun mounts and eerie subterranean bunkers are a memorable destination. The corroded skeleton of the *Peter Iredale,* a century-old English four-master ship, protrudes from the sand just west of the campground, a stark testament to the temperamental nature of the Pacific. ⊠ *Fort Stevens Hwy., from Fort Clatsop, take Alt. U.S. 101 west past U.S. 101, turn north onto Main St.–Fort Stevens Hwy., and follow signs* ☎ *503/861–2000* ⊕ *www.visitfortstevens.com* ☎ *$3 per vehicle* ☉ *Mid-May–Sept., daily 10–6; Oct.–Apr., daily 10–4.*

★ One of the Oregon coast's oldest commercial smokehouses, **Josephson's** uses alder for all processing and specializes in Pacific Northwest chinook and coho salmon. The mouthwatering fish that's smoked on the premises includes hot smoked pepper or wine-maple salmon, as well as smoked halibut, sturgeon, tuna, oysters, mussels, scallops and prawns by the pound or in sealed gift packs. ⊠ *106 Marine Dr.* ☎ *503/325–2190* ⊕ *www.josephsons.com* ☎ *Free* ☉ *Mon.–Sat. 9–6, Sun. 9–5:30.*

In a 100-year-old Colonial Revival building originally used as the city hall, the **Heritage Museum** has two floors of exhibits detailing the history of the early pioneers, Native Americans, and logging and marine industries of Clatsop County, the oldest American settlement west of the Mississippi. In the research library you can research local family and building history. ⊠ *1618 Exchange St.* ☎ *503/338–2203* ⊕ *www.cumtux.org* ☎ *$4* ☉ *May–Labor Day, daily 10–5; Labor Day–Apr., Tues.–Sat. 11–4.*

The **Astoria Riverfront Trolley,** also known as "Old 300," is a beautifully restored 1913 streetcar that travels for 4 mi along Astoria's historic riverfront. The hour-long ride gives you a close-up look at the waterfront from the Port of Astoria to the East Morring Basin; the Columbia River; and points of interest in between. ⊠ *1095 Dwayne St.* ☎ *503/325–6311* ⊕ *homepage.mac.com/cearll/trolley* ☎ *$1 per boarding, $2 all-day pass* ☉ *Memorial Day–Labor Day, Mon.–Thurs. 3–9, Fri.–Sun. noon–9; fall, winter, and spring, check trolley shelters.*

WHERE TO EAT

$$ ✕ **Bridgewater Bistro.** *Contemporary.* Next to the Columbia Pier Hotel and offering riverfront dining, Bridgewater Bistro serves inexpensive pub fare (such as burgers and fish-and-chips) as well as more refined dishes such as Moroccan chicken and duck breast. The prawns sautéed with chile

and lime and served with honey-lime aioli are a favorite. Also worth the anticipation is a bourbon-flavored pecan cheesecake. ⊠ *20 Basin St.* ☎ *503/325–6777* ⊕ *www.bridge-waterbistro.com* ⊟*AE, D, MC, V* ⊗*Mon.–Thurs. 11–9, Fri. and Sat. 11–10.*

\$\$ ✕**Cannery Cafe.** *Seafood.* Original fir-wood floors, windows, and hardware (combined with expansive views of the Columbia River make this restaurant in a renovated 1879 cannery feel rustic and nautical. Breakfast dishes, often with crab or salmon, come with potato pancakes and buttermilk biscuits. Fresh salads, large sandwiches, clam chowder, and crab cakes are lunch staples. The dinner menu emphasizes seafood, including cioppino (an Italian fish stew), and Dungeness crab Alfredo. ⊠ *1 6th St.* ☎ *503/325–8642* ⊟*AE, D, DC, MC, V* ⊗*Tues.–Sun. 8 AM–9 PM, Mon. 11–9; bar until midnight.*

★ Fodor'sChoice ✕**Clemente's.** *Seafood.* Serving some of the best
\$ seafood on the Oregon Coast, chefs Gordon and Lisa Clement have made a significant critical and popular splash in Astoria. Grounded in Mediterranean cuisine from Italy and the Adriatic Coast, Clemente's inventive specials feature the freshest catches of that day. From succulent sea bass salad to a hearty sturgeon sandwich—meals are dished up for reasonable prices. Dungeness crab cakes stuffed with crab rather than breading, and wild scallop fish and chips liven up a varied menu. Don't feel like seafood? Try the spaghetti with meatballs. ⊠ *1335 Marine Dr.* ☎ *503/325–1067* ⊟*AE, D, MC, V* ⊗*Lunch Tues. 11–6, Wed.–Sun. 11–4; dinner Wed.–Sun. 5:30–9.*

\$\$ ✕**Columbian Cafe.** *Contemporary.* Locals love this unpretentious diner with such tongue-in-cheek, south-of-the-border decor as chili-pepper-shape Christmas lights. Simple food—crepes with broccoli, cheese, and homemade salsa for lunch; grilled salmon and pasta with a lemon-cream sauce for dinner—is served by a staff that usually includes the owner. Come early; this place always draws a crowd. ⊠ *1114 Marine Dr.* ☎ *503/325–2233* ⊟No *credit cards* ⊗*Closed Sun. and Mon.*

WHERE TO STAY

\$\$–\$\$\$ ⊞**Benjamin Young Inn.** On the National Register of Historic Places, this handsome 5,500-sq-ft Queen Anne inn is surrounded by century-old gardens. Among the ornate original details are faux graining on frames and molding, shutterblinds in windows, and Povey stained glass. The spacious guest rooms mix antiques with contemporary pieces and have views of the Columbia River from their tall windows. City tennis courts are right next door. There's a two-night minimum on holiday and July, August, and September weekends. **Pros:** each room has a private bathroom; a piano in the living room is available for guests' use. **Cons:** no pets allowed; no elevator. ⊠ *3652 Duane St.* ☎ *503/325–6172 or 800/201–1286* ⊕ *www.benjaminyounginn.com* ⇨ *4 rooms, including 1 2-bedroom suite* ⚷ *In-room: no a/c, no TV (some)* ⊟ *AE, D, MC, V* ⚹*BP.*

★ **Fodor's**Choice ☆ **Cannery Pier Hotel.** Every room has a gorgeous
$$$$ river view where you can watch tugboats shepherding barges to and fro. Built upon century-old pilings where the Columbia River meets the Pacific Ocean, the hotel is in the restored Union Fisherman's Cooperative Packing Company building, an integral part of the town's history. The interior is modern and bright with a liberal use of glass and polished wood, including hardwood floors in the rooms. The property sits on the Astoria Riverwalk and on the Trolley Line, and good restaurants are within walking distance. **Pros:** river views; gas fireplaces in the rooms. **Cons:** rooms don't necessarily have good noise insulation. ⊠ *10 Basin St.* ☎ *503/325–4996 or 888/325–4996* ⊕ *www.cannerypierhotel.com* ⇨ *3 rooms, 9 suites* ⚷ *In-room: no a/c, kitchen, DVD, Wi-Fi. In-hotel: gym, spa, bicycles, laundry facilities, some pets allowed* ⊟ *AE, D, MC, V* ⚹*CP.*

$$$–$$$$ ☆ **Hotel Elliott.** This upscale, five-story downtown hotel is in
★ the heart of Astoria's historic district. Updated with modern comforts, the property nevertheless retains the elegance of yesteryear. On the rooftop, you can relax in the garden and enjoy views of the Columbia River and the Victorian homes dotting the hillside. Warm your feet on the heated stone floors in your bathroom. Downstairs you can sample fine wines in the Cabernet Room or enjoy a cigar in the tucked-away Havana Room. **Pros:** in the middle of town; walking distance to all shops and restaurants. **Cons:** no restaurant; no Wi-Fi in rooms. ⊠ *357 12th St.* ☎ *877/378–1924* ⊕ *www.hotelelliott.com* ⇨ *32 rooms* ⚷ *In-room: DVD, Internet. In-hotel: bar, Wi-Fi hotspot, some pets allowed* ⊟ *AE, D, MC, V.*

SEASIDE

12 mi south of Astoria on U.S. 101.

Seaside has grown up around the spot where the Lewis and Clark expedition finally reached the Pacific Ocean. A bronze statue of the two explorers commemorates the end of their trail, facing the ocean at the center of Seaside's historic Promenade. The Prom, built in 1908 as a wooden walkway, was extended in 1920 to its current length, 1½ mi, with concrete sidewalks.

As a resort town Seaside has brushed off its former garish, arcade-filled past and now supports a bustling tourist trade with hotels, condominiums, and restaurants surrounding a long beach. It still has fun games and noise to appeal to young people, but it has added plenty of classy getaways for adults. Only 90 mi from Portland, Seaside is often crowded, so it's not the place to come if you crave solitude. Peak times include February, during the Trail's End Marathon; mid-March, when hordes of teenagers descend on the town during spring break; and July, when the annual Miss Oregon Pageant is in full swing.

Just south of town, waves draw surfers to the Cove, a spot jealously guarded by locals.

It's a 2½-mi hike from the parking lot of **Saddle Mountain State Park** to the summit of Saddle Mountain. It's much cooler at that elevation. The campground, 14 mi north of Seaside, has 10 primitive sites. ⊠ *Off U.S. 26* ☎ *800/551–6949* 🖃 *$10 for overnight camping, first-come, first-served. Hiking is free* ☉ *Mar.–Nov., daily dawn–dusk.*

WHERE TO EAT

$$ ✕ **Girtle's Seafood & Steaks.** *Steak and Seafood.* Huge portions at reasonable prices is the strategy of this family-oriented restaurant. Here you can find juicy steaks, fresh local seafood, and plenty of simple selections for kids. It also lays out a substantial, classic breakfast spread. ⊠ *311 Broadway* ☎ *503/738–8417* ⊕ *www.girtles.com* ▭ *AE, D, MC, V* ☉ *Daily 9 AM–1:30 AM.*

$$ ✕ **Guido & Vito's Italian Eatery.** *Italian.* In a sea of family-
★ oriented fish restaurants sits this pleasant, quiet restaurant, which cooks Italian food right—be it a zesty Caeser, sausage and beef meatballs, or a belly-warming, mushroom-slathered veal marsala. ⊠ *604 Broadway* ☎ *503/717–1229* ▭ *D, MC, V* ☉ *Sun.–Fri. 4–9, Sat. 4–10.*

$ ✕ **Yummy Wine Bar & Bistro.** *Contemporary.* In his warm, fun wine bar, owner Corey R. Albert serves dishes such as paninis and fresh seafood that blend well with fine Pacific Northwest wines. No children under 16 admitted. ⊠ *831 Broadway* ☎ *503/738–3100* ⊕ *www.yummywinebarbistro. com* ▭ *AE, MC, V* ☉ *Sun., Mon., Thurs. 3–10, Fri. and Sat. 3–midnight; closed Tues. and Wed.*

8

WHERE TO STAY

$–$$ ☒ **Hillcrest Inn.** Friendliness, cleanliness, and convenience are bywords of the Hillcrest, which is one block from both the beach and the convention center, and three blocks from the downtown area's restaurants and shops. You're welcome to use the picnic tables, lawn chairs, and even the barbecue on the grounds. **Pros:** variety of rooms, including cottages. **Cons:** thin walls make neighbor noise hard to avoid. ☒ *118 N. Columbia St.* ☎ *503/738–6273 or 800/270–7659* ⊕ *www.seasidehillcrest.com* ⤳ *19 rooms, 4 suites, 3 2-bedroom cottages, 1 6-bedroom house* ♿ *In-room: a/c (some), kitchen, refrigerators, Wi-Fi. In-hotel: Wi-Fi hotspot, laundry facilities* ▤ *AE, D, MC, V.*

$$$$ ☒ **Rivertide Suites.** This hotel may not be right on the beach,
☺ but its splendid accommodations are within walking dis-
★ tance of the town's best cuisine, shopping, and beach activities. Offering one- and two-bedroom suites and studios, Rivertide gives you different packages that appeal to golfers, whale-watchers, or romantic couples. All units have their own laundry facilities. **Pros:** spacious rooms; breakfast included. **Cons:** no good views. ☒ *102 N. Holladay* ☎ *877/871–8433* ⊕ *www.rivertidesuites.com* ⤳ *45 suites* ♿ *In-room: a/c (some), kitchen, DVD. In-hotel: pool, gym, Internet terminal, Wi-Fi hotspot, some pets allowed* ▤ *AE, D, MC, V* ⦿ *BP.*

¢–$ ☒ **Royale.** This small motel in the center of downtown is on the Necanicum River, 3½ blocks from the beach and within walking distance of shopping and restaurants. Some rooms have river views. There's ample off-street parking. **Pros:** microwaves in rooms. **Cons:** older property with dated furnishings; no elevator. ☒ *531 Ave. A* ☎ *503/738–9541* ⤳ *26 rooms* ♿ *In-room: refrigerators, Wi-Fi* ▤ *D, DC, MC, V.*

A BRISK 2-MI HIKE FROM U.S. 101 south of Seaside leads to the 1,100-foot-high viewing point atop **Tillamook Head.** The view from here takes in the Tillamook Rock Light Station, which stands a mile or so out to sea. The lonely beacon, built in 1881 on a straight-sided rock, towers 41 feet above the surrounding ocean. In 1957 the lighthouse was abandoned, and for a time in the 1990s it was used to hold funerary urns.

Eight miles south of Seaside, U.S. 101 passes the entrance to **Ecola State Park,** a playground of sea-sculpted rocks, sandy shoreline, green headlands, and panoramic views. The park's main beach can be crowded in summer, but the Indian Beach area contains an often-deserted cove and explorable tidal pools. ☎ *503/436–2844 or 800/452–5687* ⬛ *$3 per vehicle* ☉ *Daily dawn–dusk.*

CANNON BEACH

10 mi south of Seaside on U.S. 101, 80 mi west of Portland on U.S. 26.

Cannon Beach is a mellow and trendy place to enjoy art, wine, fine dining, and to take in the sea air. In what's one of the most charming towns on the coast, there are beachfront homes and hotels, and a weathered-cedar downtown shopping district. On the other hand, Cannon Beach can be more expensive and crowded than other towns along Highway 101's shoreline.

Towering over the broad, sandy beach is **Haystack Rock,** a 235-foot-high monolith that is one of the most-photographed natural wonders on Oregon coast. △ **The rock is temptingly accessible during some low tides, but the coast guard regularly airlifts stranded climbers from its steep sides, and occasionally some falls from it are fatal.** Every May the town hosts the Cannon Beach Sandcastle Contest, for which thousands throng the beach to view imaginative and often startling works in this most transient of art forms.

Shops and galleries selling kites, upscale clothing, local art, wine, coffee, and food line **Hemlock Street,** Cannon Beach's main thoroughfare.

WHERE TO EAT AND STAY

$$ ✕ **The Bistro.** *Contemporary.* Flowers, candlelight, and classical music convey romance at this 11-table restaurant. The menu includes imaginative Continental renditions of local seafood and pasta dishes as well as specialty salads. The signature dish is the fresh seafood stew. ✉ *263 N. Hemlock St.* ☎ *503/436–2661* ▭ *MC, V* ☉ *Closed Tues. and Wed. Nov.–Jan. No lunch.*

¢ ✕ **Sleepy Monk.** *Coffeehouse.* In a region famous for its
★ gourmet coffee, one small roaster brews a cup more memorable than any chain. Sleepy Monk attracts java aficionados on caffeine pilgrimages from all over the Pacific Northwest; and it's not unusual to see a line outside the door. Its certified organic and fair trade beans are roasted without adding water, which adds unnecessary weight. There's a variety of teas, too. Fresh pastries are stacked high and deep. If you're a coffee fan, it's well worth the visit. ✉ *1235 S. Hemlock*

8

☏ *503/436–2796* ⊕ *www.sleepymonkcoffee.com* ▤ *MC, V* ☉ *Fri., Sat., and Sun. 8–5.*

$–$$ ▦ **Grey Whale Inn.** This small, charming inn dates from 1948. It is in a very quiet residential neighborhood, a five-minute walk to the beach or a 20-minute walk to Haystack Rock. All the rooms are furnished with original artwork, done either by the family or local artists. **Pros:** reasonable rates. **Cons:** no bathtubs in rooms. ✉ *164 Kenai St.* ☏ *503/436–2848* ⌨ *5 rooms* ☐ *In-room: kitchen (some) refrigerators, Wi-Fi. In-hotel: no pets* ▤ *MC, V.*

★ **Fodor's Choice** ▦ **Ocean Lodge.** To celebrate special occasions,
$$$$ create new memories, or enjoy first-rate service, this is the place—it was designed to capture the feel of a 1940s beachfront resort. Most of the rooms have oceanfront views, and all have open wood beams, simple but sophisticated furnishings, gas fireplaces, and balconies or decks. The lobby floor is made of reclaimed spruce wood, and the stairs were fashioned from old stadium bleachers. A massive rock fireplace anchors the lobby, and there's a second fireplace in the second-floor library with a large selection of games for the whole family at your disposal. **Pros:** lots of extras, including extensive book and DVD collection for borrowing and complimentary fresh-baked cookies throughout the day. **Cons:** the bungalows (across the street) don't have oceanfront views. ✉ *2864 S. Pacific St.* ☏ *503/436–2241 or 888/777–4047* ⊕ *www.theoceanlodge.com* ⌨ *45 rooms* ☐ *In-room: a/c (some), kitchen, DVD. In-hotel: Wi-Fi hotspot, some pets allowed* ▤ *AE, D, MC, V.*

$$$$ ▦ **Stephanie Inn.** With a stunning view of Haystack Rock,
★ this splendid hotel keeps its focus on romance, superior service, and luxurious rooms. Impeccably maintained, with country-style furnishings, fireplaces, large bathrooms with whirlpool tubs, and balconies, the rooms are so comfortable you may never want to leave—except perhaps to enjoy the four-course prix-fixe dinners of innovative Pacific Northwest cuisine. The restaurant ($$$$) serves a delectable rack of lamb. **Pros:** generous country breakfasts and evening wine and hors d'oeuvres included in rates. **Cons:** no laundry service; not family-friendly. ✉ *2740 S. Pacific St.* ☏ *503/436–2221 or 800/633–3466* ⊕ *www.stephanie-inn.com* ⌨ *50 rooms* ☐ *In-room: DVD, refrigerator, Wi-Fi. In-hotel: restaurant, no kids under 12, no pets* ▤ *AE, D, DC, MC, V* ⊚*BP.*

EN ROUTE. South of Cannon Beach, U.S. 101 climbs 700 feet above the Pacific, providing dramatic views and often hair-raising curves as it winds along the flank of **Neahkahnie Mountain.** Cryptic carvings on beach rocks near here and centuries-old Native American legends of shipwrecked Europeans gave rise to a tale that the survivors of a sunken Spanish galleon buried a fortune in doubloons somewhere on the side of the 1,661-foot-high mountain.

OSWALD WEST STATE PARK

10 mi south of Cannon Beach on U.S. 101.

One of the best-kept secrets on the Pacific coast, **Oswald West State Park,** at the base of Neahkahnie Mountain is a great destination if you're adventurous. Park in one of the two lots on U.S. 101 and use a park-provided wheelbarrow to trundle your camping gear down a ½-mi trail. An old-growth forest surrounds the primitive campsites (reservations not accepted), and the spectacular beach contains caves and tidal pools.

The trail to the summit, on the left about 2 mi south of the parking lots for Oswald West State Park (marked only by a HIKERS sign), rewards the intrepid with unobstructed views over surf, sand, forest, and mountain. Come in December or March and you might spot pods of gray whales. The 30 walk-in tent sites are first-come, first-served. ⊠ *Ecola Park Rd.* ☎ *503/368–5943 or 800/452–5687* ⊕ *www.oregon-stateparks.org* ⊠ *Day-use free, tent site $16* ⊙ *Day-use daily dawn–dusk; camping Mar.–Oct.*

8

EN ROUTE. After passing through several small fishing, logging, and resort towns, U.S. 101 skirts around **Tillamook Bay,** where the Miami, Kilchis, Wilson, Trask, and Tillamook rivers enter the Pacific. The sportfishing's good here, with quarry that includes sea-run cutthroat trout, bottom fish, and silver, chinook, and steelhead salmon, along with mussels, oysters, clams, and the delectable Dungeness crab. Charter-fishing services operate out of the **Garibaldi** fishing harbor 10 mi north of Tillamook. For some of the best rock fishing in the state, try Tillamook Bay's North Jetty.

MANZANITA

20 mi south of Cannon Beach on U.S. 101.

Manzanita is a secluded seaside community with roughly 600 full-time residents. It's on a sandy peninsula peppered with tufts of grass on the northwestern side of Nehalem Bay. It's a tranquil small town, but its restaurants, galleries, and 18-hole golf course have increased its appeal to tourists. Manzanita and Nehalem Bay both have become popular windsurfing destinations.

Established in 1974, **Nehalem Bay Winery** is known for its pinot noir, chardonnay, blackberry, and plum fruit wines. The winery also has a busy schedule of events, with concerts, barbecues, an occasional pig roast, children's activities, performances at the Theatre Au Vin, and a bluegrass festival the third week of August. ✉ *34965 Hwy. 53, Nehalem* ☎ *503/368–9463 or 888/368–9463* ⊕ *www. nehalembaywinery.com* ⊙ *Daily 9–6.*

WHERE TO STAY

$$$–$$$$ ⚏ **Inn at Manzanita.** This 1987 Scandinavian structure, filled with light-color woods, beams, and glass, is half a block from the beach. Shore pines on the property give upper-floor patios a tree-house feel; all rooms have decks, and two have skylights. A nearby café serves breakfast, and area restaurants are nearby. In winter the inn is a great place for storm-watching. There's a two-day minimum stay on weekends. There are three child-friendly rooms as well as a penthouse suite. A 20-day cancellation notice is required. **Pros:** rooms have jetted baths and down comforters on the beds. **Cons:** no elevator; some guests complain about street noise in summer months. ✉ *67 Laneda Ave., Box 243* ☎ *503/368–6754* ⊕ *www.innatmanzanita.com* ⇗ *13 rooms, 1 penthouse suite* ⚏ *In-room: no a/c, no phone (some), kitchen (some), refrigerator (some), DVD, Wi-Fi.* ⊟ *AE, D, MC, V.*

⚏ **Nehalem Bay State Park.** Close enough to the ocean that you might be lulled to sleep by the waves, the park is on the edge of Nehalem Bay, which is popular for kayaking, crabbing, and fishing. ✉ *Off U.S. 101, 3 mi south of Manzanita Junction* ☎ *800/452–5687 reservations, 800/551–6949 information* ⊕ *www.oregonstateparks.org* ⇗ *265 electrical sites, 18 yurts, 17 sites with corrals* ⚏ *Flush toilets, partial hookups, dump station, drinking water, showers, fire pits, picnic tables, electricity, swimming (ocean)* ⊟ *MC, V* ⚏ *Reservations essential.*

TILLAMOOK

30 mi south of Oswald West State Park and Neahkahnie Mountain on U.S. 101.

More than 100 inches of annual rainfall and the conflu-ence of three rivers contribute to the lush green pastures around Tillamook, probably best known for its thriving dairy industry and cheese factory. The Tillamook County Cheese Factory ships about 40 million pounds of cheese around the world every year.

Just south of town is the largest wooden structure in the world, one of two gigantic buildings constructed in 1942 by the U.S. Navy to shelter blimps that patrolled the Pacific Coast during World War II. Hangar A was destroyed by fire in 1992, and Hangar B was subsequently converted to the Tillamook Naval Air Station Museum.

The **Three Capes Loop** over Cape Meares, Cape Lookout, and Cape Kiwanda offers spectacular views of the ocean and coastline. A lighthouse and an old Indian burial Sitka spruce, Octopus Tree, are worth the trip to Cape Meares; as for Cape Lookout, it's one of the Northwest's best places to watch whales. Along the route from Tillamook's small resort area of Oceanside, take a look at Three Arch Rocks, a National Wildlife Refuge, with hundreds of seals and nesting habitat for as many as 200,000 birds.

The **Pioneer Museum** in Tillamook's 1905 county courthouse has an intriguing if old-fashioned hodgepodge of Native American, pioneer, logging, and natural-history exhibits, along with antique vehicles and military artifacts. ⊠ *2106 2nd St.* ☎ *503/842–4553* ✉ *www.tcpm.org* ☎ *$4* ⊙ *Tues.– Sat. 10–4.*

The **Latimer Quilt and Textile Center** is dedicated to the pres-ervation, promotion, creation, and display of the fiber arts. Spinners, weavers, beaders, and quilters can be found working on projects in the Quilting Room and may engage you in hands-on demonstrations. Rotating exhibits include costumes, cloth dolls, crocheted items from the 1940s and 1950s, exquisite historical quilts dating from the early to mid-1800s, basketry, and weavings. ⊠ *2105 Wilson River Loop Rd.* ☎ *503/842–8622* ⊕ *www.latimerquiltandtextile. com* ✉ *$3* ⊙ *May–Sept., daily 10–5; Oct.–Apr., Tues.–Sat. 10–4.*

8

More than 750,000 visitors annually journey through the **Tillamook County Creamery,** the largest cheese-making plant on the West Coast. Here the rich milk from the area's thousands of Holstein and brown Swiss cows becomes ice cream, butter, and cheddar and Monterey Jack cheeses. There's a self-guided cheese-making tour and an extensive shop where tasty cheeses and smoked meats are sold: you'll probably want some ice cream in a waffle cone— try the marionberry, a blackberry hybrid. ⊠ *4175 U.S. 101 N, 2 mi north of Tillamook* ☎ *503/815–1300* ⊕ *www. tillamookcheese.com* ☒ *Free* ⊙ *Mid-Sept.–May, daily 8–6; June–mid-Sept., daily 8–8.*

☾ The **Blue Heron French Cheese Company** specializes in French-style cheeses such as Camembert and Brie. The complex includes a free petting zoo for kids, a sit-down deli, wine and cheese tastings, and a gift shop that carries wines and jams, mustards, and other products from Oregon. ⊠ *2001 Blue Heron Dr., watch for signs from U.S. 101* ☎ *503/842– 8281* ⊕ *www.blueheanonoregon.com* ☒ *Free* ⊙ *Memorial Day–Labor Day, daily 8–8; Labor Day–Memorial Day, daily 8–6.*

In the world's largest wooden structure, a former blimp hangar south of town, the **Tillamook Naval Air Station Museum** displays one of the finest private collections of vintage aircraft from World War II, including a B-25 Mitchell and an ME-109 Messerschmidt. The 20-story building is big enough to hold half a dozen football fields. ⊠ *6030 Hangar Rd., ½ mi south of Tillamook; head east from U.S. 101 on Long Prairie Rd. and follow signs* ☎ *503/842–1130* ⊕ *www. tillamookair.com* ☒ *$9* ⊙ *Daily 9–5.*

WHERE TO EAT AND STAY

$ ✕ **Artspace.** *Eclectic.* You'll be surrounded by artwork as you enjoy homemade creations at Artspace, 6 mi north of Tillamook. The menu may include garlic-grilled oysters, vegetarian dishes, and other specials, all beautifully presented, often with edible flowers. Breakfast is a big draw; there's a $1 menu that includes biscuits and gravy, scones, French toast, and grilled potatoes. ⊠ *9120 5th St., Bay City* ☎ *503/377–2782* ▭ *No credit cards* ⊙ *Mon. breakfast only.*

$$ ✕ **Roseanna's.** *Seafood.* Nine miles west of Tillamook, Rose-anna's is in a rustic 1915 building on the beach opposite Three Arch Rock—you might be able to watch sea lions and puffins while you eat. The calm of the beach is complemented in the evening by candlelight and fresh flowers.

Have halibut or salmon half a dozen ways, or try the poached baked oysters or Gorgonzola seafood pasta. ⊠ *1490 Pacific Ave., Oceanside* ☎ *503/842–7351* ⚓ *www. roseannascafe.com* 🗐 *Reservations not accepted* ▭ *MC, V* ☉ *Sun. and Mon. 10–8, closed Tues. and Wed., Thurs. 10–8, Fri. and Sat. 10–9.*

$$–$$$ 🖭 **Hudson House.** The son of the original owner of this 1906 farmhouse was a photographer who captured the area's rough beauty on postcards. The larger suite is downstairs, with a parlor and private porch overlooking the Nestucca Valley. The more popular, upstairs suite has a bedroom in the house's turret. The two guest rooms are under the high-gabled roof. **Pros:** the wraparound porch has a view of the surrounding woods. **Cons:** no children under 12. ⊠ *37700 U.S. 101 S, Cloverdale* ☎ *503/392–3533 or 888/835–3533* ⊕ *www.hudsonhouse.com* ⇖ *2 rooms, 2 suites* ⚭ *In-room: no phone, no TV, Wi-Fi. In-hotel: No kids under 12* ▭ *MC, V* ⊚ *BP.*

$$$–$$$$ 🖭 **Sandlake Country Inn.** Surrounded by old roses on 2 acres, this bed-and-breakfast is in a farmhouse built of timbers that washed ashore from a shipwreck in 1890. It's listed on the Oregon Historic Registry and filled with antiques. The Timbers Suite has a massive, king-size wood canopy bed, wood-burning fireplace, and two-person jetted tub; the Starlight Suite occupies four rooms on the second floor and includes a canopy queen bed and double-sided fireplace. **Pros:** four-course breakfast delivered to the door. **Cons:** no children under 12 or pets are allowed; no elevator. ⊠ *8505 Galloway Rd., Pacific City* ☎ *503/965–6745 or 877/726–3525* ⊕ *www.sandlakecountryinn.com* ⇖ *1 room, 2 suites, 1 cottage* ⚭ *In-room: no a/c, no phone (some), kitchen (some), DVD, Wi-Fi. In-hotel: no kids under 12* ▭ *D, MC, V* ⊚ *BP.*

THREE CAPES LOOP

Starts south of downtown Tillamook off 3rd St.

The Three Capes Loop, a 35-mi byway off U.S. 101, is one of the coast's most thrilling driving experiences. The loop winds along the coast between Tillamook and Pacific City, passing three distinctive headlands—Cape Meares, Cape Lookout, and Cape Kiwanda. Bayocean Road heading west from Tillamook passes what was the thriving resort town of Bay Ocean. Back in 1940, the houses, a post office, a bowling alley, and everything else that made up Bayocean washed into the sea during a raging Pacific storm.

Nine miles west of Tillamook, trails from the parking lot at the end of Bay Ocean Spit lead through the dunes to a usually uncrowded and highly walkable white-sand beach.

Cape Meares State Park is on the northern tip of the Three Capes Loop. Cape Meares was named for English navigator John Meares, who voyaged along this coast in 1788. The restored **Cape Meares Lighthouse,** built in 1890 and open to the public May–September, provides a sweeping view over the cliff to the caves and sea-lion rookery on the rocks below. A many-trunked Sitka spruce known as the Octopus Tree grows near the lighthouse parking lot. Legend states that this tree was used for Native American burials. The dead were placed in canoes that were then positioned in the boughs of trees. Branches of normal forest trees grow toward the light, but such trees were forced at a young age into a horizontal position, beyond which they grew upward. ✉ *Three Capes Loop 10 mi west of Tillamook* ☎ *800/551–6949* ⊕ *www.oregonstateparks.org* 🎫 *Free* ⊙ *Park daily dawn–dusk. Lighthouse Apr.–Oct., daily 11–4.*

Cape Lookout State Park lies south of the beach towns of Oceanside and Netarts. A fairly easy 2-mi trail—marked on the highway as WILDLIFE VIEWING AREA—leads through giant spruces, western red cedars, and hemlocks to views of Cascade Head to the south and Cape Meares to the north. Wildflowers, more than 150 species of birds, and migrating whales passing by in early April make this trail a favorite with nature lovers. The park has a picnic area overlooking the sea and a year-round campground. ✉ *Three Capes Loop 8 mi south of Cape Meares* ☎ *800/551–6949* ⊕ *www. oregonstateparks.org* 🎫 *Day-use $3* ⊙ *Daily dawn–dusk.*

Huge waves pound the jagged sandstone cliffs and caves at **Cape Kiwanda State Natural Area.** The much-photographed, 235-foot-high **Haystack Rock** juts out of Nestucca Bay just south of here. Surfers ride some of the longest waves on the coast, hang gliders soar above the shore, and beachcombers explore tidal pools and take in unparalleled ocean views. ✉ *Three Capes Loop 15 mi south of Cape Lookout* ☎ *800/551–6949* ⊕ *www.oregonstateparks.org* 🎫 *Free* ⊙ *Daily dawn–dusk.*

THE WILLAMETTE VALLEY AND WINE COUNTRY

Updated by Janna Mock-Lopez

During the 1940s and 1950s, researchers at Oregon State University concluded that the climate of Willamette Valley—the wet, temperate trough between the Coast Range to the west and the Cascade Range to the east—was unsuitable for growing varietal wine grapes. Evidently, they were wrong, as the current success of the wine industry here proves.

More than 100 wineries dot the Willamette (pronounced "wil-*lam*-it") Valley, with the bulk of them in Yamhill County in the northern part of the state. Their products—mainly cool-climate varietals like pinot noir, chardonnay, and Johannisberg Riesling—have won gold medals in blind tastings against the best wines of California and Europe.

GETTING HERE AND AROUND

I–5 runs north–south the length of the Willamette, and many Willamette Valley attractions lie fairly close to it. Highway 22 travels west from the Willamette National Forest through Salem to the coast. Highway 99 travels parallel to I–5 through much of the Willamette Valley. Highway 34 leaves I–5 just south of Albany and heads west, past Corvallis and into the Coast Range, where it follows the Alsea River. Highway 126 heads east from Eugene toward the Willamette National Forest; it travels west from town to the coast.

VISITOR INFORMATION

Contacts Chehalem Valley Chamber of Commerce (Newberg, Dundee, and St. Paul) (✉ 415 E. Sheridan ☎ 503/538–2014 ⊕ www. chehalemvalley.org). **McMinnville Chamber of Commerce** (✉ 417 N.W. Adams St. ☎ 503/472–6196 ⊕ www.mcminnville.org). **Oregon Wine Country/ Willamette Valley Visitors Association** (✉ 553 N.W. Harrison Blvd., Corvallis ☎ 866/548–5018 ⊕ www.oregonwine-country.org). **Yamhill Valley Visitors Association** (✉ Box 774, McMinnville 97128 ☎ 503/883–7770 ⊕ www.yamhillvalley.org).

Points of interest can be found on the Willamette Valley and Wine Country map.

FOREST GROVE

24 mi west of Portland on Hwy. 8.

Named for a large grove of Oregon white oak trees on a knoll above the Tualatin Plains, Forest Grove is also surrounded by stands of Douglas firs and giant sequoia, including the largest giant sequoia in the state. Originally inhabited by the Tualatin tribe, the site was settled by pioneers in 1840, and the town incorporated in 1872. If you want to head to the wineries from here, head south from Forest Grove on Highway 47 and watch for the blue road signs between Forest Grove, Gaston, and Yamhill.

With 1,800 students, **Pacific University** is on a shady campus that provides a respite from sightseeing. It was founded in 1849, making it one of the oldest educational institutions in the western United States. Concerts and special events are held in McCready Hall in the Taylor-Meade Performing Arts Center. The school also has a College of Optometry. ⊠ *2043 College Way* ☎ *503/357–6151* ⊕ *www.pacificu.edu* ▨ *Free* ⊙ *Daily*.

In the wake of a forest fire, the Oregon Department of Forestry created **Forest Grove Educational Arboretum**, a facility on 364,000 acres that addresses how the environment can be salvaged following devastating natural disasters. ⊠ *801 Gales Creek Rd.* ☎ *503/357–2191* ⊕ *www.oregon.gov/odf* ⊙ *Tours on request*.

Just southeast of Forest Grove, **Fernhill Wetlands,** on 243 acres, is a haven for waterfowl. For a guided tour of the Fernhill Wetlands, contact the **Friends of Fernhill Wetlands** (☎ *503/357–5890*).

A beautiful area in the Coast Range foothills, **Scoggin Valley Park and Henry Hagg Lake** has a 15-mi-long hiking trail that surrounds the lake. Bird-watching is best in spring. Recreational activities include fishing, boating, water-skiing, and picnicking, and a well-marked 10½-mi bicycle lane parallels the park's perimeter road. ⊠ *Scoggin Valley Rd.* ☎ *503/846–8715* ⊕ *www.co.washington.or.us* ▨ *$5* ⊙ *Daily dawn–dusk Mar.–Nov.*

WHERE TO STAY

$$–$$$ 🏨 **McMenamins Grand Lodge.** On 13 acres of pastoral countryside, this converted Masonic rest home has accommodations that run from bunk-bed rooms to a three-room fireplace suite. The lodge's sturdy 1922 brick buildings also include pubs that serving McMenamins beers on draft. Rooms are furnished with period antiques such as oak nightstands and porcelain sinks. For those not staying in the bunkhouse, rates include use of the European-style soaking pool, Continental breakfast during the week, and

a full breakfast on weekends. At the Compass Room Theater, feature films are screened nightly; kids accompanied
by a guardian are permitted at the early show. ⊠ *3505
Pacific Ave.* ☎ *503/992–9533 or 877/992–9533* ⊕ *www.
thegrandlodge.com* ↝ *77 rooms* ⚒ *In-room: Wi-Fi. In-hotel:
bars, spa, Wi-Fi hotspot* ⊟ *AE, D, DC, MC, V.*

LAKE OSWEGO

9 mi south of Portland.

Contrary to the intentions of its early founders, who built
iron smelters in an effort to turn the area into "the Pitts-
burgh of the West," Lake Oswego is an affluent residential
community. It's immediately south of Portland, between
the Willamette and Tualatin rivers. The Willamette Shore
Trolley, operated by the Oregon Electric Railway Historical
Society, carries passengers along the Willamette between
downtown Lake Oswego and the Riverplace area at the
south end of Portland's downtown.

Framed by an open fireplace on one end and a reflecting
pond on the other, **Millennium Plaza Park** is the site of many
community events as well as a Saturday farmer's market.
⊠ *200 1st St.* ☎ *503/675–2549* ⊗ *Mid-May–mid-Oct., Sat.
8–1.*

Cooks Butte Park consists of 42 acres of informal pathways
and undeveloped land. ⊠ *Delenka La.* ☎ *No phone.*

Originally built in 1887, the **Willamette Shore Trolley**—one
standard and one double-decker trolley, both of museum
quality—carries passengers on a 45-minute ride to Portland
along a scenic 7-mi route, which you can travel one-way or
round-trip; you'll take in Mt. Hood and the wooded banks
of the Willamette River. In summer there are four departures
daily from Lake Oswego. Reservations are recommended.
In December there are special excursions to see the Christmas lights along the river. ⊠ *311 State St.* ☎ *503/697–7436*
⊕ *www.oerhs.org* ⊠ *$10 round-trip* ⊗ *Early May–Memorial
Day, weekends; Memorial Day–Labor Day, Thurs.–Sun.;
Labor Day–late Sept., Fri.–Sun.; Oct., Sat.*

WHERE TO EAT

$$$ ✕**Tucci.** *Continental.* This small Italian option serves suc-
culent, fresh scallops and tasty local meats dressed with
tantalizing sauces. A full-service lounge offers a bounty of
wines and spirits, and the warm chocolate polenta cake is
silky and delicious. Reserve a table overlooking the river,

8

select a bottle of wine, and settle in for a memorable experience. ✉ *220 A Ave.* ☎ *503/697–3383* ⊕ *www.tucci.biz*
🖃 *AE, D, DC, MC, V* ⊗ *Dinner daily. Lunch Tue.–Fri.*

OREGON CITY

6 mi southwest of Newberg on Hwy. 99 W.

Historic Oregon City was the destination for thousands
of pioneer families, who traveled the Oregon Trail from
St. Louis, Missouri, to the promised land on the western
frontier. Several of Oregon's prominent early residents
built homes in Oregon City on the Willamette River's east
bank, where the river plunges 40 feet over a basaltic ridge
at Willamette Falls. The End of the Oregon Trail Interpretive Center debuted in 1993 to commemorate the Trail's
150th anniversary. Dozens of historic homes, churches, and
other buildings have been restored and now offer tours into
times past. More than 26,000 people live here today; the
city is the seat of Clackamas County, one of three counties
that make up the Portland metro area.

Waterfowl are part-time residents at the ½-acre **John Inskeep
Environmental Learning Center** on the Clackamas Community College campus. The property has a trail that circles
two ponds at the headwaters of Newell Creek. ✉ *19600 S.
Molalla* ☎ *503/657–6958 Ext. 2644* ⊕ *www.depts.clack-
amas.edu.cc.or.us/elc* 🖃 *$2 donation suggested* ⊗ *Daily
sunrise–sunset.*

Built in 1845, **Ermatinger House** was the first frame house
built in Oregon City and the only two-story Federal-style
house in the state with a flat roof. The McLoughlin Memorial Association moved the house to save it from development, and then in 1986 it was moved again to 6th and John
Adams. For groups, hosts will present a Living History Tea.
✉ *619 6th St.* ☎ *503/650–1851* 🖃 *$4* ⊗ *Fri.–Sun. 11–4. Dur-
ing winter months call ahead to ensure they're open.*

An officer for a fur-trading company, Dr. John McLoughlin
lost his job when he forwarded supplies to needy Oregon
Trail pioneers, but his presence and deeds in the area are
remembered at **McLoughlin House National Historic Site,** the
mansion he moved to with his family in 1846. The site
is perhaps the key historic home in the city. ✉ *713 Center
St.* ☎ *503/656–5146* ⊕ *www.mcloughlinhouse.org* 🖃 *Free*
⊗ *Wed.–Sat. 10–4, Sun. 1–4.*

Stevens Crawford Heritage House celebrates the contributions of two Oregon City natives. Harley Stevens joined the Emigrant Escort Service to help protect pioneers on the Oregon Trail, and he went on to become the first telegraph operator in Oregon City. Mary Crawford was an important member of the Woman's Christian Temperance Union. When the house was built in 1908, it was one of the first homes to have indoor plumbing and both gas and electric light fixtures. Special events such as tea and luncheon are also a living-history lesson, as the hosts wear era-specific attire. ✉ *603 6th St.* ☎ *503/655–2866* 🖃 *$4* 🕓 *Wed.–Sat. noon–4.*

Artifacts dating back 10,000 years are on display at the **Museum of the Oregon Territory.** One such display examines the ways different tribes of the Northwest gathered to trade with the Chinooks; another exhibit takes up the history of wedding fashion. ✉ *211 Tumwater Dr.* ☎ *503/655–5574* 🖃 *$4* 🕓 *Daily 11–4.*

Along the Clackamas River and only 45 minutes from Portland, **Milo McIver State Park** is a popular rafting, canoeing, and kayaking area. There's also a 27-hole disc golf course. An annual Civil War reenactment is staged here in April; 300 actors participate. Camping is permitted: 44 electrical $17; 9 walk-in tent $15. ✉ *Hwy. 213 N to Hwy. 212 and Hwy. 211 SE* ☎ *503/630–7150 or 800/551–6949* ⊕ *www.oregonstateparks.org/park_142.php* 🖃 *Day use $3 per vehicle* 🕓 *Mar.–Nov., daily.*

The Willamette Falls are created when the Willamette River at Oregon City spills 40 feet over a basaltic ridge. The **Willamette Falls Locks** were built in the early 1870s to move river traffic around the falls. ✉ *On Willamette River, in West Linn* ☎ *503/656–3381* 🕓 *Daily; information center June–Oct., daily 9:30–4.*

WHERE TO EAT

¢ ✕**McMenamins Pub.** *American.* At this bustling family favorite you can order a Communication Breakdown Burger— Tillamook cheddar, onions, mushrooms, and peppers— among others, including a few vegetarian options. Couple your burger or sandwich with a creative ale such as chocolaty Black Rabbit Porter or raspberry Ruby Ale. Kid-pleasing comfort foods include grilled cheese, corn dogs, and peanut butter and jelly. The pub becomes more of a bar scene after 10 PM. ✉ *102 9th St.* ☎ *503/655–8032* 🕓 *Closed Mon.–Wed.* ▭ *AE, D, MC, V.*

NEWBERG

25 mi southwest of Portland on Hwy. 99 W.

Fertile fields of the Willamette Valley surround the community of Newberg, named by the first postmaster for his Bavarian hometown, Newburgh. Many of its early settlers were Quakers from the Midwest who founded the school that has become George Fox University. Newberg's most famous resident, likewise a Quaker, was Herbert Hoover, the 31st president of the United States. For about five years during his adolescence, he lived with an aunt and uncle at the Hoover-Minthorn House, now a museum listed on the National Register of Historic Places. In addition to numerous well-reputed wineries, the Newberg area also offers slightly more out-of-the-ordinary entertainment, with tours of nine llama ranches (see ⊕ *www.thellamaranch.com*) and Vista Balloon Adventures, the Pacific Northwest's largest hot-air-balloon company. St. Paul, a historic town with a population of about 325, is about 8 mi south of Newberg and 20 mi north of Salem. Every July, St. Paul holds a professional rodeo.

George Fox University, founded by the Quakers in 1884, is on a 75-acre shady campus in a residential neighborhood. Centennial Tower is surrounded by a campus quad and academic buildings, the library, and the student commons. Hess Creek Canyon cuts through the campus. ✉ *414 N. Meridian St.* ☎ *503/538–8383* ⊕ *www.georgefox.edu* ⊠ *Free* ⊙ *Daily.*

The oldest and most significant of Newberg's original structures is the **Hoover-Minthorn House Museum,** the boyhood home of President Herbert Hoover. Built in 1881, the preserved frame house still has many of its original furnishings. Outside is the woodshed that may have played an important role in shaping young "Bertie" Hoover's character. ✉ *115 S. River St.* ☎ *503/538–6629* ⊠ *$3* ⊙ *Mar.–Nov., Wed.–Sun. 1–4; Dec. and Feb., weekends 1–4.*

The drive-in is a perpetual novelty, and **99W Drive-in** is a good bet for a double feature. Ted Francis built this one in 1953 and operated it until his death at 98; the business is now run by his grandson. The first film begins at dusk. Kids 6–11 get in for $4, and children 5 and under are free. ✉ *Hwy. 99 W, Portland Rd., just west of Springbrook Rd. intersection* ☎ *503/538–2738* ⊕ *www.99w.com* ⊠ *$7 per person, $11 minimum vehicle charge* ⊙ *Fri.–Sun.*

SPORTS AND THE OUTDOORS

BALLOONING

If you're intrigued by what it might feel like to have the Earth gently moving toward you, book a ride with **Vista Balloon Adventures** (⌖ *701 S.E. Sherk Pl., Sherwood 97140* ☏ *503/625–7385 or 800/622–2309* ⊕ *www.vistaballoon. com*). Several balloons take off daily from Sportsman Airpark in Newberg. April through October except Tuesday, FAA-licensed pilots take the balloons about 1,500 feet over Yamhill County's wine country. Rates are $189 per person ($160 for a group of four or more).

DUNDEE AND YAMHILL

6 mi southwest of Newberg on Hwy. 99 W.

William Reid traveled to Oregon from Dundee, Scotland. As he became interested in the railway business, he got support from his homeland to finance the Oregon Railway Co., Ltd. After the city was incorporated in 1895, Dundee was named after Reid's hometown in recognition of its support.

The lion's share (more than 90%) of the U.S. hazelnut crop is grown in Dundee, a haven of produce stands and wine-tasting rooms. The 25 mi of Highway 18 between Dundee and Grande Ronde, in the Coast Range, roll through the heart of the Yamhill Valley wine country. What used to be a pleasant drive through quaint Dundee is now a traffic bottleneck nightmare—its main road is the main artery from Lincoln City to suburban Portland. Until the Dundee bypass is built, weekday visits are best.

WINERIES

Merlot, chardonnay, and gewürztraminer are among the wines made at **Duck Pond Cellars** (✉ *23145 Hwy. 99 W* ⌖ *Box 429* ☏ *503/538–3199 or 800/437–3213* ⊕ *www.duckpond-cellars.com*). Select free tastings and other vintages for $2. Picnicking in the outdoor seating area is encouraged. The winery is open October–April, daily 11–5, and May–September, daily 10–5.

Pinot noir, chardonnay, and sparkling wines are among the specialties at **Argyle Winery** (✉ *691 Hwy. 99 W* ☏ *503/538–8520 or 888/427–4953* ⊕ *www.argylewinery.com*). The winery is open daily 11–5.

Sokol Blosser (✉ *5000 Sokol Blosser La., 3 mi west of Dundee off Hwy. 99 W* ☏ *503/864–2282 or 800/582–6668* ⊕ *www. sokolblosser.com*), one of Oregon's oldest and largest wineries, has a tasting room and walk-through vineyard. A self-guided tour explains the grape varieties—pinot noir and chardonnay, among others. Open daily 10–4.

WHERE TO EAT

$$ ✕**Dundee Bistro.** *Contemporary.* This highly regarded, 80-seat restaurant by the Ponzi wine family uses local ingredients, including wines, Draper Valley chicken, nuts, and fish. Vaulted ceilings provide an open feeling inside, warmed by abundant fresh flowers and artworks by local Oregon artists. ✉ *100-A S.W. 7th St., Dundee* ☏ *503/554–1650* ▭ *AE, DC, MC, V.*

★ **Fodor'sChoice** ✕**Tina's.** *French.* Chef–proprietors Tina and
$$$ David Bergen bring a powerful one-two punch to this Dundee favorite, which often lures Portlanders. The couple shares cooking duties—Tina does the baking and is often on hand to greet you—and David brings his experience as a former caterer and employee of nearby Sokol Blosser Winery to the table, ensuring that you have the right glass of wine to match your course. Fish and game vie for attention on the country French menu—entrées might include grilled Oregon salmon or Alaskan halibut, or a braised rabbit, local lamb, or tenderloin. Avail yourself of any of the special soups, particularly if there's corn chowder on hand. A lunch menu includes soup, sandwiches, and Tina's grilled hamburger, made with free-range beef. Service is as intimate and laid-back as the interior. A double fireplace divides the dining room, with heavy glass brick shrouded by bushes on the highway side, so you're not bothered by the traffic on Highway 99. ✉ *760 Hwy. 99 W* ☏ *503/538–8880* ⊕ *www.tinasdundee.com* ⊘ *No lunch Sat.–Mon.* ▭ *AE, D, MC, V.*

CHAMPOEG STATE PARK

9 mi from Newberg, south on Hwy. 219 and east on Champoeg Rd.

Pronounced "sham-*poo*-ee," this 615-acre state park on the south bank of the Willamette River is on the site of a Hudson's Bay Company trading post, granary, and warehouse that was built in 1813. This was the seat of the first provisional government in the Northwest. The settlement was abandoned after a catastrophic flood in 1861, then rebuilt and abandoned again after the flood of 1890. The park's wide-open spaces, groves of oak and fir, modern visitor center, museum, and historic buildings yield vivid insight into pioneer life. Tepees and wagons are displayed here, and there are 10 mi of hiking and cycle trails. ☎ *503/678–1251 Ext. 225, 800/551–6949 ⊕ www.oregonstateparks.org/ park_113.php* ⛺ *12 full hookup $20, 67 electrical $20; 6 yurts $27; 6 cabins $32; 3 group tent sites $61; group RV area $81; 6 walk-in tent sites $16; hiker/biker camp $4. Day use $3.* Robert Newell was among the inaugural American settlers in the Willamette Valley and helped establish the town of Champoeg; a replica of his 1844 home, what is now the **Newell House Museum** (✉ *8089 Champoeg Rd. NE, St. Paul* ☎ *503/678–5537*), was rebuilt inside the park grounds in 1959 and paid for by the Oregon State Society Daughters of the American Revolution. Admission is $4. It's open March through October, Friday–Sunday 1–5. The first floor is furnished with 1860s antiques. Pioneer quilts and a collection of gowns worn by the wives of Oregon governors at inaugurations are displayed on the second floor. There's also a pioneer jail and schoolhouse. Also on park grounds is the historic **Pioneer Mother's Memorial Log Cabin** (✉ *8035 Champoeg Rd. NE, St. Paul* ☎ *503/633–2237*), with pioneer artifacts from the Oregon Trail era. Admission is $4, and it's open March through October, Friday–Sunday 1–5. ✉ *8239 Champoeg Rd. NE, St. Paul* ☎ *800/551–6949* ⛁ *$3 per vehicle.*

OLD AURORA COLONY. A fascinating slice of Oregon's pioneer past, the colony was the only major 19th-century communal society in the Pacific Northwest. Created by Germans in 1856, this frontier society espoused a "Love thy neighbor" philosophy, shared labor and property, and was known for its hospitality. Aurora retains many white frame houses dating from the 1860s and 1870s. Several structures have been incorporated into the **Old Aurora Colony Museum**, which provides an overview of the colony's way of life. The colony is about 14 mi from Champoeg State Park; take Champoeg Rd. east to Arndt Rd.; pass under I–5 and turn south onto Airport Rd., then east onto Ehlen Rd. ✉ *2nd and Liberty Sts.* ☎ *503/678–5754 for museum* ⊕ *www.auroracolonymuseum.com* ⛁ *Museum $6* ⊙ *Feb.–Dec., Tues.–Sat. 11–4, Sun. noon–4.*

MCMINNVILLE

14 mi south of Newberg on Hwy. 99 W.

The Yamhill County seat, McMinnville, lies at the center of Oregon's burgeoning wine industry. There's a larger concentration of wineries in Yamhill County than in any other area of the state, and the vineyards in the McMinnville area, including some in the town of Dayton to the east, also produce the most award-winning wines. Among the varieties are chardonnay, pinot noir, and pinot gris. Most of the wineries in the area offer tours and tastings. McMinnville's downtown area, with a pleasantly disproportionate number of bookstores and art galleries for its size, is well worth exploring; most of the historic district buildings, erected 1890–1915, are remarkably well-maintained.

★ **Fodor'sChoice** The claim to fame of the **Evergreen Aviation Museum** is the Hughes (H-4) HK-1 Flying Boat, better known as the *Spruce Goose*. On permanent display here, the famous plane was moved to Portland in 1992 from Long Beach, California, and eventually shipped to McMinnville in pieces. Eccentric millionaire Howard Hughes flew it only once—on November 2, 1947. If you can take your eyes off the Spruce Goose there are also more than 45 historic planes and replicas here from the early years of flight and World War II, as well as the postwar and modern eras. Among the aircraft are a Spitfire, a C-47 "Gooney Bird," a Messerschmitt Bf 109, and the sleek SR-71 Blackbird, which set both speed and high-altitude records as "the world's fastest spy plane." Among the replicas is a Wright 1903—the craft the Wright brothers used for the first sustained powered flight. If you're curious to know which of these planes are still flyable, look for the telltale oil pan resting on the floor underneath the aircraft. There's a museum store and café, as well as and there are ongoing educational programs and special events. ✉ *500 N.E. Michael King Smith Way* ☎ *503/434–4180* ⊕ *www.spruce-goose.org* ⚏ *$13* ⊙ *Daily 9–5, closed holidays.*

A perennial football powerhouse in NCAA Division III, **Linfield College** is an outpost of brick and ivy amid McMinnville's farmers'-market bustle. The college, founded in 1849 and the second oldest in Oregon, hosts the **International Pinot Noir Celebration** (☎ *503/883–2200*) at the end of July and beginning of August (⊕ *www.ipnc.org*). ✉ *900 S.E. Baker St.* ⊕ *www.linfield.edu.*

NEED A BREAK? Try Tillamook ice cream on a waffle cone at Ser-endipity Ice Cream (✉ *502 N.E. 3rd St.* ☎ *503/474–9189*), an old-fashioned ice-cream parlor in the former Cook's Hotel; the building was constructed in 1886.

WINERIES

Its original tasting area was the back of a 1952 Ford pickup. Its gamay noir label notes that the wine gives "more enjoy-ment to hamburgers [and] fried chicken." And the winery's current architecture still includes a trailer affectionately referred to as the "mobile chateau," already on the property when winemaker Myron Redford purchased the winery in 1974. These modest and whimsical touches underscore what seems to be Redford's philosophy for **Amity Vineyards** (✉ *18150 Amity Vineyards Rd. SE, Amity* ☎ *503/835–2362* ⊕ *www.amityvineyards.com*): take your winemaking a lot more seriously than you take yourself. Taste the pinot blanc for Redford's take on the grape, and also linger in the tast-ing room to sample the pinot noir and the gewürztraminer, among other varieties. Chocolates made with Amity's pinot noir and other products are available for sale. Hours are daily, October–May noon–5 and June–September 11–5.

In Dundee's Red Hills, **Domaine Serene** (✉ *6555 N.E. Hilltop La., Dayton* ☎ *503/864–4600* ⊕ *www.domaineserene.com*) is a world-class five-level winery—it's well-regarded for its pinot noir, as well as chardonnay and Syrah. It's open Wednesday–Monday 11–4.

WHERE TO EAT AND STAY

$$$ ✕ **Joel Palmer House.** *Contemporary.* The 1857 house of Oregon pioneer Joel Palmer, now a restaurant, is on the National Register of Historic Places. There are three small dining rooms, each seating about 15 people. The chef spe-cializes in wild-mushroom dishes; a popular starter is a three-mushroom tart. Entrées include rib eye au poivre, rack of lamb, breast of duckling, and coq au vin; desserts include apricot-walnut bread pudding and crème brûlée. Or, if you really, really like mushrooms, have your entire table order Jack's Mushroom Madness Menu, a five-course extravaganza for $75 per person. ✉ *600 Ferry St., Dayton* ☎ *503/864–2995* ⊕ *www.joelpalmerhouse.com* ▭ *AE, D, DC, MC, V* ⊘ *Closed Sun. and Mon. No lunch.*

$$$ ✕ **Nick's Italian Cafe.** *Italian.* Modestly furnished but with a voluminous wine cellar, Nick's is a favorite of area wine makers. The food is spirited and simple, reflecting the owner's northern Italian heritage. A five-course prix-fixe

menu that changes nightly is $45, but à la carte options are also available. ⊠ *521 N.E. 3rd St.* ☎ *503/434–4471* ⊕ *www.nicksitaliancafe.com* ⚑ *Reservations essential* ⊟ *AE, MC, V* ⊙ *Closed Sun. and Mon. No lunch.*

$–$$ ▣ **Hotel Oregon.** Built in 1905, this historic facility—the former Elberton Hotel—was rescued from decay by the McMenamins chain, renovated in 1998, and reopened the following year. It's four stories of brick; rooms have tall ceilings and high windows. The hotel is outfitted in late Victorian furnishings, but its defining design element is its art. The hotel is whimsically decorated by a half-dozen staff artists: around every corner, even in the elevator, you'll find art—sometimes serene, often times bizarre and haunting—as well as photos and sayings scribbled on the walls. The Oregon has a first-floor pub serving three meals a day, a rooftop bar with an impressive view of Yamhill County, and a cellar wine bar, resembling a dark speakeasy, that serves only area vintages. **Pros:** great central location and close to town's shops. **Cons:** some rooms have shared bathrooms. ⊠ *310 N.E. Evans St.* ☎ *503/472–8427 or 888/472–8427* ⊕ *www.mcmenamins.com* ⇀ *42 rooms* ⚑ *In room: Wi-Fi. In-hotel: bars* ⊟ *AE, D, DC, MC, V.*

★ **Fodor's**Choice ▣ **The Joseph Mattey House Bed & Breakfast.** Built
$$–$$$ in 1982 by English immigrant Joseph Mattey, a local butcher, this Queen Anne Victorian mansion—on the National Register of Historic Places—has several cheerful areas that define it. Downstairs is a cozy living room jammed with antiques, dual dining areas—a parlor with white wicker and a dining room with elegant furniture—and a porch with a swing. The four upstairs rooms are named after locally grown grape varieties and are decorated in keeping with the character of those wines: the chardonnay room, for instance, has tall windows and crisp white furnishings, and pinot noir has dark-wood pieces and reddish wine accents. A small balcony off the upstairs landing is perfect for sipping a glass of wine on a cool Yamhill Valley evening. Proprietors Jack and Denise will make sure you're comfortable, getting a glass of wine in your hand as they fill you in on local history, the vineyards, and the antiquing scene. If you're imprudent enough to duck out before the fine full breakfast, Denise or Jack will have pastry and hot coffee on hand before you set off. **Pros:** friendly, personable service; house is bound by 10 acres that include an orchard and its own vineyard. **Cons:** no pets allowed. ⊠ *10221 N.E. Mattey La., off Hwy. 99 W, ¼ mi south of Lafayette* ☎ *503/434–5058* ⊕ *www.matteyhouse.com* ⇀ *4*

rooms ♿ *In-room: no phone, no TV, Wi-Fi. In-hotel: no kids under 10* ⊟ *AE, MC, V* ⊚ *BP.*

THE COLUMBIA GORGE AND MT. HOOD AREA

Updated by Janna Mock-Lopez

Volcanoes, lava flows, Ice Age floodwaters, and glaciers were Nature's tools of choice to carve the breathtaking 80-mi landscape that's now the Columbia River Gorge. Proof of human civilization here reaches back 31,000 years, and excavations near the Dalles have uncovered evidence that salmon fishing is a 10,000-year-old tradition in these parts.

In 1805 Lewis and Clark discovered the Columbia River to be the only waterway that led to the Pacific. Their first expedition was a treacherous route through wild, plunging rapids, but their successful navigation set a new exodus in motion. By the 1850s, almost 12,000 new settlers arrived in the Oregon Territory.

Sightseers, hikers, and skiers have long found contentment in this robust region, officially labeled a National Scenic Area in 1986. Highlights of the Columbia River Gorge include Multnomah Falls, Bonneville Dam, and the rich orchard land of Hood River—a windsurfing hub. To the south of Hood River are all the alpine attractions of the 11,245-foot-high Mt. Hood. From Portland, the Columbia Gorge–Mt. Hood Scenic Loop is the easiest way to see the gorge and the mountain. Take I–84 east to Troutdale and follow U.S. 26 to Bennett Pass (near Timberline), where Highway 35 heads north to Hood River; then follow I–84 back to Portland. Or make the loop in reverse.

Winter weather in the Columbia Gorge and the Mt. Hood area is much more severe than in Portland and western Oregon. At times I–84 may be closed because of snow and ice. If you're planning a winter visit, be sure to carry plenty of warm clothes. Chains are a requirement for traveling over mountain passes. In spring the Gorge's 77 waterfalls, including 11 that cascade over 100 feet, are especially energetic—and photogenic. In early fall, look for maple, tamarack, and aspen trees fairly bursting with brilliant red and gold color. But no matter the season, the basalt cliffs, the acres of lush forest, and that glorious expanse of water make the Gorge worth visiting time and again.

8

Points of interest can be found on the Columbia Gorge map.

GETTING HERE AND AROUND

I–84 is the main east–west route into the Columbia River Gorge. U.S. 26, heading east from Portland and northwest from Prineville, is the main route into the Mt. Hood area. Portions of I–84 and U.S. 26 that pass through the mountains pose winter-travel difficulties, though the state plows these roadways regularly. The gorge is closed frequently during harsh winters due to ice and mud slides. Extreme winds can also make driving hazardous and potentially result in highway closures.

The Historic Columbia River Highway (U.S. 30) from Troutdale, to just east of Oneonta Gorge, passes Crown Point State Park and Multnomah Falls. I–84/U.S. 30 continues on to the Dalles. Highway 35 heads south from the Dalles to the Mt. Hood area, intersecting with U.S. 26 at Government Camp.

VISITOR INFORMATION

Contacts Columbia River Gorge Visitors Association (⊠ *404 W. 2nd St., The Dalles* ☎ *800/984–6743* ⊕ *www.crgva.org*). **Hood River County Chamber of Commerce** (⊠ *405 Portway Ave.* ☎ *541/386–2000 or 800/366–3530* ⊕ *www.hoodriver.org*). **Mt. Hood Chamber of Commerce** (⊠ *24403 E. Welches Rd., Welches* ☎ *503/622–3017* ⊕ *www.mthood.org*). **Mt. Hood National Forest Ranger Stations** (⊠ *6780 Hwy. 35, Mt. Hood* ☎ *541/352–6002* ⊠ *Superintendent, 16400 Champion Way, off U.S. 26, Sandy* ☎ *503/668–1700*). **Oregon Tourism Commission** (⊠ *775 Summer St. NE, Salem* ☎ *800/547–7842* ⊕ *www.traveloregon.com*).

TROUTDALE

13 mi east of Portland on I–84.

Troutdale's nomenclature comes courtesy of captain of industry and sea, John Harlow, who bought a substantial portion of the town's original land claim in 1872 to build his country home. Harlow raised trout in the ponds surrounding his estate and called his place "Troutdale." But Captain John was also a farmer who needed to transport his produce, so he convinced the railroad to build a depot near his home. Or, rather, at the exact site of his home. Therefore, when the train pulled up to its new destination, it would always be known as Troutdale. Called the gateway to the Columbia River Gorge, Troutdale is still known for its great fishing spots, as well as antique stores and the Columbia Gorge Premium Outlets.

Continuing eastward, as the Gorge widens, is the 22-mi-long **Historic Columbia River Highway,** U.S. 30 (also known as the Columbia River Scenic Highway and the Scenic Gorge Highway). The oldest scenic highway in the U.S., it's a construction marvel that integrates asphalt path with cliff, ocean, and forest landscapes. Paralleling the highway on the south side of I–84, the road climbs to forested riverside bluffs high above the Interstate. Completed in 1922, the serpentine highway was the first paved road in the Gorge built expressly for automotive sightseers. (Keep an eye out for five waterfalls along the way.)

A few miles east of Troutdale on U.S. 30 is **Crown Point State Scenic Corridor,** a 730-foot-high bluff with an unparalleled 30-mi view down the Columbia River Gorge. **Vista House,** the two-tier octagonal structure on the side of the cliff, opened its doors to visitors in 1916; the rotunda has displays about the Gorge and the highway. Vista House's architect, Edgar Lazarus, was the brother of Emma Lazarus, the author of the poem quoted on the base of the Statue of Liberty. ⊠ *U.S. 30* ☎ *503/695–2261 or 800/551–6949* ⊕ *www.oregonstateparks.org/park_150.php* ⊒ *Free* ⊙ *Daily* ⟁ *ADA accessible.*

About 4 mi east of the Troutdale bridge, **Dabney State Park** has boating, hiking, and fishing. There's also a popular summer swimming hole and an 18-hole disc golf course. A boat ramp is open year-round. ⊠ *U.S. 30, 4 mi east of Troutdale* ☎ *800/551–6949* ⊕ *www.oregonstateparks.org/park_151. php* ⊒ *Day-use $3 per vehicle* ⊙ *Daily dawn–dusk.*

The most famous beach lining the Columbia River, **Rooster Rock State Park** is below Crown Point; access is from the Interstate only. Three miles of sandy beaches, panoramic cascades, and a large swimming area makes this a popular spot. True naturists appreciate that one of Oregon's two designated nude beaches is at the east end of Rooster Rock, and that it's not visible to conventional sunbathers. ⊠ *I–84, 7 mi east of Troutdale* ☎ *503/695–2261* ⊕ *www.oregonstateparks.org/park_175.php* ⊒ *Day-use $3 per vehicle* ⊙ *Daily 7–dusk.*

8

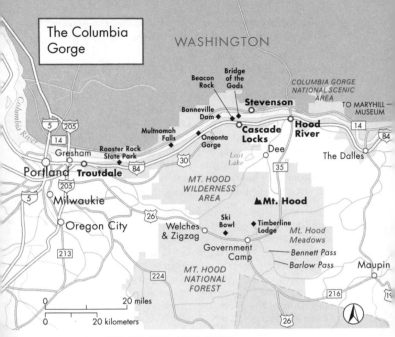

The Columbia Gorge

WASHINGTON

Beacon Rock
Bridge of the Gods
COLUMBIA GORGE NATIONAL SCENIC AREA
Bonneville Dam
Stevenson
TO MARYHILL MUSEUM
Multnomah Falls
Cascade Locks
Hood River
Oneonta Gorge
Lost Lake
Dee
The Dalles
Rooster Rock State Park
Gresham
Portland
Troutdale
Milwaukie
MT. HOOD WILDERNESS AREA
Oregon City
▲Mt. Hood
Welches & Zigzag
Ski Bowl
◆Timberline Lodge
Mt. Hood Meadows
Government Camp
Bennett Pass
Barlow Pass
Maupin
MT. HOOD NATIONAL FOREST

Columbia River

0   20 miles
0   20 kilometers

WHERE TO EAT AND STAY

$$$ ✕**Black Rabbit Restaurant & Bar.** *Contemporary.* Chef John Zenger's grilled rib-eye steak, old-fashioned roasted chicken, and sesame-crusted salmon are popular entrées at this hotel restaurant. Vivid murals depicting the Gorge's history enrich your view as you linger over dinner in a high-backed wooden booth. Enjoy an Edgefield wine or any one of five McMenamins brews (made on-site, approximately 50 yards away). Patio seating is available, with plenty of heaters to handle the unpredictable Oregon weather. Top off your meal with a homemade dessert and a house-roasted cup of coffee. ⊠*McMenamins Edgefield, 2126 S.W. Halsey St.* ☎*503/492–3086* ⊕*www.mcmenamins.com* ▬*AE, D, DC, MC, V.*

★ **Fodor'sChoice** ▥**McMenamins Edgefield.** As you explore the
$–$$ grounds of this Georgian Revival house, you'll feel like you've entered a European village filled with activity and beauty. Wander through 38 acres of gardens, orchards, and vineyards with a drink in your hand. Enjoy complimentary movies in the Edgefield theater, live music in the Winery, and golf at the 17-hole course. There are three restaurants and six bars to choose from, as well as a pool hall, distillery,

and a spa. Be sure to make reservations ahead of time for the Black Rabbit restaurant and the spa. **Pros:** plenty of choices for eating and drinking; large variety of rooms. **Cons:** crowds can get large at this busy place. ✉ *2126 S.W. Halsey St.* ☎ *503/669–8610 or 800/669–8610* ⊕ *www. mcmenamins.com* ⤳ *114 rooms, 24 beds in men's/women's hostels* ♿ *In-room: a/c (some), no phone, no TV. In-hotel: 3 restaurants, bars, golf course, spa, Wi-Fi hotspot, parking (free)* ▭ *AE, D, DC, MC, V.*

EN ROUTE. From Crown Point, the Columbia River Highway winds through quiet forest glades, heading downhill over graceful stone bridges built by Italian immigrant masons. More than a dozen waterfalls pour over fern- and lichen-covered cliffs in a 10-mi stretch. Latourell, Bridal Veil, Wahkeena, and Horsetail falls are the most impressive. All have parking areas and hiking trails.

MULTNOMAH FALLS

20 mi east of Troutdale on I–84 or Historic Columbia River Hwy. (U.S. 30).

Multnomah Falls, a 620-foot-high double-decker torrent, the second highest year-round waterfall in the nation, is by far the most spectacular of those east of Troutdale. The scenic highway leads down to a parking lot; from there, a paved path winds to a bridge over the lower falls. A much steeper trail climbs to a viewing point overlooking the upper falls.

WHERE TO EAT

$$ ✕ **Multnomah Falls Lodge.** *Contemporary.* Vaulted ceilings, stone fireplaces, and exquisite views of Multnomah Falls are complemented by wonderful service and an extensive menu at this restaurant, which is listed on the National Register of Historic places. Consider the halibut fish-and-chips, the lemon and herb roasted wild salmon, or ancho chile– and espresso-cured flat iron steak. Breakfast favorites include blueberry, buttermilk, or huckleberry pancakes. A champagne Sunday brunch, a particular pleaser for out-of-towners, is held 8–2. For a treat during warmer months, sit on the patio and get close to the Falls without feeling a drop. ✉ *Exit 31 off I–84, 50000 Historic Columbia River Hwy., Bridal Veil* ☎ *503/695–2376* ⊕ *www.multnomah-fallslodge.com* ▭ *AE, D, MC, V.*

ONEONTA GORGE

2 mi east of Multnomah Falls on Historic Columbia River Hwy.

Following the old highway east from Multnomah Falls, you come to a narrow, mossy cleft with walls hundreds of feet high. Oneonta Gorge is most enjoyable in summer, when you can walk up the streambed through the cool green canyon, where hundreds of plant species—some found nowhere else—flourish under the perennially moist conditions. At other times of the year, take the trail along the west side of the canyon. The clearly marked trailhead is 100 yards west of the gorge, on the south side of the road. The trail ends at Oneonta Falls, about ½ mi up the stream. Bring boots or submersible sneakers—plus a strong pair of ankles—because the rocks are slippery. East of Oneonta Gorge, the scenic highway returns to I–84.

CASCADE LOCKS

7 mi east of Oneonta Gorge on Historic Columbia River Hwy. and I–84, 30 mi east of Troutdale on I–84.

In pioneer days, boats needing to pass the bedeviling rapids near here had to be portaged (carried overland) around them. The town's namesake locks were completed in 1896, allowing waterborne passage for the first time. Native Americans still use the locks for their traditional dip-net fishing.

The first federal dam to span the Columbia, **Bonneville Dam** was dedicated by President Franklin D. Roosevelt in 1937. Its generators (visible from a balcony during self-guided powerhouse tours) have a capacity of nearly a million kilowatts, enough to supply power to more than 200,000 single-family homes. There's a modern visitor center on Bradford Island, complete with underwater windows for viewing migrating salmon and steelhead as they struggle up fish ladders. The best viewing times are between April and October. In recent years the dwindling runs of wild Columbia salmon have made the dam a subject of much environmental controversy. ✉ *Bonneville Lock and Dam, U.S. Army Corps of Engineers, from I–84 take Exit 40, head northeast, and follow signs 1 mi to visitor center, Cascade Locks* 🌐 *www.nwp.usace.army.mil/op/b/home.asp* ☎ *541/374–8820* 🎟 *Free* ⏲ *Visitor center daily 9–5.*

Below Bonneville Dam, the ponds at the **Bonneville Fish Hatchery** teem with fingerling salmon, fat rainbow trout, and 6-foot-long sturgeon. The hatchery raises chinook and coho salmon; from mid-October to late November, you can watch as staff members spawn the fish, beginning a new hatching cycle—you can also feed the trout with food pellets from a coin-operated machine. ✉ *From I–84 take Exit 40 and follow signs northeast 1 mi to Hatchery, 70543 N.E. Herman Loop* ☎ *541/374–8393* ✇ *Free* ☉ *Hatchery grounds daily dawn–dusk, spawning room daily 7:30–4:30.*

☾ Cascade Locks is the home port of the 600-passenger stern-wheeler **Columbia Gorge, built in 1983.** Between mid-June and early October the ship churns upriver, then back again, on two-hour excursions through some of the Columbia River Gorge's most impressive scenery. The ship's captain will talk about the gorge's fascinating 40-million-year geology and about pioneering spirits and legends, such as Lewis and Clark, who once triumphed over this very same river. Group bookings and private rentals available. Call sales department at 800/224–3901 for rates. ✉ *Cruises leave from Marine Park in Cascade Locks. Marine Park, 355 Wanapa St.* ☎ *541/374–8427 or 800/224–3901* ⊕ *www.sternwheeler.com* ⚓ *Reservations essential* 🏷 *Prices vary, depending on choice of excursion: sightseeing, brunch, dinner, or Landmarks of the Gorge cruises, $28–$80* ▭ *AE, MC, V* ☉ *Cruises mid-June–early Oct., call for cruise schedule.*

WHERE TO EAT AND STAY

8

$ ✕ **Pacific Crest Pub.** *American.* In this woodsy tavern with cedar-shake walls, old photos, and a stone fireplace, you get hearty servings of dishes that include chowder (made of salmon smoked on-site) and oven-roasted chicken accompanied by house-specialty horseradish. If you like feta cheese with your pizzas, try the house favorite, the Greek "pizza of the gods." During warmer months, sit outside in the adjacent courtyard and take in mountain and river views while sipping one of 13 featured micro-brews, including Full Sail and Walking Man. ✉ *500 Wanapa St.* ☎ *541/374–9310* ▭ *D, MC, V* ☉ *Closed Mon.*

$–$$ 🛏 **Bridge of the Gods Motel and RV Park.** One block from the historic Bridge of the Gods and within walking distance of Cascade Locks activities, this locally owned business provides spacious rooms with modest furnishings, including microwaves. There are also new cabins on the property which offer kitchenettes, flat screen TVs, and jetted tubs. **Pros:** some rooms have kitchenettes, patios, and balconies. **Cons:** outdated decor. ✉ *630 Wanapa St., Box 278*

☎ 541/374–8628 🛏 15 rooms plus 3 cabins ♿ In-room: kitchen (some). In-hotel: laundry facilities, some pets allowed ▭ AE, D, MC, V.

STEVENSON, WASHINGTON

Across the river from Cascade Locks via the Bridge of the Gods and 4 mi east on Hwy. 14.

For a magnificent vista 135 feet above the Columbia, as well as a speedy route between Oregon and Washington, $1 will pay your way over the grandly named **Bridge of the Gods** (⊕ *www.portofcascadelocks.org/bridge.htm*). Slightly west of the bridge, hikers gain access to the Oregon-Washington link of the Mexico-to-Canada **Pacific Crest Trail.** Travel east on Highway 14 for about 10 minutes to reach the small town of Stevenson, with several antiques shops and good places to grab a bite.

For several hundred years, 848-foot **Beacon Rock** was a landmark for river travelers, including Native Americans, who recognized this point as the last rapid of the Columbia River. Lewis and Clark are thought to have been the first white men to see the volcanic remnant. Picnic atop old lava flows after hiking a 1-mi trail, steep but safe, which leads to tremendous views of the Columbia Gorge and river. A round-trip hike takes 45–60 minutes. The site is a few miles west of the Bridge of the Gods.

NEED A BREAK? Hippie Haight-Ashbury meets Native American art at the funky and fun **Bahma Coffee Bar,** the place in Stevenson for Wi-Fi (with purchase) and, of course, coffee. Or choose from grilled panini sandwiches, soups, fresh carrot juice, wine, sake, tea, and tasty homemade pastries. Scrabble tournaments, games aplenty, reading material, and live music on some weekends. All this, and a super staff. ✉ 256 S.W. 2nd St., Hwy. 14 ☎ 509/427–8700 ⊕ www.bahmacoffeebar.com ▭ MC, V ⊙ Daily 8:30–5.

� A petroglyph whose eyes seem to look straight at you, "She Who Watches" or "Tsagaglalal" is the logo for the **Columbia Gorge Interpretive Center.** Sitting among the dramatic basaltic cliffs on the north bank of the Columbia River Gorge, the museum explores the life of the Gorge: its history, culture, architecture, legends, and much more. Kids may enjoy the reenactment of the Gorge in the Creation Theatre. Or a 37-foot-high fishwheel from the 19th century. Historians will appreciate studying the water route of the Lewis &

Clark Expedition. There's also an eye-opening exhibit that examines current environmental impacts on the area. ⊠ *990 S.W. Rock Creek Dr., Stevenson WA ✛ 1 mi east of Bridge of the Gods on Hwy. 14* ☎ *509/427–8211 or 800/991–2338* ⊕ *www.columbiagorge.org* ⚏ *$7* ⊙ *Daily 10–5* ☞ *Handicapped accessible.*

WHERE TO EAT AND STAY

$$ ✕ **The Cascade Room at Skamania Lodge.** *Contemporary.* Gaze at the perfect fusion of sky, river, and cliffscapes through the Cascade Room's expansive windows during an exquisite dining experience. Alder-plank potlatch salmon and oat-crusted trout stuffed with Northwest potatoes and herbs are signature dishes; also try the garlic sizzling shrimp and sautéed forest mushrooms. Melt-in-your-mouth chocolate soufflé and fresh mixed-berry cobbler are grand finales. Breakfast specialties include hazelnut pancakes and fresh-berry crepes. The Gorge Harvest Buffet brunch is offered on Sunday, and the seafood, salads, sushi, and pasta draw patrons from miles around. ⊠ *Skamania Lodge Way north of Hwy. 14, 2 mi east of the Bridge of the Gods* ☎ *509/427–2508* ⊟ *AE, D, DC, MC, V.*

$$$ ✕ **Pacific Crest Dining Room.** *Contemporary.* After a rejuvenating spa treatment or hike, the fresh healthy cuisine at this resort's restaurant is a special treat. You can dine in the low light of the muted main room (metal pine tree light fixtures are custom made), or in the adjoining lounge, its 12-foot-high glass wall overlooking the manicured courtyard and the forest beyond. The pastry chef works through the night, ensuring fresh-baked breads and pastries by sunrise. Healthy never tasted so good with crisp salads, Pacific Northwest fish (great ahi tuna), Cascade-area beef, and tasty vegetarian fare. Late afternoons, the lounge serves goodies such as hazelnut-crusted Brie and Walking Man beer–battered halibut and chips. ⊠ *1252 E. Cascade Dr., North Bonneville, WA* ☎ *509/427–9711* ⊕ *www.bonnevilleresort.com* ⊟ *AE, D, MC, V.*

GRAPE EXPECTATIONS? Representing three different wine regions, there's a 40-sq-mi area within the Gorge that varies in soil and climate, supporting more than 22 wineries. Though vintners state that in Europe, a similar variety of wines would encompass 1,200 square mi, they swear that the Gorge can do it all, including rieslings to nebbiolos, pinot noirs, and pinot gris.

$$$-$$$$ ⊡ **Bonneville Hot Springs Resort and Spa.** Enter a wonderland of wood, iron, rock, and water, water everywhere. Owner Pete Cam and his five sons built the resort to share their love of these historic mineral springs with the public, especially those seeking physical renewal. The three-story lobby, with its suspended black-iron trestle, Paul Bunyan–size river-rock fireplace, and floor-to-ceiling arched windows, is magnificent to behold. The unique redwood-paneled, 25-meter indoor lap pool is adjacent to an immaculate European spa, where more than 40 candlelighted treatments (mineral baths, body wraps, massages) are available. Rooms are spacious, with upscale furnishings. **Pros:** glorious grounds; amazing architectural detail; attentive and knowledgeable spa staff. **Cons:** must reserve spa appointments separately from room reservations; dull, boxy exterior. ⊠ *1252 E. Cascade Dr., North Bonneville, WA ✛ 3 mi west of Bridge of the Gods on Hwy. 14, right on Hot Springs Way, right on E. Cascade Dr. follow for ½ mi* ☎ *509/427–7767 or 866/459–1678* ⊕ *www. bonnevilleresort.com* ⤳ *78 rooms* ♿ *In-room: refrigerator, Wi-Fi. In-hotel: restaurant, bar, pool, spa, concierge, Wi-Fi hotspot* ⊟ *AE, D, MC, V.*

$$$$ ⊡ **Skamania Lodge.** "Skamania," the Chinook word for "swift water," overlooks exactly that: its 175 acres sit to the north of the Columbia River Gorge. So big you need a map to get around, the Lodge impresses with its multitude of windows that take in the surrounding forests and Gorge, Montana slate tiles, Native American artwork, and an immense word-burning fireplace. Outstanding recreational facilities include an 18-hole, par-70 golf course, three hiking trails, large indoor pool and even a sand volleyball court. The accommodating staff will pack you a lunch if you're going out to explore for the day. **Pros:** works for active guests as well as the kids; U.S. Forest Service has a kiosk in the lobby; good for large events. **Cons:** expensive for a large family; can get crowded, sometimes there's a wait for a table in the dining room. ⊠ *Skamania Lodge Way north of Hwy. 14, 1½ mi east of Bridge of the Gods. 1131 S.W. Skamania Lodge Way* ☎ *509/427–7700 or 800/221– 7117* ⊕ *www.skamania.com* ⤳ *254 rooms* ♿ *In-room: Wi-Fi, Internet. In-hotel: 3 restaurants, bars, golf course, tennis courts, pool, gym, spa, bicycles, concierge, executive floor, Wi-Fi hotspot, parking (no fee), some pets allowed* ⊟ *AE, D, DC, MC, V.*

HOOD RIVER

17 mi east of Cascade Locks on I–84.

For years the incessant easterly winds blowing through the town of Hood River were just a nuisance. Then somebody bolted a sail to a surfboard, waded into the fat part of the Gorge, and a new recreational craze was born. A fortuitous combination of factors—mainly the reliable gale-force winds blowing against the current—has made Hood River the self-proclaimed boardsailing capital of the world. Especially in summer, this once-sleepy town swarms with colorful "boardheads" who come from as far as Europe and Australia. Not just content to surf the water, others are boosting their hang time with another craze, the kiteboard. In winter many of these same athletes stay in town, but turn south to ski on mountain slopes that are only a short drive away. Other outdoor enthusiasts find the area's fishing, boating, swimming, and hiking venues the best in the region.

Hood River's rich pioneer past is reflected in its downtown historic district. The City of Hood River publishes a free self-guided walking tour (available through the City of Hood River government office or the Hood River Chamber of Commerce ⊕ *www.hoodriver.org*), which will take you on a tour of more than 40 civic and commercial buildings dating from 1893 to the 1930s, some of which are listed in the National Register of Historic Places.

Either by car or bicycle, tour Hood River valley's **Fruit Loop,** whose vast orchards surround the Hood River. You'll see apples, pears, cherries, and peaches that grow through volcanic soil, pure glacier water, and good weather. Along the 35 mi of farms are a host of delicious baked goods, wines, flowers, and nuts. Festive farm activities from April to November also give a taste of the agricultural life. While on the loop, consider stopping at the town of **Parkdale** to lunch, shop, and snap a photo of Mt. Hood's north face. There are well-marked signs on the entire 35-mi loop. ✉ *Rte. begins on Hwy. 35* ⊕ *www.hoodriverfruitloop.com.*

On a 2-acre National Historic Site, the **Hutson Museum** exhibits Native American dolls, taxidermy, and a rare rock collection, which includes thousands of rough specimens, polished slabs, spheres, and eggs. More than 2,500 arrow and spear points, stone bowls, mortars, grinding tools, and specialized tools are prized for their regional geological and historical value. The Mt. Hood excursion train, mentioned below, ends at the museum. ✉ *4967 Baseline Dr., Parkdale* 🕿 *541/352–6808* ⛵*Free, donations accepted* ☉ *Apr.–Oct., Wed.–Fri. 11–2; Apr.–June, weekends 11–4; July and Aug., Tues.–Fri. 11–2; July–Oct., weekends 11–5:30.*

On the river downtown, **Columbia Gorge Sailpark** has a boat basin, swimming beach, jogging trails, picnic tables, and restrooms. ✉ *Port Marina, Exit 64 off I–84, 97031* 🕿 *541/386–1645.*

An efficient and relaxing way to survey Mt. Hood and the Hood River, the **Mt. Hood Scenic Railroad and Dinner Train** was established in 1906 as a passenger and freight line. Chug alongside the Hood River through vast fruit orchards before climbing up steep forested canyons, glimpsing Mt. Hood along the way. There are four trip options: a four-hour excursion (serves light concessions with two daily departures, morning and afternoon), dinner, brunch, and a themed murder-mystery dinner. Choose from brunch fare such as raspberry crepes, omelets, and eggs Benedict. Favorite dinner selections include huckleberry-sauced salmon, sun-dried tomato ravioli, and chicken picatta. The service is as impressive as the scenery. ✉ *110 Railroad Ave.* 🕿 *541/386–3556 or 800/872–4661* ⊕ *www.mthoodrr.com* ⊟ *AE, D, MC, V* ⛵ *$25–$80* ☉ *Apr.–Dec., check Web site for schedule.*

NEED A BREAK? A glass-walled microbrewery with a windswept deck overlooking the Columbia, the **Full Sail Tasting Room and Pub** (✉ *506 Columbia St.* 🕿 *541/386–2247*) has won major awards at the Great American Beer Festival. Savory snack foods complement fresh ales. The Taster Tray, seven 4-ounce samples for $5, is a great way to explore the many varieties of Full Sail brews. On-site brewery tours available.

Half art museum, half theater, the **Columbia Center for the Arts** promotes professional and novice artists alike, both visual and theatrical. The successful blend of the 28-year-old Columbia Arts Stage Troupe (CAST) and the Columbia Art Gallery happened by coincidence, when both realized they were looking for a home in 2003. Combining their efforts and fundraising, they renovated a 10,000-sq-ft American Legion Hall, and opened in 2005, calling themselves the Columbia Center for the Arts. Call or check the Web site for updates on exhibits and theater. ✉ *215 Cascade*

Ave. ☎ *541/387–8877* ⊕ *www.columbiaarts.org* ☉ *Sept. 30–Memorial Day, Wed.–Sun. 11–5. Memorial Day–Sept. 30, daily 11–5.*

Awarded the Oregon Winery of the Year in 2007 by the Northwest Wine Press, **Cathedral Ridge Winery** has a 6-acre vineyard. Popular varietals include Riesling, pinot gris, and Syrah. The tasting room is open 11–5 daily. ✉ *4200 Post Canyon Dr.* ☎ *800/516–8710* ⊕ *www.cathedralridgewinery. com* ✆ *Free* ☉ *Daily 11–5.*

Sauvignon blanc, cabernet sauvignon, and merlot are among the varieties produced at the 12-acre, family-owned **Hood River Vineyards,** which overlook the Columbia River Gorge and the Hood River valley. Bottles are sold individually; best sellers are the pinot noir and chardonnay. ✉ *4693 Westwood Dr.* ☎ *541/386–3772* ⊕ *www.hoodrivervineyards.us* ✆ *Free* ☉ *Apr.–Oct., daily 11–5; Nov.–Mar., Wed.–Sun. 11–5.*

**OFF THE BEATEN PATH. One of the most photographed sights in the Pacific Northwest, the waters of Lost Lake reflect towering Mt. Hood and the thick forests that line its shore. Cabins are available for overnight stays, and because no motorboats are allowed on Lost Lake, the area is blissfully quiet. ✉ *Lost Lake Rd., take Hood River Hwy. south from Hood River to town of Dee and follow signs; also accessible from Lolo Pass* ☎ 541/386-6366 ✆ *Day use $5.*

WHERE TO EAT AND STAY

★ **Fodor's**Choice ✕ **Stonehedge Gardens.** *Contemporary.* It's not
$$$ just the cuisine that's exceptional—Stonehedge is of another time and place, surrounded by 7 acres of lush English gardens that frame its many stone terraces and trickling fountains. Each of the four dining rooms in the restored 1898 home has a distinct personality, from cozy to verdant to elegant. The curry shiitake mushroom soup is a favorite of the *Bite of the Gorge food festival.* Other highlights include the homemade pecan vinaigrette dressing and the fresh seafood and meat, served with light sauces and spices that heighten rather than smother the taste. Just when you think your meal is complete, along comes the flaming bread pudding. ✉ *3405 Cascade Ave.* ☎ *541/386–3940* ▭ *AE, MC, V* ☉ *No lunch.*

$$$ ⊡ **Columbia Gorge Hotel.** One selling point of this grande dame of Gorge hotels is the view of a 208-foot-high water-

fall. Rooms with plenty of wood, brass, and antiques over-look the formal gardens. Rates include a hearty breakfast (the Sunday brunch is available to nonguests for $19). While watching the sun set on the Columbia River, you can dine in the hotel's restaurant ($-$$$), also open to nonguests, where selections might include breast of pheasant with pear wine, hazelnuts, and cream, as well as grilled venison, breast of duck, Columbia River salmon, or sturgeon. **Pros:** great views; beautiful setting. **Cons:** limited room service. ⊠ *4000 Westcliff Dr.* ✤ *off I–84 Exit 62* ☎ *541/386–5566 or 800/345–1921* ⊕ *www.columbiagorge-hotel.com* ✍ *46 rooms* ⌂ *In room: refrigerator, Wi-Fi. In-hotel: restaurant, bar, laundry service, Wi-Fi hotspot, some pets allowed.* ⊟ *AE, D, DC, MC, V* ⊺◎ *BP.*

$$$ 🛏 **Lakecliff Bed & Breakfast.** On a cliff overlooking the Columbia Gorge, this beautiful 1908 summer house has long been a favorite spot for weddings. Designed by architect A.E. Doyle (who also created the Multnomah Falls Lodge), and surrounded by three acres of ferns, firs, and water, it's a stunner. Pluses here include a deck at the back of the house, fireplaces and river views in three of the rooms, and top-notch service, including hot coffee right outside your door in the morning. "Large, spoiling breakfasts," says the owner, referring to her poached pears, blueberry pancakes, and butterscotch pecan rolls. For summer, make reservations as far ahead as possible. **Pros:** glorious views; friendly and accommodating staff. **Cons:** no king-size beds; small number of rooms means you must book months in advance; no elevator. ⊠ *3820 Westcliff Dr., head east from I–84 Exit 62* ☎ *541/386–7000* ⊕ *www.lakecliffbnb.com* ✍ *4 rooms* ⌂ *In-room: no phone, no TV. In-hotel: no kids under 18* ⊟ *MC, V.*

THE DALLES

20 mi east of Hood River on I–84.

The Dalles lies on a crescent bend of the Columbia River where the river narrows and once spilled over a series of rapids, creating a flagstone effect. French voyagers christened it *dalle,* or "flagstone." The Dalles is the seat of Wasco County and the trading hub of north-central Oregon. It gained fame early in the region's history as the town where the Oregon Trail branched, with some pioneers departing to travel over Mt. Hood on Barlow Road and the others continuing down the Columbia River. This may account for the small-town, Old West feeling that still permeates the area. Several historical Oregon moments as they relate to the Dalles's past are magnificently illustrated on eight murals painted by renowned Northwest artists, located downtown within short walking distance of one another.

Outstanding exhibits at the 130-year-old **Original 1859 Wasco County Courthouse** illustrate the trials and tribulations of those who traveled the Oregon Trail. ⊠*410 W. 2nd Pl.* ☎*541/296–4798* ⊕*www.wascochs.org/wcch.htm* ☎*Free* ⊘*June–Aug., Wed.–Sat. 11–3.*

The 1856-vintage Fort Dalles Surgeon's Quarters is the site of the **Fort Dalles Museum,** the oldest history museum in Oregon. Originally a military base, the museum's first visitors came through the doors in 1905. On display in authentic hand-hewn log buildings are the personal effects of some of the region's settlers and a collection of early automobiles. The entrance fee gains you admission to the **Anderson House** museum across the street, which also has pioneer artifacts. ⊠*500 W. 15th St., at Garrison* ☎*541/296–4547* ⊕*www.historicthedalles.org/fort_dalles/home.htm* ☎*$5* ⊘*Thurs.–Mon. 11–4* ⊘*Closed Nov.–Mar.*

A favorite of windsurfers, **Celilo Park** also has swimming, sailboarding, and fishing. It's 7 mi east of The Dalles. ⊠*Exit 99 off I-84* ☎*541/296–1181* ☎*Free* ⊘*Daily.*

⟳ Exhibits at **Columbia Gorge Discovery Center–Wasco County Historical Museum** highlight the geological history of the Columbia Gorge, back 40 million years when volcanoes, landslides, and floods carved out the area. The museum focuses on 10,000 years of Native American life and exploration of the region by white settlers. ⊠*5000 Discovery Dr.* ☎*541/296–8600* ⊕*www.gorgediscovery.org* ☎*$8* ⊘*Daily 9–5.*

At the **Dalles Lock and Dam,** a hydroelectric dam just east of the Bonneville Dam, you can ride the free Dalles Dam Tour Train to the fish ladder and powerhouse. There's also a sturgeon pond at the visitor center. ⊠*Exit 87 in summer or Exit 88 other times off I-84, 2 mi east of the Dalles at Lake Celilo* ☎*541/296–1181* ⊕*corpslakes.usace.army.mil/visitors/projects.cfm?Id=G204400* ☎*Free* ⊘*Varied hrs, call ahead.*

Built in 1897, **Old St. Peter's Landmark** is a Gothic brick church with brilliant stained glass, hand-carved pews, marble altars, and an immense pipe organ. Steamboat captains once used the 176-foot steeple as a navigational benchmark.

CLOSE UP Hood River Fruit Loop

A remarkable combination of natural occurrences makes this 15,000-acre region of the world a delicious hub for growing fruit including pears, cherries, apples, and peaches. Fertile volcanic soil yielded from numerous Mt. Hood eruptions over thousands of years is complemented by centuries of decomposed organic materials. Add pure glacier water and warm sunny days into the mix, and results are 220,000 tons of harvested apples, cherries, and pears every year. Half of the nation's winter pears are picked off these trees, and the highest grade of Pippens are found here.

The Dalles is the largest cherry-growing district in Oregon, with 7,500 acres producing two-thirds of the state's sweet cherry output. There are ample, seasonal opportunities to pick fruit and, depending upon where you live, fruit may be shipped to meet specific government regulations and personal travel requirements. For details, visit ⊕ www.hood-riverfruitloop.com.

The landmark now functions as a nondenominational, non-profit organization available for tours, weddings, and other private functions. ⊠ 3rd and Lincoln Sts. ☎ 541/296–5686 ⊕ www.oldstpeterslandmark.org ☑ Free, donation suggested ☉ Feb.–Dec., Tues.–Fri. 11–3, weekends 1–3.

View the lower part of **Mayer State Park** from the top of Rowena Crest. Recreational activities include swimming, boating, fishing, and picnicking. ⊠ Exit 77 off I–84, ☎ 800/551–6949 ⊕ www.prd.state.or.us ☑ Day use $3 per vehicle ☉ Daily.

WHERE TO EAT AND STAY

$ ✕ **Cousin's Restaurant.** *American.* Home cooking rules the roost at this family restaurant with a frontier motif. Try the home-style pot roast, old-fashioned meat loaf or Tom Turkey supper with all the trimmings. In a goofy move, all the wait-staff goes by "Cousin." The ample menu includes plenty of vegetarian choices, breakfast that's served all day, and plenty of kids' choices. ⊠ 2114 W. 6th St. ☎ 541/298–2771 ⊕ www.cousinsthedalles.com ▭ AE, D, DC, MC, V.

¢ ✕ **Petite Provence.** *Cafe.* On offer here are eggs, crepes, and croissants for breakfast; hot and cold sandwiches and salads for lunch, and fresh-baked pastries and breads (you can take a loaf home). The sparkling display case tempts with a goodly selection of napoleons, éclairs, tarts, and mousses.

A spinoff from the main site in the Portland suburb of Lake Oswego ("La Provence"), this branch successfully retains the charms of its big sister. ✉ *408 E. 2nd St.* ☎ *541/506–0037* �'*AE, D, MC, V* ⊗ *No dinner.*

$ 🏨 **Cousins Country Inn.** Renovated in 2009, this property does its best to make travelers feel welcome. Rooms are spacious and clean, with simple and new furnishings. All rooms also have large-screen TVs and DVD players, and some have kitchenettes. **Pros:** homemade cookies on arrival; free movie rentals; indoor Jacuzzi. **Cons:** no room service; pool is outdoors. ✉ *2114 W. 6th St.* ☎ *800/848–9378* ⊕ *www.cousinscountryinn.com* ➲ *97 rooms* ⌂ *In-room: a/c, refrigerator (some), DVD, Wi-Fi (some). In-hotel: restaurant, bar, laundry facilities, Wi-Fi hotspot, some pets allowed* �' *AE, D, MC, V.*

MT. HOOD

About 60 mi east of Portland on I–84 and U.S. 26, 65 mi from the Dalles, west on I–84 and south on Hwy. 35 and U.S. 26.

Majestically towering 11,245 feet above sea level, Mt. Hood is what remains of the original north wall and rim of a volatile crater. Although the peak no longer spews ash or fire, active steam vents can be spotted high on the mountain. Native Americans in the area named it Wy'east, after a great chief who mystically became the mountain. In anger, Wy'east spouted flames and threw rocks toward the sky. The name was changed in 1792 when a crew of the British Royal Navy, the first recorded Europeans to sail down the Columbia River, spotted the mountain and named it after a famed British admiral, Samuel Hood. Mt. Hood offers the only year-round skiing in the lower 48 states, with three major ski areas and 26 lifts, as well as extensive areas for cross-country skiing and snowboarding. Many of the ski runs turn into mountain bike trails in summer. The mountain is also popular with climbers and hikers. In fact, some hikes follow parts of the Oregon Trail—some signs of the pioneers' passing, such as wagon ruts, are still evident.

★ The highest peak in Oregon, "the Mountain" is a focal point of the 1.1-million-acre **Mt. Hood National Forest,** an all-season playground attracting more than 7 million visitors annually. Twenty miles southeast of Portland, it extends south from the Columbia River Gorge for more than 60 mi and includes 189,200 acres of designated wilderness. These woods are perfect for hikers, horseback riders, mountain climbers, and cyclists. Within the forest are more than 80 campgrounds and 50 lakes stocked with brown, rainbow, cutthroat, brook, and steelhead trout. The Sandy, Salmon, and other rivers are known for their fishing, rafting, canoeing, and swimming. Both forest and mountain are crossed by an extensive trail system for hikers, cyclists, and horseback riders. The **Pacific Crest Trail**, which begins in British Columbia and ends in Mexico, crosses at the 4,157-foot-high Barlow Pass. As with most other mountain destinations within Oregon, weather can be temperamental, and snow and ice may affect driving conditions as early as October and as late as May. Bring tire chains and warm clothes as a precaution.

For a glimpse into the area's vivid history stop at the **Mt. Hood Information Center** (⊠*24403 E. Welches Rd., Welches*) and pick up a copy of *The Barlow Road*. This is a great navigational map of the first emigrant road over the Cascades, where pioneers traveled west via ancient Indian trails to avoid the dangers of the mighty Columbia River. Since this forest is close to the Portland metro area, campgrounds and trails are often crowded over the summer months, especially on weekends. If camping, contact the forest service desk while you're at the Mt. Hood Information Center. Prepare yourself by gathering information about the more than 80 campgrounds, including a string of neighboring campgrounds that rest on the south side of Mt. Hood: Trillium Lake, Still Creek, Timothy Lake, Little Crater Lake, Clackamas Lake, Summit Lake, Clear Lake, and Frog Lake. Each varies in what it offers and in price. The mountain is overflowing with day-use areas, and passes can be obtained for $5. There are also Mt. Hood National Forest maps with details about well-marked trails. ⊠ *70220 E. Hwy. 26* ☎ *503/622–3191 or 888/622–4822* ⊕ *www.fs.fed.us* ⊠ *Day-use free–$5, campsites $12–$14 Zigzag Ranger Station Mon.–Sat. 7:45–noon and 1–4:30, most campgrounds open year-round.*

WHERE TO EAT AND STAY

$$$$ ✕ **Cascade Dining Room.** *Contemporary.* If the wall of windows isn't coated with snow, you may get a good look at some of the neighboring peaks. Vaulted wooden beams and a wood-plank floor, handcrafted furniture, handwoven drapes, and a lion-size stone fireplace set the scene. Executive chef Leif Benson has been going strong since 1979,

incorporating Mt. Hood–grown morels in his "campfire spice" wild salmon, pistachios in his basmati rice, and truffles with his pheasant. A four-course tasting menu (including house favorite, crème brûlée) is always a tasty option. Open for breakfast, lunch, and dinner, this elegant spot serves a clever mix of lobster with macaroni and cheese at the noon hour. The Sunday brunch buffet, an all-you-can-eat affair, is almost as big as the fireplace. ⊠ *Timberline Rd., Timberline* ☎ *503/272–3104 or 800/547–1406* ⊕ *www.timberlinelodge.com/dining/cascade-dining-room* ⊟ *AE, D, MC, V.*

$$$–$$$$ ⌕ **Timberline Lodge.** The approach alone, an unforgettable
  ⌚ 6-mi ascent that circles Mt. Hood, is reason enough to visit
  ★ the magnificent Timberline Lodge. Now you see it, now you don't: Mt. Hood teases you the whole way up, then quite unexpectedly, the Lodge materializes out of the mist and you momentarily forget about the snow-capped peak. It's no wonder that Stanley Kubrick used the lodge for exterior shots in "The Shining." Built to complement the size and majesty of Mt. Hood, the massive structure was built from the timber and rock on the mountain itself. More than 500 men and women toiled in 1936–37 as part of the Works Project Administration, forging metal for furniture and fixtures, sculpting old telephone poles into beams and banisters, weaving, looming, sawing. Here, the historical artifacts are not displayed behind a glass wall—they're the chairs you sit on, the doors you walk through, the floors you step on. Enjoy the restaurants, the snow sports, the hiking paths; relax by the lobby's massive fireplace with a 96-foot stone chimney. But also make time for the detailed 22-minute film (on the lower level) to learn about the building's genesis. **Pros:** it's thrilling to stay on the mountain itself; plush feather beds; amazing architecture throughout; fun dining places. **Cons:** rooms are small; no a/c; carloads of tourists. ⊠ *Timberline, Timberline Lodge, OR* ☎ *503/231–5400 or 800/547–1406* ⊕ *www.timberlinelodge.com* ⟿ *60 rooms* ⌂ *In-room: no a/c. In-hotel: restaurant, bar, pool, gym, elevator, concierge, parking (no fee)* ⊟ *AE, D, MC, V.*

SPORTS AND THE OUTDOORS

SKIING

One of the longest ski and snowboard seasons in North America unfolds at **Timberline Lodge Ski Area** (⊠ *Off U.S. 26, Timberline* ☎ *503/272–3311* ⊕ *www.timberlinelodge. com*). The U.S. ski team conducts summer training at this full-service ski area. It's the only ski area in the lower 48 states that's open year-round (except for two weeks in late September). Timberline is famous for its Palmer chairlift, which takes skiers to a high glacier for summer skiing. The top elevation is 8,500 feet, with a 3,600-foot vertical drop, and the longest run is 3 mi. Facilities include a day lodge with fast food and a ski shop; lessons and equipment rental and repair are available. Parking requires a Sno-Park permit. Lift tickets per day are $54 peak, $49 regular. The area is open Sunday–Tuesday 9–5 and Wednesday–Saturday 9 AM–10 PM; the lift is also open June–August, daily 7 AM–1:30 PM.

Travel Smart Portland

WORD OF MOUTH

"We stayed in Portland . . . without a car. It was very easy to get around."

—ltr

GETTING HERE AND AROUND

We're proud of our Web site: Fodors.com is a great place to begin any journey. Scan Travel Wire for suggested itineraries, travel deals, restaurant and hotel openings, and other up-to-the-minute info. Check out Booking to research prices and book plane tickets, hotel rooms, rental cars, and vacation packages. Head to Talk for on-the-ground pointers from travelers who frequent our message boards. You can also link to loads of other travel-related resources.

Geographically speaking, Portland is relatively easy to navigate. It's mapped out into quadrants with the Willamette River dividing east and west into halves and Burnside Street separating the north from south. "Northwest" refers to the area north of Burnside and west of the river; "Southwest" refers to the area south of Burnside and west of the river; "Northeast" refers to the area north of Burnside and east of the river; "Southeast" refers to the area south of Burnside and east of the river. As you travel around the Portland metropolitan area, keep in mind that named east and west streets intersect numbered avenues, run north–south and begin at each side of the river. For instance, Southwest 12th Avenue is 12 blocks west of the Willamette. Most of downtown's streets are one-way.

■TIP→ Ask the local tourist board about hotel and local transportation packages that include tickets to major museum exhibits or other special events.

▮ BY AIR

It takes about 5 hours to fly non-stop to Portland from New York, 4 hours from Chicago, and 2½ hours from Los Angeles. Flying from Seattle to Portland takes just under an hour; flying from Portland to Vancouver takes an hour and 15 minutes.

Even if your final destination is in another city in Oregon, you may choose to fly into Portland and rent a car to get there, because all other airports in the state are small regional airports with limited service. It is possible, however, to get a connecting flight from Portland International Airport (PDX) to smaller cities in Oregon. Portland Airport is served by all major airlines as well as by several smaller regional carriers.

Airlines and Airports Airline and Airport Links.com (⊕ www. airlineandairportlinks.com) has links to many of the world's airlines and airports.

Airline-Security Issues Transportation Security Administration (⊕ www.tsa.gov) has answers for almost every question that might come up.

AIRPORTS

Portland International Airport (PDX) is a sleek, modern airport with service to many national and international destinations. It's easily accessible from downtown Portland.

Contacts Portland International Airport (✉ *N.E. Airport Way at I–205* ☎ *877/739–4636* ⊕ *www.flypdx. com/*).

GROUND TRANSPORTATION

TriMet trains and buses serve the airport. A 5½-mi extension of the MAX light-rail system runs from the Gateway Transit Center (at the intersection of I–84 and I–205) directly to and from the airport. Trains arrive at and depart from inside the passenger terminal near the south baggage-claim area. The trip takes about 35 minutes from downtown. TriMet Bus 12, which runs about every 15 minutes, also serves the airport. The fare to or from the airport on MAX or the bus is $2.30.

Contacts TriMet/MAX (✉ *6th Ave. and Morrison St., Downtown* ☎ *503/238–7433* ⊕ *www.trimet.org*).

FLIGHTS

Airlines that serve Portland include Alaska Airlines, Continental, Delta, and United. JetBlue has daily flights from New York's JFK airport to Portland. US Airways flies from Portland to Las Vegas, Phoenix, Charlotte, and Philadelphia. Frontier Airlines, Horizon Air, and United Express provide frequent service between cities in Washington, Oregon, Idaho, Montana, and California. Southwest Airlines has frequent service to Portland from cities in California, Nevada, Idaho, and Utah as well as some other parts of the country.

Airline Contacts Alaska Airlines/ Horizon Air (☎ *800/252–7522 or 206/433–3100* ⊕ *www. alaskaair.com*). **American Airlines** (☎ *800/433–7300* ⊕ *www. aa.com*). **Continental Airlines** (☎ *800/523–3273 for U.S. and Mexico reservations, 800/231–0856 for international reservations* ⊕ *www.continental.com*). **Delta Airlines** (☎ *800/221–1212 for U.S. reservations, 800/241–4141 for international reservations* ⊕ *www. delta.com*). **Frontier Airlines** (☎ *800/432–1359* ⊕ *www.frontierairlines.com*). **jetBlue** (☎ *800/538– 2583* ⊕ *www.jetblue.com*). **Southwest Airlines** (☎ *800/435– 9792* ⊕ *www.southwest.com*). **Spirit Airlines** (☎ *800/772–7117 or 586/791–7300* ⊕ *www.spiritair.com*). **United Airlines** (☎ *800/864–8331 for U.S. reservations, 800/538–2929 for international reservations* ⊕ *www.united.com*). **US Airways** (☎ *800/428–4322 for U.S. and Canada reservations, 800/622–1015 for international reservations* ⊕ *www. usairways.com*).

▌ BY BOAT

From Portland, the *Portland Spirit, Willamette Star,* and *Crystal Dolphin* make sightseeing and dinner cruises on the Willamette and Columbia rivers. America West also uses paddle-wheel boats for overnight historic tours along the Columbia and Snake rivers. Departing from Cascade Locks, Oregon (45 minutes east of Portland), the sternwheeler *Columbia Gorge* cruises the Columbia Gorge and the Willamette River (December only). To view the rich wildlife along the western edge of the Columbia River, you can take an ecologically focused cruise or an estuary tour, both of which depart from Astoria, Oregon.

Contacts Columbia Gorge (☎ 503/224–3900 or 800/224–3901 ⊕ www.sternwheeler.com). **Portland Spirit** (☎ 503/224–3900 or 800/224–3901 ⊕ www.portland-spirit.com).

▮ BY BUS

Greyhound is a good way to get between destinations in Oregon for a reasonable price if you don't have a car at your disposal. Portland is the main hub for nearly all routes in the state, making it the most practical starting and ending point for most bus excursions. Keep in mind that many small towns in Oregon may not be regularly accessible by bus and that there may be no public transportation or car-rental locations in many towns you visit. Buses arrive at and depart from the Greyhound terminal next to the Amtrak station in Old Town.

Greyhound's domestic and international Discovery Passes allow unlimited bus travel in North America—including Canada and Mexico—for periods of 7 to 60 days.

For bus travel within the city, see ⇨ *By TriMet/MAX*, below.

Contacts Greyhound Terminal (✉ 550 N.W. 6th Ave., Old Town ☎ 503/243–2310 or 800/231–2222, 503/243–2337 baggage, 503/243–2361 customer service).

▮ BY CAR

I–5 enters Portland from the north and south. I–84, the city's major eastern corridor, terminates in Portland. U.S. 26 and U.S. 30 are primary east–west thoroughfares. Bypass routes are I–205, which links I–5 and I–84 before crossing the Columbia River into Washington, and I–405, which arcs around western downtown. Most city-center streets are one-way only, and Southwest 5th and 6th avenues between Burnside and Southwest Madison streets are limited to bus traffic.

From the airport to downtown, take I–205 south to westbound I–84. Drive west over the Willamette River and take the City Center exit. If going to the airport, take I–84 east to I–205 north; follow I–205 to the airport exit.

Traffic on I–5 north and south of downtown and on I–84 and I–205 east of downtown is heavy between 6 AM and 9 AM and between 4 and 8 PM. Four-lane U.S. 26 west of downtown can be bumper-to-bumper any time of the day going to or from downtown.

GASOLINE

Gas stations are plentiful in major metropolitan areas and along major highways like I–5. Most stay open late, except in rural areas, where Sunday hours are limited and where you may drive long stretches without a refueling opportunity. This is particularly true in Oregon, where you are not allowed to pump your own gas, and therefore won't be able to find an automated pump in an emergency.

■TIP→ **Keep an eye on the gauge when traveling to national parks and off-the-beaten-path trails, particularly if you'll be heading down Forest Service roads. A good rule of thumb is to fill up before you get off (or too far away) from a major highway like I–5 or I–90.**

PARKING
Though there are several options, parking in downtown Portland can be tricky and expensive. If you're parked for more than several hours, your most affordable and accessible option is to park in one of seven city-owned "Smart Park" lots. Rates start at $1.50 per hour (short-term parking, four hours or less) to $3–$5 per hour (long-term parking, weekdays 5 AM–6 PM), with a $15 daily maximum; weekends and evenings have lower rates. The best part about Smart Park is that hundreds of participating merchants will validate tickets and cover the first two hours of parking when you spend at least $25 in their stores.

There are numerous privately owned lots around the city as well; fees for those vary and add up quickly.

Street parking is metered only and requires you to visibly display a sticker on the inside of your curbside window. The meters that dispense the stickers take coins or credit cards (though you'll be charged a bank fee for using a debit card). Metered spaces are mostly available for 90 minutes to three hours; parking tickets for exceeding the limit are regularly issued.

Once you get out of downtown and into residential areas, there's plenty of nonmetered street parking available.

RENTAL CARS
It's possible to get around Portland by public transportation and taxis, but once you go outside city limits, your options are limited. National lines like Greyhound do provide service between major towns, and Amtrak has limited service between Washington and Oregon (allowing you to get from, say, Portland to Seattle, by train), but it's nearly impossible to get to and around the major recreation areas and national parks of each state without your own wheels.

Rates in Portland begin at $30 a day and $138 a week, not including the 17% Multnomah County tax if you rent in this county, which includes the airport.

All the major agencies are represented in the region. If you're planning to cross the U.S.–Canadian border with your rental car, discuss it with the agency to see what's involved.

In the Pacific Northwest you must be 21 to rent a car. Car seats are compulsory for children under four years *and* 40 pounds; older children are required to sit in booster seats until they're eight years old *and* 80 pounds. In the United States nonresidents need a reservation voucher, passport, driver's license, and insurance for each driver.

When you reserve a car, ask about cancellation penalties, taxes, drop-off charges (if you're planning to pick up the car in one city and leave it in another), and surcharges (for being under or over a certain age, for additional drivers, or for driving across state or country borders or beyond a specific distance from your point of rental). All these things can add substantially to your costs. Request car seats and extras such as GPS when you book.

Rates are sometimes—but not always—better if you book in advance or reserve through a rental agency's Web site. There are other reasons to book ahead, though: for popular destinations, during busy times of the year, or to ensure that you get certain types of cars (vans, SUVs, exotic sports cars).

■TIP➔ **Make sure that a confirmed reservation guarantees you a car. Agencies sometimes overbook, particularly for busy weekends and holiday periods.**

Automobile Associations U.S.: American Automobile Association (*AAA* ☎ *315/797–5000* ⊕ *www. aaa.com*); most contact with the organization is through state and regional members. **National Automobile Club** (☎ *650/294–7000* ⊕ *www. thenac.com*); membership is open to California residents only.

Major Agencies Alamo (☎ *800/462–5266* ⊕ *www.alamo. com*). **Avis** (☎ *800/331–1212*

⊕ *www.avis.com*). **Budget** (☎ *800/527–0700* ⊕ *www.budget. com*). **Hertz** (☎ *800/654–3131* ⊕ *www.hertz.com*). **National Car Rental** (☎ *800/227–7368* ⊕ *www. nationalcar.com*).

RENTAL CAR INSURANCE

Everyone who rents a car wonders whether the insurance that the rental companies offer is worth the expense. No one—including us—has a simple answer. It all depends on how much regular insurance you have, how comfortable you are with risk, and whether or not money is an issue.

If you own a car and carry comprehensive car insurance for both collision and liability, your personal auto insurance will probably cover a rental, but read your policy's fine print to be sure. If you don't have auto insurance, then you should probably buy the collision- or loss-damage waiver (CDW or LDW) from the rental company. This eliminates your liability for damage to the car.

Some credit cards offer CDW coverage, but it's usually supplemental to your own insurance and rarely covers SUVs, minivans, luxury models, and the like. If your coverage is secondary, you may still be liable for loss-of-use costs from the car-rental company (again, read the fine print). But no credit-card insurance is valid unless you use that card for *all* transactions, from reserving to paying the final bill.

■TIP➔ **Diners Club offers primary CDW coverage on all rentals reserved and paid for with the card. This means that Diners Club's** company—not your own car insurance—pays in case of an accident. It *doesn't* mean that your car-insurance company won't raise your rates once it discovers you had an accident.

You may also be offered supplemental liability coverage; the car-rental company is required to carry a minimal level of liability coverage insuring all renters, but it's rarely enough to cover claims in a really serious accident if you're at fault. Your own auto-insurance policy will protect you if you own a car; if you don't, you have to decide whether you are willing to take the risk.

U.S. rental companies sell CDWs and LDWs for about $15 to $25 a day; supplemental liability is usually more than $10 a day. The car-rental company may offer you all sorts of other policies, but they're rarely worth the cost. Personal accident insurance, which is basic hospitalization coverage, is an especially egregious rip-off if you already have health insurance.

■TIP→ **You can decline the insurance from the rental company and purchase it through a third-party provider such as Travel Guard (⊕ www.travelguard.com)—$9 per day for $35,000 of coverage. That's sometimes just under half the price of the CDW offered by some car-rental companies.**

ROADSIDE EMERGENCIES
In case of an accident, dial 119. On the major roads such as the North Coast Highway, you can call a garage in one of the larger towns. In rural areas, you'll probably have

to rely on the help of locals to get your car up and running as far as one of the larger towns.

To report a car theft, call 119. You also need to call your rental-car agency.

For emergencies and for an ambulance, dial 911.

Emergency Services Oregon State Police (☎ 503/378–3720 or 800/452–7888).

ROAD CONDITIONS
Winter driving can present challenges. In coastal areas the mild, damp climate contributes to frequently wet roadways. Snowfalls generally occur only once or twice a year, but when it does fall, traffic grinds to a halt and roadways become treacherous and stay that way until the snow melts.

Tire chains, studs, or snow tires are essential equipment for winter travel in mountain areas. If you're planning to drive into high elevations, be sure to check the weather forecast beforehand. Even the main highway mountain passes can close because of snow conditions. In winter state and provincial highway departments operate snow advisory telephone lines that give pass conditions.

▌BY TAXI
Taxi fare is $2.50 at flag drop plus $2.30 per mi. The first person pays by the meter, and each additional passenger pays $1. Cabs cruise the city streets, but it's better to phone for one. The major companies are Broadway Cab, New Rose City Cab, Portland Taxi Company,

and Radio Cab. The trip between downtown Portland and the airport takes about 30 minutes by taxi. The fare is about $35.

Taxi Companies Broadway Cab (☎ 503/227–1234). **New Rose City Cab** (☎ 503/282–7707). **Portland Taxi Company** (☎ 503/256–5400). **Radio Cab** (☎ 503/227–1212).

▌ BY TRAIN

Amtrak, the U.S. passenger rail system, has daily service to Union Station from the Midwest and California. The *Empire Builder* takes a northern route through Minnesota and Montana from Chicago to Spokane, from where separate legs continue to Seattle and Portland. The *Coast Starlight* begins in Los Angeles; makes stops throughout California, western Oregon, and Washington; and terminates in Seattle.

Amtrak's *Cascades* trains travel between Seattle and Vancouver and between Seattle, Portland, and Eugene. The trip from Seattle to Portland takes roughly 3½ hours and costs $28–$44 for a coach seat; this is a pleasant alternative to a mind-numbing drive down I–5. The *Empire Builder* travels between Portland and Spokane (7 hours, $75), with part of the route running through the Columbia River gorge. From Portland to Eugene, it's a 3-hour trip; the cost is $21–$35.

▌TIP➔ **Book Amtrak tickets at least a few days in advance, especially if you're traveling between Seattle and Portland on the weekend.**

Information Amtrak (✉ 800 N.W. 6th Ave., Old Town ☎ 800/872–7245).

▌ BY TRIMET/MAX

TriMet operates an extensive system of buses, streetcars, and light-rail trains. The Central City streetcar line runs between Legacy Good Samaritan hospital in Nob Hill, the Pearl District, downtown, and Portland State University. To Nob Hill it travels along 10th Avenue and then on Northwest Northrup; from Nob Hill it runs along Northwest Lovejoy and then on 11th Avenue. Trains stop every few blocks.

Metropolitan Area Express, or MAX, links the eastern and western Portland suburbs with downtown, Washington Park and the Oregon Zoo, the Lloyd Center district, the Convention Center, and the Rose Quarter. From downtown, trains operate daily 5:30 AM–1 AM, with a fare of $2 for travel through one or two zones, $2.30 for three zones, and $4.75 for an unlimited all-day ticket. A seven-day visitor pass is also available for $22.50. Trains run about every 10 minutes Monday–Saturday and every 15 minutes on Sunday and holidays.

Bus, MAX, and streetcar fare is $2 for one or two zones, which covers most places you'll have cause to go, and $2.30 for three zones, which includes all of the outlying areas of the city. Ask the driver if you're uncertain whether you're traveling within Zones 1 and 2. A "fareless square" extends from downtown all the way to the Lloyd Center on the east side. If you're riding only within this area, your ride is free.

Day passes for unlimited system-wide travel cost $4.75. Three-day and monthly passes are available. As you board the bus, the driver will hand you a transfer ticket that is good for one to two hours, depending on the time of day, on all buses and MAX trains. Be sure to hold on to it whether you're transferring or not; it also serves as proof that you have paid for your ride. MAX trains run every 10 minutes Monday–Saturday before 8 PM and every 15 minutes after 8 PM and all day Sunday and holidays. Buses can operate as frequently as every five minutes or once an hour. Bikes are allowed on designated areas of MAX trains, and there are bike racks on the front of all buses that everyone is free to use.

Contacts TriMet/MAX (✉ *6th Ave. and Morrison St., Downtown* ☎ *503/238-7433* ⊕ *www.trimet.org*).

ESSENTIALS

■ COMMUNICATIONS

INTERNET

Portland is well wired, and it's difficult to find a hotel that doesn't offer either Ethernet connections, Wi-Fi, or both. (Whether those services are free, however, is another issue.)

Coffeehouses almost always have reliable Wi-Fi and the service is often free (assuming, of course, that you at least buy a cup of coffee); a few have a communal computer or two if you didn't bring the laptop, but often your best bet for dedicated computer stations is either your hotel's business center or public library branches.

For a list of wired coffee shops in Portland, check out ⊕ *oregon.com* and click on "Metro Portland." For more Portland hot spots, check out ⊕ *www.wifipdx.com.*

Contacts Cybercafes (⊕ *www.cybercafes.com*) lists more than 4,000 Internet cafés worldwide.

■ DAY TOURS AND GUIDES

BOAT TOURS

Sternwheeler Riverboat Tours' *Columbia Gorge* departs year-round from Tom McCall Waterfront Park on two-hour excursions of the Willamette River; there are also Friday-night dinner cruises. In summer the sternwheeler travels up the Columbia River. For the more adventurous, Willamette Jet-boat Excursions offers whirling, swirling one- and two-hour tours along the Willamette River that include an up-close visit with Willamette Falls.

Contacts Sternwheeler Riverboat Tours (✉ *S.W. Naito Pkwy. and Stark St., Riverfront Park* ☎ *503/224–3900*). **Willamette Jetboat Excursions** (✉ *S.E. Marion St.* ☎ *888/538–2628*).

BUS TOURS

Gray Line operates City of Portland and Pacific Northwest sightseeing tours, including service to Chinook Winds Casino in Lincoln City, from April through October; call for departure times and tours.

Contacts Raz/Gray Line (☎ *503/684–3322 Ext. 2* ⊕ *www.grayline.com*).

TROLLEY TOURS

The Willamette Shore Trolley company operates vintage double-decker electric trolleys that provide scenic round-trips between suburban Lake Oswego and downtown, along the west shore of the Willamette River. The 7-mi route, which the trolley makes in 45 minutes, passes over trestles and through Elk Rock tunnel along one of the most scenic stretches of the river. The line, which opened in 1885, was electrified in 1914, and Southern Pacific Railway operated dozens of trips daily along this route in the 1920s. Passenger service ended in 1929, and the line was taken over by the Oregon Electric Railway Historical Society. Reservations are recommended. The trolley ($10 round-trip) departs Lake Oswego at noon and 2:30 PM and Portland at 1 and 3:15 on weekends from May through October. Charters are available year-round.

Contacts Willamette Shore Trolley (⊠ *311 N. State St., Lake Oswego* ⊠ *South of RiverPlace Marina, at Sheridan and Moody Sts., Portland* ☎ *503/697–7436*).

WALKING TOURS

Travel Portland (⇨ Visitor Information), which is open weekdays 9–5 and Saturday 9–4, has brochures, maps, and guides to art galleries and select neighborhoods.

▌ HOURS OF OPERATION

In Oregon, store hours can be erratic, a testament to the laid-back nature of the region. Major department stores or shops generally follow the 10-to-6 rule, but you should always phone ahead if you have your heart set on visiting a smaller shop. Never assume a store is open on Sunday; many smaller shops have truncated Saturday hours as well. To make matters more confusing, most smaller stores close one day during the week (usually Monday or Tuesday, but it varies), and some stores don't open until 11 AM, noon, or even 1 PM. Thankfully, coffeehouses tend to keep regular and long hours, so you'll have no problem finding one to kill time in if you have to wait for a store to open.

Bars in Oregon close at 2 AM, with last call coming as early as 1:30.

▌ MONEY

Meals in Portland are generally a little less expensive than in other major North American regions. Prices for first-class hotel rooms are high in summer ($250–$400), though the same rooms become more affordable in low season ($100 to $200 a night). Unless you're willing to stay in rundown motels, the cheapest rooms you'll find start at $75–$90 a night. Though you'll get some great deals on food and other on-the-ground expenses (fewer sights charge prohibitive fees), you'll find that some urban "necessities," like taxi rides, are frustratingly expensive.

Debit cards and major credit cards are accepted almost everywhere—some cafés will even let you charge a single cup of coffee—so don't worry about carrying around wads of cash. It's a good idea to keep handy a few small bills and coins for parking meters.

ITEM	AVERAGE COST
Cup of Coffee	$1.50
Glass of Wine	$6–$9
Glass of Beer	$4–$6
Sandwich	$5–$8
One-Mile Taxi Ride	$4.50
Museum Admission	$10–$15

ATMS AND BANKS

ATMs are common and can be found all over Portland.

CREDIT CARDS

Throughout this guide, the following abbreviations are used: **AE,** American Express; **D,** Discover **DC,** Diners Club; **MC,** MasterCard; and **V,** Visa.

It's a good idea to inform your credit-card company before you travel, especially if you're going abroad and don't travel internationally very often. Otherwise, the credit-card company might put a hold on your card owing to unusual activity—not a good thing halfway through your trip. Record all your credit-card numbers—as well as the phone numbers to call if your cards are lost or stolen— in a safe place, so you're prepared should something go wrong. Both MasterCard and Visa have general numbers you can call (collect if you're abroad) if your card is lost, but you're better off calling the number of your issuing bank, since MasterCard and Visa usually just transfer you to your bank; your bank's number is usually printed on your card.

If you plan to use your credit card for cash advances, you'll need to apply for a PIN at least two weeks before your trip. Although it's usually cheaper (and safer) to use a credit card abroad for large purchases (so you can cancel payments or be reimbursed if there's a problem), note that some credit-card companies *and* the banks that issue them add substantial percentages to all foreign transactions, whether they're in a foreign currency or not. Check on these fees before leaving home, so there won't be any surprises when you get the bill.

Reporting Lost Cards American Express (☎ *800/528–4800 in U.S., 336/393–1111 collect from abroad* ⊕ *www.americanexpress.com*). **MasterCard** (☎ *800/627–8372 in U.S., 636/722–7111 collect from abroad* ⊕ *www.mastercard.com*). **Visa** (☎ *800/847–2911 in U.S., 410/581–9994 collect from abroad* ⊕ *www.visa.com*).

▍SAFETY

The Pacific Northwest is generally a safe place to visit. Portland is the least gentrified of the three major cities, though it doesn't necessarily have more problems with crime than Seattle or Vancouver. You'll often see people in coffeehouses leave laptops and bags unattended when they head up to the counter for a refill. That said, it's better to be safe than sorry, so keep an eye on your belongings in public places.

Always lock rental cars. Try not to leave any valuables inside the car; if you must do so, put them in the trunk. Car break-ins are common in Portland, even in seemingly peaceful residential areas.

The Great Outdoors pose the most dangerous element of the Northwest. Don't hike alone, and make sure you bring enough water plus basic first-aid items. If you're not an experienced hiker, stick to tourist-friendly spots like the more accessible parts of the national parks; if you have to drive 30 mi down a

Forest Service road to reach a trail, it's possible you might be the only one hiking on it.

TAXES

Oregon has no sales tax, although many cities and counties levy a tax on lodging and services. Room taxes, for example, vary from 6% to 9½%.

TIME

Portland is in the Pacific time zone. Daylight savings time is observed from early April to late October.

TIPPING

Tips and service charges are usually not automatically added to a bill. If service is satisfactory, customers generally give waitstaff 15%–20% of the total bill. Hairdressers, taxi drivers, and other service specialists receive 10%–20%. Bellhops, doormen, and porters at airports and railway stations are generally tipped $1–$2 for each item of luggage.

When visiting coffeehouses, throw your change or $1 into the tip jar on the counter—like waiters, baristas depend on tips to supplement their wages.

VISITOR INFORMATION

At Montego Bay's Sangster International Airport, arriving passengers will find a Jamaica tourist Board booth in the customs hall. This desk can help with a limited number of brochures and maps and can

also make hotel arrangements for travelers who arrive with reservations. The airport information desk is open 6 AM to 10 PM daily.

The Oregon Coast Visitors Association provides information on coastal towns as well as a helpful FAQ on driving tours and beach etiquette at ⊕ *www.visittheoregoncoast.com*. The Columbia River Gorge Visitors Association Web site, ⊕ *www.crgva.org*, has tons of links to help you find outfitters, events, and accommodations in Oregon's most-popular recreation area. Before you head to Mt. Hood to hike or ski, go to ⊕ *www.mthoodterritory.com* for driving tour maps, agritourism suggestions, and more. Oregon's wine country is a big attraction, and the Willamette Valley Visitor's Association does a good job of cataloging the state's sizable number of wineries by region or by experience at ⊕ *www.oregonwinecountry.org*.

Contacts Travel Portland (✉ *1000 S.W. Broadway, Suite 2300,* ☎ *800/962-3700* ⊕ *www.travelportland.com*). Travel Portland Information Center (✉ *701 S.W. 6th Ave., Pioneer Courthouse Sq.* ☎ *503/275-8355 or 877/678-5263*).

INDEX